HOLT McDOUGAL

The Americans

RECONSTRUCTION TO THE 21ST CENTURY

Guided Reading Workbook

HOLT McDOUGAL
a division of Houghton Mifflin Harcourt

ISBN   978-0-547-52136-7

11   0982   16 15

4500531740

Contents

Guided Reading Workbook

Guided Reading Workbook

How to Use This Book

The purpose of this *Guided Reading Workbook* is to help you read and understand your history textbook, *The Americans: Reconstruction to the 21st Century*. You can use this *Guided Reading Workbook* in two ways.

1. **Use the *Guided Reading Workbook* side-by-side with your history book.**

- Turn to the section that you are going to read in the textbook. Then, next to the book, put the pages from the *Guided Reading Workbook* that accompany that section. All of the heads in the *Guided Reading Workbook* match the heads in the textbook.

- Use the *Guided Reading Workbook* to help you read and organize the information in the textbook.

2. **Use the *Guided Reading Workbook* to study the material that will appear in the chapter tests.**

- Reread the summary of every chapter.

- Review the definitions of the **Terms and Names** in the *Guided Reading Workbook*.

- Review the graphic organizer that you created as you read the summaries.

- Review your answers to questions.

Strategy: Read the **Terms and Names** and the definition of each. The **Terms and Names** are in dark type in the section.

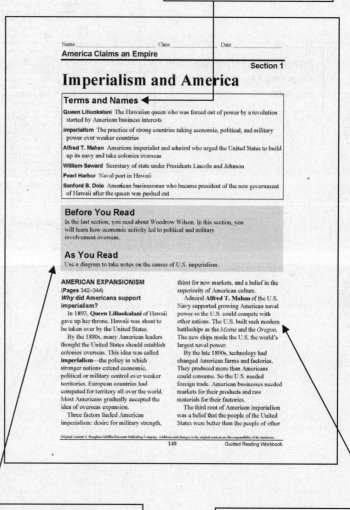

Name _____ Class _____ Date _____
America Claims an Empire

Section 1

Imperialism and America

Terms and Names

Queen Liliuokalani The Hawaiian queen who was forced out of power by a revolution started by American business interests

imperialism The practice of strong countries taking economic, political, and military power over weaker countries

Alfred T. Mahan American imperialist and admiral who urged the United States to build up its navy and take colonies overseas

William Seward Secretary of state under Presidents Lincoln and Johnson

Pearl Harbor Naval port in Hawaii

Sanford B. Dole American businessman who became president of the new government of Hawaii after the queen was pushed out

Before You Read

In the last section, you read about Woodrow Wilson. In this section, you will learn how economic activity led to political and military involvement overseas.

As You Read

Use a diagram to take notes on the causes of U.S. imperialism.

AMERICAN EXPANSIONISM
(Pages 342–344)
Why did Americans support imperialism?

In 1893, **Queen Liliuokalani** of Hawaii gave up her throne. Hawaii was about to be taken over by the United States.

By the 1880s, many American leaders thought the United States should establish colonies overseas. This idea was called **imperialism**—the policy in which stronger nations extend economic, political or military control over weaker territories. European countries had competed for territory all over the world. Most Americans gradually accepted the idea of overseas expansion.

Three factors fueled American imperialism: desire for military strength,

thirst for new markets, and a belief in the superiority of American culture.

Admiral **Alfred T. Mahan** of the U.S. Navy supported growing American naval power so the U.S. could compete with other nations. The U.S. built such modern battleships as the *Maine* and the *Oregon*. The new ships made the U.S. the world's largest naval power.

By the late 1800s, technology had changed American farms and factories. They produced more than Americans could consume. So the U.S. needed foreign trade. American businesses needed markets for their products and raw materials for their factories.

The third root of American imperialism was a belief that the people of the United States were better than the people of other

Original content © Houghton Mifflin Harcourt Publishing Company. Additions and changes to the original content are the responsibility of the instructor.

140   Guided Reading Workbook

Strategy: Use a graphic organizer to help you organize information in the section.

Strategy: Read the summary. It contains the main ideas and the key information under the head.

Name_____ Class _____ Date _____

Section 1, *continued*

countries. This racist belief came from people's pride in their Anglo-Saxon (Northern European) heritage. People sometimes felt they had a duty to spread their culture and Christian religion among other people.

1. What were three reasons Americans supported imperialism?

_____

_____

THE UNITED STATES ACQUIRES ALASKA; THE UNITED STATES TAKES HAWAII (Pages 344–345)
How **did the Hawaiian Islands become a U.S. territory?**

William Seward was Secretary of State for presidents Lincoln and Andrew Johnson. In 1867 he purchased Alaska from Russia for $7.2 million. Some opponents in Congress made fun of the deal calling it "Seward's Icebox" or "Seward's Folly."

The Hawaiian Islands, in the Pacific Ocean, had been important to the United States since the 1790s. Merchants had stopped there on their way to China and India. In the 1820s, American missionaries founded Christian schools and churches on the islands.

A number of Americans had established sugar plantations in Hawaii. In the mid-1800s, these large farms accounted for about three-quarters of the wealth in the islands. Plantation owners brought thousands of laborers to Hawaii from Japan, Portugal, and China. This weakened the influence of the native Hawaiians. By 1900, the foreign laborers outnumbered the Hawaiians three to one.

In 1875, the United States agreed to import Hawaiian sugar duty-free. Over the next 15 years, Hawaiian sugar production increased nine times. Then the McKinley Tariff caused a crisis for Hawaiian sugar growers. With the duty on their sugar, Hawaiian growers faced stiff competition from other growers. The powerful Hawaiian sugar growers called for the U.S. to annex Hawaii. The U.S. military had already understood the value of Hawaii. In 1887, the U.S. forced Hawaii to let it build a naval base at **Pearl Harbor**, Hawaii's best port.

When the Hawaiian king died in 1891, his sister became queen. Queen Liliuokalani wanted a new constitution that would give voting power back to ordinary Hawaiians. American business interests did not want this to happen.

American business groups organized a revolt against the queen. The U.S. ambassador John L. Stevens helped them. The planters took control of the island. They established a temporary government and made American businessman **Sanford B. Dole** the president.

Stevens urged the U.S. government to annex the Hawaiian Islands. President Grover Cleveland refused to take over the islands unless a majority of Hawaiians favored that. In 1897, however, William McKinley became president. He favored annexation. In 1898, Hawaii became a U.S. territory.

2. How did Hawaiians lose control of their islands?

_____

_____

Strategy: Underline the main ideas and key information as you read.

Strategy: Answer the question at the end of each part.

The last page of each section of the *Guided Reading Workbook* ends with a graphic organizer that will help you better understand the information in the section. Use the graphic organizer to take notes as you read. The notes can help you to prepare for the section quiz and chapter tests.

Name _____ Class _____ Date _____
Section 1, *continued*

As you read this section, fill out the chart below by summarizing reasons why the United States became an imperial power.

The Roots of American Imperialism		
1. Economic roots	2. Political and military roots	3. Racist roots

↓

4. What did Admiral Mahan urge the United States to do to protect its interests?

For each year on the time line below, identify one important event in the history of U.S. involvement in Hawaii.

U.S. Imperialism in Hawaii	
1875	
1887	
1890	
1891	
1897	
1898	

142   Guided Reading Workbook

Exploration and the Colonial Era

The Americas, West Africa, and Europe

Terms and Names

nomadic Moving from place to place in search of food and water

Aztecs People who built an empire in Mexico, beginning in the 1200s

Anasazi Native Americans of the Southwest, about A.D. 100 to 1300

Pueblo Native American group in the Southwest

Iroquois Native American group in Eastern North America

Benin African kingdom around the Niger River known for metalworking

Kongo Small kingdoms on the lower Congo River united under one ruler

Islam Religion founded by Muhammad in the 600s

Christianity A religion based on the life and teachings of Jesus

Reformation Split in the Christian Church that led to Protestantism

Renaissance A term meaning "rebirth" of the kind of interest in the physical world that had characterized ancient Greece and Rome

Before You Read

In this section, you will learn about the people who lived in North America, West Africa, and Europe in the 1400s. In the next section, you will see how these people came together in the Americas.

As You Read

Use a web diagram to take notes on how trade and commerce affected regions in different time periods.

ANCIENT CULTURES IN THE AMERICAS (Pages 4-6)
Who lived in the Americas first?

The first humans came to the Americas from Asia about 22,000 years ago. Over thousands of years, these **nomadic** people moved from place to place, spreading out across North and South America. They lived by hunting animals and gathering wild plants.

Between 10,000 and 5,000 years ago (800 to 3000 B.C.), people living in

Mexico discovered a new way to get food. They began to raise plants or to farm. The practice of farming spread. Because people who farmed no longer had to search for plant foods, they could stay in one place. They could turn their attention to learning crafts and to building settled communities. In this way, farming made possible the growth of civilizations.

Beginning about 3,000 years ago (1000 B.C.), a number of rich and complex Native American civilizations developed. The

Aztecs settled in Mexico in the 1200s. The **Anasazi** farmed the dry areas of the Southwest between 300 B.C. and A.D. 1400.

1. Who were the first people to live in the Americas?

_____

_____

NATIVE AMERICAN SOCIETIES OF THE 1400S (Pages 6-8)
How did Native Americans live?

Native American people lived in many kinds of environments. For example, the **Pueblo** people lived in the dry Southwest (today's Arizona and New Mexico). They built adobe houses and grew corn and beans. In the forests of the Northeast (today's New York state), the **Iroquois** hunted, fished, and gathered fruits and nuts.

Trade routes across North America linked Native American groups that lived far apart. Trade allowed them to share both goods and ideas.

Native Americans did not buy and sell land. They treated the land as a resource for all groups to share. They felt that the world was filled with spirits. For instance, the spirit of a relative who had died might still serve as a guide to the living.

The family was the basic unit. Groups of families, or clans, got together for special events. By the time Europeans arrived in North America, Native American cultures were thousands of years old.

2. How did Native American people in different environments get their food?

_____

_____

WEST AFRICAN SOCIETIES OF THE 1400S (Pages 8-10)
What was life like in a West African kingdom?

Three powerful kingdoms with strong rulers played important roles in West Africa. Songhai controlled trade across the Sahara Desert. **Benin** was a powerful nation in the forests of the southern coast. In central Africa, the kingdom of the **Kongo** united smaller areas under one ruler.

Most West Africans lived with their families in small villages. They farmed, herded, hunted, and fished. The oldest people in the family had the most influence over the others.

Religious rituals were important in daily life. West Africans respected the spirits of living and non-living things. Many also believed in a single Creator.

By the 1400s, some West African leaders had accepted a new religion called Islam. **Islam** was founded by Muhammad in Arabia in 622. It taught that there is only one God, called Allah. Islam later spread among ordinary people.

The kingdoms of West Africa were connected to North Africa, Europe, and Asia by trade. Sailors and traders arrived from Portugal in the 1400s. Some Portuguese settled on islands off Africa. They started large farms, or plantations, to grow sugar cane. The Portuguese started the use of African slaves for field labor.

3. What were two ways of earning a living in a West African kingdom?

_____

_____

EUROPEAN SOCIETIES OF THE 1400S (Pages 10-13)
What was happening in Europe?

In European societies, everyone had a rank or position. Rulers and nobles owned the most land and were the most powerful. Leaders of the church, or clergy, were also important. At the bottom were the peasants, who worked in the fields. Most Europeans lived in small farming villages.

European society was beginning to change. **Christianity,** a religion based on the life and teachings of Jesus, was the dominant religion in Western Europe. In the early 1500s, reformers called for changes in the Church. Some of these reformers broke away from the Roman Catholic Church and formed Protestant churches. This movement was called the **Reformation.**

The Reformation led to a split in Europe between Catholics and Protestants. In this time four powerful nations arose: Portugal, Spain, France, and England.

The 1400s were the time of the **Renaissance,** a term meaning "rebirth" of the kind of interest in the physical world characterized by ancient Greece and Rome. The new learning led to inventions like the printing press and new ways to navigate with new sailing technology.

4. What were two important changes in Europe?

_____

_____

As you read about the cultures of the Americas, Africa, and Europe, fill out the chart below by writing notes that describe the achievements of those cultures.

	Achievements
1. Ancient Americans	
2. Native Americans	
3. West Africans	
4. Europeans	

Exploration and the Colonial Era

Section 2

Spanish North America

Terms and Names

Christopher Columbus Italian explorer who sailed to North America for Spain

Taino Native Americans who lived where Columbus first landed

Treaty of Tordesillas Agreement between Spain and Portugal to explore different lands

Columbian Exchange Trade across the Atlantic Ocean

conquistador Spanish explorer

Hernándo Cortés Conquistador who defeated the Aztecs

Montezuma The Aztec emperor

mestizo Person of mixed Spanish and Native American blood

encomienda Brutal Spanish system of using Native Americans for labor

New Spain Spanish colonies in Mexico and Central America

New Mexico Spanish colonies in North America

Before You Read

In the last section, you learned about the people living in North America, West Africa, and Europe. In this section, you will learn about what happened when the Spanish came to North America from Europe.

As You Read

Use a time line to record the major events of Columbus's voyages and the Spanish exploration of the New World.

COLUMBUS CROSSES THE ATLANTIC (Pages 14-15)
How did Columbus change people's lives?

Christopher Columbus was an Italian sailor. He believed he could find a new trade route to Asia by sailing west, across the Atlantic, instead of east. He asked the rulers of Spain to give him money and supplies. In exchange, he would claim new lands for Spain and convert the people he found to Christianity.

In 1492, Columbus sailed across the Atlantic. He landed on an island between North and South America, now called Hispaniola. He called the native people there **Taino,** from their word for "noble ones." He made three more voyages to the Americas, bringing soldiers, priests, and people to settle the land.

The arrival of the Spanish was a disaster for Native Americans. Many died from the harsh working conditions. Others caught diseases brought by Europeans. Because they had no resistance to these diseases, tens of thousands of Native Americans died.

Because of the Native American deaths, the Spanish needed more laborers. So they began to bring Africans to the New World as slaves. From the 1500s to the 1800s, about 10 million Africans were taken to the Americas.

Many European countries wanted to claim American land for themselves. In 1494, Spain and Portugal signed the **Treaty of Tordesillas.** It divided the Western Hemisphere north to south. Spain could explore and start colonies in areas west of the line. Portugal could have lands to the east.

After Columbus, ships carried trade goods between the Americas and Europe. This ongoing transfer of goods came to be known as the **Columbian Exchange.**

1. How did Columbus's arrival in the Americas affect Native Americans, Africans, and Europeans?

_____

_____

THE SPANISH CLAIM A NEW EMPIRE (Pages 16-18)
Why did Spain start colonies in the Americas?

After Columbus, many more Spanish explorers called **conquistadors** came to the Americas. They were looking for gold and silver.

The conquistador **Hernándo Cortés** heard about a rich empire in Mexico. With the help of some native people, Cortés's army conquered the Aztecs and took their gold. Then the Aztecs rebelled. **Montezuma** the Aztec emperor was killed. Finally, in 1521, the Spanish defeated the Aztecs again, partly because so many Aztecs had died of European diseases.

Most of the Spanish who settled in the Americas were men. They often married Native American women. This created a

large population of *mestizos,* people who were part Spanish and part Native American.

The Spanish forced native workers to labor under the *encomienda* system. Many workers were treated badly. Some died from overwork. In 1542, Spain ended the encomienda system because it was so brutal. Then Spanish settlers began to use African slaves.

Spain built a large empire in the Americas. The Spanish Empire in the New World included **New Spain,** which is what the Spanish called Mexico and part of Guatemala. Other parts of the Spanish Empire included Central America, and the land of the Incas in Peru. They also settled the American Southwest and Florida.

2. What was the result of Spain's outlawing the *encomienda* system?

_____

_____

SPAIN EXPLORES THE SOUTHWEST AND WEST (Pages 18-20)
Where did Spain send missionaries?

In 1540, the Spanish explorer Francisco Coronado explored the Southwest but found no gold and went home. Fifty years later the Spanish returned and founded the colony of **New Mexico** which extended throughout the southwestern United States. The capital of New Mexico was Santa Fe. New Mexico traded with New Spain. The goals of the colony were to convert the Pueblo peoples and to prevent other European nations from claiming this land.

In 1528, the Spanish began to build missions in what is now Texas. In 1769, they founded a string of missions in California. They converted Native Americans and taught them European styles and ways. The Native Americans did the work of farming and building the mission buildings.

   Some of the native people were angry at how they were treated by the Spanish. In 1680, the religious leader Popé led an uprising in New Mexico that drove the Spanish out of the area. It took the Spanish 14 years to get this area back.

3. Where did the Spanish missionaries build missions in North America?

_____

_____

As you read this section, fill out the chart below to help you better
understand the motivations and methods behind the conquests of the
conquistadors.

Columbus's Exploration of the Americas

Motivations	Methods
1. Why did Columbus come to the Americas?	2. How did European contact change the Americas?

Conquistadors' Conquest of Central and North America

Motivations	Methods
3. What motivated Spain's conquest?	4. How were the Spanish able to succeed?

Spanish Establishment of Missions

Motivations	Results
5. Why did the missionaries come to North America?	6. What resulted from the spread of missions?

Section 3

Early British Colonies

Terms and Names

John Smith Leader of Jamestown

Jamestown First permanent English settlement in North America

joint-stock companies Groups of investors who pooled their wealth in support of a colony they hoped would yield a profit

indentured servants Workers who exchanged labor for a home and food

Puritan Member of a religious group known for its strict beliefs

John Winthrop Leader of the first settlers at Massachusetts Bay Colony

King Philip's War Conflict between settlers and Native Americans

William Penn Founder of the colony of Pennsylvania

Quaker Member of a religious group known for tolerance

mercantilism Belief that nations should get gold and silver and can do so by having colonies

Navigation Acts Laws passed by the British to control colonial trade

---

Before You Read

In the last section, you learned how the Spanish claimed an empire in the Americas. In this section, you will learn how the British came to North America and founded their own colonies.

As You Read

Use a chart to identify the effects of events in the colonies.

THE ENGLISH SETTLE AT JAMESTOWN (Pages 21-23)
What happened at Jamestown?

In 1607, English settlers sent by the Virginia Company, led by **John Smith,** founded the colony of **Jamestown** in Virginia. The Virginia Company was one of a number of **joint-stock companies**— groups of investors who pooled their wealth in support of a colony they hoped would yield a profit.

Many colonists wanted to get rich quick by finding gold or furs. But Smith forced them to farm. He also got help from the native Powhatan people. After Smith returned to England, the colonists almost starved. They were saved when more colonists and supplies arrived from England.

Then the colonists discovered they could sell tobacco in Europe for a big profit. They hired **indentured servants** to work on tobacco plantations. These workers traveled to America from Europe. They received food and a place to live. In exchange, they agreed to work on a plantation.

The Jamestown colony grew and needed more land for farming. The

---

Guided Reading Workbook

English settlers took Powhatan land, and the Powhatan fought back.

The settlers also fought among themselves. Poor farmers complained about being taxed and governed without being able to vote. But their rebellion failed.

1. What were two problems Jamestown faced?

_____

_____

PURITANS CREATE A "NEW ENGLAND" (Pages 24-26)
Why did the Puritans come to America?

The **Puritans** were a religious group that wanted to purify the Church of England by removing some of the practices that were more like the Catholic Church. They had been punished in England. In 1620, a small group of Puritans came to North America and founded the colony of Plymouth.

In 1630, Puritans started the Massachusetts Bay Colony. Unlike the settlers in Jamestown, the Puritans were well prepared with people and supplies. **John Winthrop** was their first governor.

Puritans controlled the colony. They did not like dissent, or the expression of other points of view. Dissenters like Roger Williams and Anne Hutchinson both had to leave Massachusetts. They settled in what is now Rhode Island.

Native Americans helped the Puritans at first. As the colony grew, however, settlers began to take their lands. Native Americans died of European diseases. And the settlers wanted the Native Americans to accept Puritan laws and religion.

In 1675, **King Philip's War** began. A chief the English called King Philip led an

alliance of Native Americans against the settlers. The brutal war lasted over a year, until the English finally won.

2. What did the Puritans want to find in America?

_____

_____

SETTLEMENT OF THE MIDDLE COLONIES (Pages 26-28)
How were New Netherland and Pennsylvania alike?

Dutch settlers founded the colony of New Netherland in 1621. The capital of New Netherland was New Amsterdam. To encourage settlers to come and stay, the colony practiced religious tolerance and welcomed all ethnic groups and religions.

The Dutch had friendly relations with the Native Americans. In 1664, England took over the colony and renamed it New York.

The colony of Pennsylvania was founded by **William Penn.** Penn was a **Quaker.** The ideals of this religious group were equality, cooperation, and religious tolerance. Pennsylvania gave land to all adult men and had a representative assembly. Penn also treated Native Americans fairly.

3. What two things did New Netherland and Pennsylvania have in common?

_____

_____

ENGLAND AND ITS COLONIES PROSPER (Pages 28-30)
How did the colonies thrive?

Trade was the main reason England wanted colonies. The theory of **mercantilism** said that a nation becomes

Guided Reading Workbook

rich and powerful two ways: (1) by getting gold and silver, and (2) by selling more goods than it buys.

England's American colonies provided raw materials to England. They also bought goods made in England. Under this system, both England and its colonies gained wealth. In 1651, England's Parliament passed the **Navigation Acts.** Their purpose was to control trade with the colonies.

By 1732, there were 13 English colonies. Governors appointed by the king headed most colonial governments. Only white men who owned land could vote. Colonial assemblies had the right to raise taxes and make laws.

4. How did England benefit from its colonies?

_____

_____

As you read about Jamestown, the Massachusetts Bay Colony, New Netherland, and Pennsylvania, fill out the chart below by writing notes that describe aspects of each colony.

JAMESTOWN	
1. Settlers	2. Leaders
3. Motives for Settlement	4. Relations with Native Americans

MASSACHUSETTS BAY	
5. Settlers	6. Leaders
7. Motives for Settlement	8. Relations with Native Americans

NEW NETHERLAND	
9. Settlers	10. Motives for Settlement
11. Relations with Native Americans	12. Relations with England

PENNSYLVANIA	
13. Settlers	14. Leaders
15. Motives for Settlement	16. Relations with Native Americans

Exploration and the Colonial Era

The Colonies Come of Age

Terms and Names

triangular trade The pattern of shipping trade across the Atlantic

middle passage The voyage that brought slaves to America

Enlightenment Intellectual movement that started in Europe

Benjamin Franklin Philadelphia inventor, writer, and political leader

Great Awakening Religious revival movement in the colonies

Jonathan Edwards Forceful preacher in the Great Awakening

French and Indian War War that gave the British control of North America

William Pitt British leader in the French and Indian War

Pontiac Native American leader who fought the British

Proclamation of 1763 Law limiting the area of English settlement

Before You Read

In the last section, you learned how the British founded colonies in the Americas. In this section, you will learn about the growth of those colonies in the North and South.

As You Read

Use a web diagram to take notes on how trade and commerce affected regions in different time periods.

A PLANTATION ECONOMY ARISES IN THE SOUTH (Pages 31-33)
How did people farm in the South?

Colonists in the South created a society based on farming. A typical large Southern farm, or plantation, grew a single cash crop, such as tobacco or rice. Plantations often had their own warehouses and docks.

Most Southerners worked small farms. But the wealthy plantation owners, or planters, controlled the economy. They also controlled the social and political life of the South.

Planters used enslaved Africans as workers. Africans were brought to the Americas by a route across the Atlantic called the **middle passage.** This was one leg of the **triangular trade,** which had three main parts: (1) Merchants carried rum and other goods from New England to Africa; (2) they brought slaves from Africa to the West Indies, where they sold them for sugar and molasses; (3) finally, they sold those goods in New England.

Africans were brought to America on crowded ships. They were treated cruelly, and many died. Once in America, slaves tried to hold onto their African culture. Many resisted slavery, and some led revolts. This resulted in even harsher slave laws.

Guided Reading Workbook

1. What were two main features of farming in the South?

_____

_____

COMMERCE GROWS IN THE NORTH (Pages 33-34)
How did people earn a living in the North?

The economy of the North was based on small farms, manufacturing, and trade. Bustling port cities developed. Ship-building was important, and traders sailed all over the world. Merchants became wealthy and important. The Northern colonies attracted many immigrants from Europe.

Farms in the North usually produced several cash crops. They did not depend on slave labor. However, slavery and racial prejudice did exist in the North.

2. What are three kinds of work people did in the North?

_____

_____

THE ENLIGHTENMENT; THE GREAT AWAKENING
(Pages 34-36)
What new ideas and beliefs spread in the colonies?

The **Enlightenment** was a philosophical movement that said you could use reason and science to find truth. It began in Europe and spread to the colonies. **Benjamin Franklin** was one of its leaders. He conducted scientific experiments and made several practical inventions.

The Enlightenment had two important effects: (1) its emphasis on science as a source of truth weakened the authority of the church, and (2) the idea that people have natural rights which governments must respect challenged the authority of the British rulers.

The **Great Awakening** was a series of religious revivals that spread through the colonies. **Jonathan Edwards** was one of its most powerful preachers. By awakening renewed religious feelings, the Great Awakening challenged the authority of existing churches. New Christian denominations became popular.

3. How did the Enlightenment and the Great Awakening change people's beliefs?

_____

_____

THE FRENCH AND INDIAN WAR
(Pages 37-39)
What caused the French and Indian War?

Like Britain, France also had colonies in the Americas. France's vast empire included eastern Canada, the Great Lakes region, and the upper Mississippi River.

Most French settlers were fur traders or Catholic priests who wanted to convert the Native Americans. The French had better relations with the Native Americans than the English did.

The British and French fought over the western lands. In 1754, the **French and Indian War** began. At first, the British and the colonies were losing the war. Then the English king appointed **William Pitt** to the government. Under Pitt's leadership, the British began to win battles. After they took the city of Quebec, the British had won the war. In 1763, France gave up Canada and all of North America east of the Mississippi to Britain.

Native Americans did not like British settlers moving west onto their lands. Led by **Pontiac,** an Ottawa chief, they attacked British forts. The British purposely gave smallpox to Native Americans who came to discuss peace. The spreading disease weakened the Native American groups, and they surrendered.

To prevent further fighting, the British banned colonists from settling west of a line along the Appalachian Mountains.

Many colonists were angered by this **Proclamation of 1763,** and continued to settle the area anyway.

4. What was the main cause of the war?

_____

_____

As you read this section, fill out the chart below with some different characteristics of the Northern and Southern colonies.

Northern Colonies	Southern Colonies

Fill out this chart by comparing the Enlightenment and the Great Awakening.

	The Enlightenment	The Great Awakening
1. What kind of movement was it (intellectual, social, political, religious)?		
2. Who were its key figures in the colonies?		
3. What ideas did it stress?		
4. What did it encourage people to do?		

Colonial Resistance and Rebellion

Terms and Names

King George III King of England during the American Revolution

Sugar Act Law passed by Parliament to try to raise money

Stamp Act Law passed by Parliament to make colonists buy a stamp to place on many items such as wills and newspapers

Samuel Adams One of the founders of the Sons of Liberty

Boston Massacre Conflict between colonists and British soldiers in which four colonists were killed

Boston Tea Party Protest against increased tea prices in which colonists dumped British tea into Boston Harbor

John Locke English philosopher who believed people had natural rights to life, liberty, and property

Common Sense Pamphlet written by Thomas Paine that attacked monarchy

Thomas Jefferson Main author of the Declaration of Independence

Declaration of Independence Document that said the United States was an independent nation

Before You Read

In the last section, you learned how the British and their American colonists pushed the French out of North America. In this section, you will see how the American colonists rebelled against the British and declared independence.

As You Read

Use a cluster diagram to take notes on the conflict between Great Britain and the American colonies.

THE COLONIES ORGANIZE TO RESIST BRITAIN (Pages 46-47)
Why were the colonists angry?

The French And Indian War cost Great Britain a lot of money. **King George III's** prime minister, George Grenville, was surprised to find that the Colonial customs service was losing money. Grenville was sure the Colonists were smuggling goods into the colonies to avoid paying taxes. Grenville had Parliament pass two new sets of taxes, the **Sugar Act** and the **Stamp Act,** to reform the tax system and raise money to help pay for the war. The Sugar Act raised taxes on imports and called for smugglers to be tried in British,

Guided Reading Workbook

not Colonial courts. The Stamp Act imposed a tax on many items including wills, newspapers and playing cards.

Some colonists felt that Britain had no right to tax them because colonists were not represented in Parliament. They felt this violated their rights as British citizens. Some colonists became angry at the British government.

Colonial assemblies protested the taxes as did merchants in New York, Boston, and Philadelphia who agreed to boycott British goods until the Stamp Act was repealed. Parliament did repeal the Stamp Act but replaced it with new taxes called the Townshend Acts which included a tax on tea. **Samuel Adams,** one of the founders of the Sons of Liberty, led protests.

1. How did the colonists respond to new taxes?

_____

_____

TENSION MOUNTS IN MASSACHUSETTS (Pages 48-49)
Why did the colonists stay angry?

In 1770, some British soldiers fired on a mob of colonists. Several colonists were killed. Colonial leaders called the event the **Boston Massacre.**

For a while the situation relaxed. The British repealed all the taxes except the one on tea. In 1773, Britain gave a British company the right to all the trade in tea. Colonial merchants were angry at losing business. Colonists dressed as "Indians" dumped the British tea into Boston Harbor. This was called the **Boston Tea Party.**

To punish Massachusetts, Britain passed the Intolerable Acts which closed Boston Harbor and placed Boston under martial law. Other colonies supported Massachusetts and sent representatives to the First Continental Congress. They issued a declaration of colonial rights. They said that if Britain attacked, the colonies should fight back.

2. How did Britain try to punish Boston for its protests?

_____

_____

THE ROAD TO REVOLUTION
(Pages 50-51)
How did the colonists prepare for war?

Some New England towns began to prepare for attack. Minutemen stored guns and ammunition. In 1775, the British marched to Lexington, Massachusetts, to seize these weapons. In the battle of Lexington and Concord, the colonists defeated the British.

The Second Continental Congress met. Some leaders urged independence, but others were not ready. Still, they agreed to form the Continental Army with George Washington in command. Hoping to succeed in battle, the British attacked the colonists on Breed's Hill in what became known as the Battle of Bunker Hill. It resulted in 450 casualties for the colonists and over 1,000 for the British.

The Second Continental Congress sent King George III a peace offer, but he rejected it. Instead, the king declared that the colonies were in rebellion.

3. What actions did the colonies take to prepare for war?

_____

_____

THE PATRIOTS DECLARE INDEPENDENCE (Pages 52-53)
What ideas supported rebellion?

More colonists began to object to British rule. Colonial leaders were influenced by the ideas of **John Locke**. Locke said that people have a right to life, liberty, and property. People form a social contract, or an agreement, with their government. If the government takes away the people's rights, the people can overthrow the government.

Thomas Paine argued for independence in his pamphlet *Common Sense*. Many people read it and agreed with his arguments.

Drafted by **Thomas Jefferson,** the **Declaration of Independence** was adopted by the Second Continental Congress on July 4, 1776. Jefferson used some of Locke's ideas in the Declaration. He said that people's rights to life, liberty, and the pursuit of happiness cannot be taken away. Government gets its power from the people, and the people can remove a government that threatens their rights. Then he listed the ways the British had taken away the colonists' rights.

4. What ideas of John Locke did Thomas Jefferson put in the Declaration of Independence?

   _____

   _____

Section 1, *continued*

As you read this section, trace the following sequence of events.

1a. The British Parliament passed the Stamp Act (1765) in order to . . .	b. Colonists responded to the act by . . .	c. Britain responded to the colonists by . . .
2a. The British Parliament passed the Townshend Acts (1767) in order to . . .	b. Colonists responded to the act by . . .	c. Britain responded to the colonists by . . .
3a. The British Parliament passed the Tea Act (1773) in order to . . .	b. Colonists responded to the act by . . .	c. Britain responded to the colonists by . . .
4a. The British Parliament passed the Intolerable Acts (1774) in order to . . .	b. Colonists responded to the act by . . .	c. Britain responded to the colonists by . . .

Section 2

The War for Independence

Terms and Names

Loyalists Colonists who were loyal to Britain

Patriots Colonists who wanted independence from Britain

Saratoga Battle won by the Americans in 1777

Valley Forge Place where Washington's army spent the winter of 1777–1778

inflation Rise in the price of goods

Marquis de Lafayette French noble who helped the Americans

Charles Cornwallis British general

Yorktown Battle that gave the Americans victory in the war

Treaty of Paris Treaty that officially ended the war

egalitarianism A belief in equality

Before You Read

In the last section, you learned why the colonists rebelled against the British. In this section, you will see how the Americans won the Revolutionary War and established a new nation.

As You Read

Use a chart to take notes on events of the Revolutionary War and their significance.

THE WAR BEGINS (Pages 59-60)
What **were the important battles?**

Colonists were divided equally between Loyalists and Patriots. The Revolution was both a war for independence and a civil war.

Loyalists supported the British and were loyal to the king. Some felt that the British could protect their rights better than a new government could. Others did not want to be punished as rebels. Many went to British North America, or Canada.

Patriots wanted independence. Some wanted to be free of British rule. Others saw economic opportunity in a new nation.

Many African Americans joined the Patriots. Others fought on the British side because they were offered freedom from slavery. Most Native Americans supported the British.

In March 1776, the British army seized New York City. Their aim was to isolate New England. But on Christmas night of 1776, Washington crossed the Delaware River and took Trenton, New Jersey. He soon scored another victory. These wins gave Americans hope.

In the fall of 1777, the Americans won an important victory at **Saratoga,** New York. This win proved that American forces could defeat the British army. It convinced France to support the Americans.

Later, Washington's army suffered from cold and hunger during a winter at **Valley Forge,** Pennsylvania.

Guided Reading Workbook

1. Why was the Battle of Saratoga important?

_____

_____

LIFE DURING THE REVOLUTION
(**Pages** 60-61)
How did the war affect people?

The war touched all Americans. Congress printed money to pay American troops. The more money they printed, the less the money was worth. This caused **inflation,** which is a rise in the price of goods.

As men went to war, many women took their husbands' places running homes, farms, and businesses. Some women earned money washing and cooking for the troops. A few even went into battle.

Thousands of slaves escaped to freedom during the war. About 5,000 African Americans served in the Continental Army. Their courage and loyalty impressed many white Americans.

2. How did the war affect different groups of Americans?

_____

_____

WINNING THE WAR (**Pages** 61-62)
Why did the Americans win?

In 1778, the Americans got help. The **Marquis de Lafayette,** a French nobleman, joined Washington. He helped make the American army an effective fighting force. The French also sent soldiers and their navy to help the Americans.

The British moved their war effort south. British general **Charles Cornwallis** moved his army to Yorktown, Virginia. Meanwhile, French military forces arrived in America.

French and American forces surrounded the British at **Yorktown.** French ships defeated British naval forces. Cornwallis could not get help. The British surrendered at Yorktown on October 19, 1783.

The **Treaty of Paris** was signed in 1783. Britain recognized the United States as a nation with borders from the Atlantic Ocean to the Mississippi River.

3. How did the French help the Americans win the war?

_____

_____

THE WAR BECOMES A SYMBOL OF LIBERTY (**Page** 63)
What did the Revolution mean?

The ideas that led to the Revolution influenced the new nation. The war also brought changes. Differences between rich and poor had not been important during the war. Military leaders had shown respect to their men regardless of their background or social status. These changes caused a rise in **egalitarianism,** a belief in equality. It included the idea that people should be valued for ability and effort—not wealth or family.

This egalitarianism applied only to white males. The status of women, African Americans, and Native Americans did not change. They still did not have the rights that white male property-owners did. Married women's property still belonged to their husbands, and settlers continued to encroach upon Native American tribal lands.

4. Whom did the rise in egalitarianism apply to?

_____

_____

As you read this section, write answers to the questions about each of the
Revolutionary War battles listed below.

	Who won?	Why did they win?	What were the important results?
1. New York			
2. Trenton			
3. Saratoga			
4. Yorktown			

Summarize the difficulties faced by each group of Patriots during the
Revolutionary War?

Patriots	What were some of the hardships they faced?
1. Soldiers	
2. Members of Congress	
3. Civilians	

Revolution and the Early Republic

Confederation and the Constitution

Terms and Names

republic A government in which the people elect representatives to govern

Articles of Confederation Document outlining the first form of government of the United States

Northwest Ordinance of 1787 Law that organized the Northwest Territories

Shays's Rebellion Anti-tax protest by farmers

James Madison One of the leaders of the Constitutional Convention

federalism System in which power is shared between the national government and state governments

checks and balances Powers given to separate branches of government to keep any one from getting too much power

ratification Official approval of the Constitution

Federalists Supporters of the new Constitution

Antifederalists People opposed to ratification of the new Constitution

Bill of Rights Set of amendments passed to protect individual rights

Before You Read

In the last section, you learned how the people of the United States won their independence. In this section, you will read about the early years of the young nation.

As You Read

Use a web diagram to take notes on specific issues that were debated at the Constitutional Convention.

EXPERIMENTING WITH CONFEDERATION (Pages 66-67)
What was the Confederation?

Americans wanted a **republic**—a government in which the people elect representatives to govern. But many people feared that a democracy— government directly by the people— placed too much power in the hands of the uneducated masses.

The Second Continental Congress wrote the **Articles of Confederation.** It gave much power to the states and little power to the federal government. This plan set up a Congress elected by the people. Each state had one vote in Congress.

The Confederation had some successes. One was the **Northwest Ordinance of 1787.** It organized the land west of the Appalachian Mountains into territories. It decided how new states would enter the union.

But the Confederation also had problems. States with small populations had the same power as large states. Congress did not have the power to tax. The Articles could not be changed without the agreement of all states.

There were economic problems, too. Congress had borrowed large amounts of money during the war. To pay these debts, the states raised taxes. High taxes were a problem for many Americans.

Farmers were losing their land because they could not pay the high taxes. In 1787, a tax protest by farmers, which was called **Shays's Rebellion,** led to violence. The Massachusetts militia killed four protestors.

The weak national government could not solve the nation's problems. In 1787, 12 states sent delegates to Philadelphia to fix the Articles of Confederation.

1. What problems did the Confederation face?

_____

_____

CREATING A NEW GOVERNMENT
(Pages 68-69)
Who had the power in the new Constitution?

The delegates decided to form a whole new government. **James Madison,** a delegate from Virginia, was one of the leaders of the convention.

The delegates made compromises. To settle the dispute between big states and small states, they agreed on a legislature with two houses. Each state would have two members in the Senate, or upper house. In the House of Representatives, or lower house, representation would be

based on a state's population. The Three-Fifths Compromise allowed states to count three-fifths of their slaves as part of their population. Power was divided between the national government and the states in a system called **federalism.** But the central government was stronger than it was under the Articles.

The delegates agreed to a separation of powers. Congress, the legislative branch, would make the laws. The executive branch would carry out laws. The judicial branch would settle legal disputes. They created a system of **checks and balances** to prevent any branch from getting too much power. They also created a way of changing, or passing amendments to, the Constitution.

2. How was power divided in the new Constitution?

_____

_____

RATIFYING THE CONSTITUTION
(Pages 69-71)
Would you vote to ratify the Constitution?

The convention decided that **ratification,** or official approval, of the Constitution would be in state conventions. Voters elected representatives to the conventions.

Federalists supported the new Constitution. They published essays called *The Federalist Papers* to explain and defend the Constitution. **Antifederalists** opposed the Constitution. They thought it gave the central government too much power. They wanted a bill of rights, a formal, written guarantee of people's rights and freedoms, like many states had. Federalists promised to add a Bill of Rights. Because of this promise, the

Guided Reading Workbook

required nine states ratified the Constitution in 1789.

The **Bill of Rights** consisted of ten amendments that guaranteed Americans rights such as freedom of religion, speech, and the press. They protected citizens from the threat of standing armies. They protected citizens against having their homes searched and property seized. They also protected the rights of people accused of crimes. Finally, they gave all powers that were not given to the federal government to the people and the states. The Bill of Rights was ratified in 1791.

3. How did the Federalists and Antifederalists feel about the Constitution?

_____

_____

CONTINUING RELEVANCE OF THE CONSTITUTION (Page 71)
Why is the Constitution still important?

The Constitution has met the changing needs of Americans for over 200 years. That is because it is flexible.

The Constitution can be changed, or amended, when needed. But the amendment process is difficult. In over 200 years, there have been only 27 amendments to the Constitution.

4. Why has the Constitution been able to meet the changing needs of the country for so long?

_____

_____

As you read how our Constitution was developed, take notes summarizing
issues in the chart below.

1. The Virginia Plan proposed a Congress composed of:	2. The New Jersey Plan called for a Congress consisting of:

↓

3. The Virginia Plan proposed that representation in Congress be based on: Other large states agreed.	4. The New Jersey Plan proposed that congressional representation be based on: Other small states agreed.

5. How did the Great Compromise resolve this conflict?

↓

6. Northern states felt that representation in Congress should be based on the number of:	7. Southern states felt that representation should be based on the number of:

8. How did the Three-Fifths Compromise resolve this conflict?

Revolution and the Early Republic

Launching the New Nation

Terms and Names

Judiciary Act of 1789 Law that set up the national court system

Alexander Hamilton An early Federalist leader

cabinet Chief advisors of the president

two-party system Political system where two political parties compete for power

Democratic-Republican Political party led by Thomas Jefferson

protective tariff Tax on imported goods to protect domestic business

XYZ Affair American anger over bribes demanded by French diplomats

Alien and Sedition Acts Laws that made it harder to become a citizen and created harsh punishments for people who criticize the government

nullification Effort by a state to cancel a federal law

Before You Read

In the last section, you learned how the new Constitution was created. In this section, you will see how the new government acted.

As You Read

Use a chart to list the leaders, beliefs, and goals of the country's first political parties.

WASHINGTON HEADS THE NEW GOVERNMENT (Pages 74-76)
Why did Hamilton and Jefferson disagree?

George Washington was the first president of the United States. He and Congress set up the new government. The **Judiciary Act of 1789** set up a national court system.

Congress also set up three executive departments. Washington appointed **Alexander Hamilton** as secretary of the treasury, Thomas Jefferson as secretary of state, and Henry Knox as secretary of war. These men became the president's chief advisers, or **cabinet.**

Hamilton, who wanted a strong central government, wanted to create a national bank. Jefferson, who wanted a weak central government, opposed this. He and James Madison argued against Hamilton. Finally, they agreed to Hamilton's national bank. In exchange, the new capital of the nation was built in the South, in Washington, D.C.

The differences between Hamilton and Jefferson helped to give rise to the **two-party system,** in which two political parties compete for power. Federalists agreed with Hamilton. **Democratic-Republicans** agreed with Jefferson that state governments should be stronger.

Congress passed two important taxes. One was a **protective tariff.** It placed a tax on goods imported from Europe. But Hamilton wanted more tax money.

Guided Reading Workbook

He pushed through a tax on whiskey. Whiskey was made by small farmers on the frontier. They were so angry about the tax that they attacked the tax collectors.

Hamilton wanted to show that the federal government could enforce the law on the frontier. The Whiskey Rebellion was put down by federal troops.

1. What were the different views of government held by Hamilton and Jefferson?

_____

_____

CHALLENGES AT HOME AND ABROAD (Pages 76-77)
What were America's earliest foreign policy problems?

In 1789 the French overthrew their monarchy. Then the French went to war against Britain. The United States had a treaty with France. Democratic-Republicans wanted to honor the treaty and support France. Federalists wanted to back the British. Washington decided on neutrality—to support neither side.

In 1795 Spain and the United States signed the Pinckney Treaty. Spain gave up claims to land east of the Mississippi. This treaty also paved the way for the westward expansion of the United States.

Settlers streamed into the Northwest Territory. This angered the Native Americans there. They continued to claim their tribal lands. Native Americans formed a confederacy that won some battles against American troops. In 1794 federal troops defeated the confederacy.

At the same time, John Jay negotiated a treaty with Britain. The British agreed to give up their forts in the Northwest

Territory. Still, the British continued to bother American ships in the Caribbean.

2. How did the United States handle problems with France and Spain?

_____

_____

ADAMS PROVOKES CRITICISM (Pages 77-79)
Was John Adams a good president?

President Washington retired. Federalist John Adams was elected president. Thomas Jefferson, a Democratic-Republican, became vice-president.

France began to interfere with American shipping. Adams sent representatives to France. Three French officials demanded bribes from the Americans. This was called the **XYZ Affair.** Some Americans felt insulted and wanted war against France. But Adams settled the matter through diplomacy.

Adams thought the Democratic-Republicans and immigrants who supported them were dangerous. The Federalists supported the **Alien and Sedition Acts.** These acts, passed in 1798, made it harder to become an American citizen and created harsh punishment for people who criticized the government.

Democratic-Republicans opposed these laws. Kentucky and Virginia claimed that states could cancel laws that they thought were unconstitutional. This is called **nullification.**

3. How did Adams handle the fear of foreign influence at home?

_____

_____

Section 4, *continued*

Fill out the chart below, taking notes about Washington's two terms as president.

Government Organization	
1. What did the Judiciary Act of 1789 establish?	2. What departments did Washington create and whom did he appoint to head them?

Philosophies of Government	
3. How did Jefferson feel about political power and the common people?	4. How did Hamilton feel about political power and the common people?
5. Why did Jefferson and Madison oppose the national bank?	6. Why did Hamilton support the national bank?

Party Politics	
7. To which party did Jefferson belong?	8. To which party did Hamilton belong?
9. Which region in general supported the Federalists? The Democratic-Republicans?	

The Preamble and Article 1: The Legislature

Terms and Names

Preamble Introduction to the Constitution

Congress National legislature

House of Representatives Lower house of the national legislature

Senate Upper house of the national legislature

checks and balances Provisions of the Constitution that keep one branch of the government from controlling the other two branches

enumerated powers Powers specifically granted in the Constitution

implied powers Powers not specifically stated in the Constitution

elastic clauses Clause in the Constitution that allows Congress to pass laws necessary to carry out its enumerated powers

---

Before You Read

In the last section, you saw how the new government began to work under the Constitution. In this section, you will learn about the Constitution itself—how the Preamble introduces the Constitution and explains its purpose and how Article 1 sets up the Congress.

As You Read

Use an outline to take notes on the Preamble and on the powers of Congress.

PREAMBLE. PURPOSE OF THE CONSTITUTION (Page 84)
***What* does the Preamble do?**

The **Preamble,** or introduction, sets out to do two things. The first is to show the legitimacy of the new government, or its right to rule. The Preamble shows that this government is based on the agreement of those who are to be governed. It is the people themselves who have the power to create a government. That is why the Constitution begins with, "We the people of the United States . . . do ordain and establish this Constitution."

This statement also shows that the legitimacy of this government does not come from the states. Instead, it comes from the people. The Confederation was an agreement among the states, and the national government was too weak.

The second purpose of the Preamble is to state why this new government is being formed:

- to improve the structure of the government,
- to create justice and peace within the nation,
- to protect the nation from outside attack,

- to ensure the well-being of the people,
- to keep citizens and their descendants free.

1. What are the two purposes of the Preamble?

_____

_____

ARTICLE 1. SECTIONS 1–7: THE LEGISLATURE (Pages 84–86)
How are the House and Senate different?

The framers of the Constitution set up **Congress** first. It was to be the legislature, or law-making branch of government. The framers saw the Congress as the central branch of government because it represents the people most directly.

Congress is made up of two houses. The **House of Representatives** is sometimes called "the House" or "the lower house." Its members are most responsible to the people who elect them because they serve for only two years. Then they must run for reelection. The number of representatives each state can send to the House is based on population. Thus, the House reflects the will of the majority of the people of the nation.

The **Senate** is sometimes called the "upper house." To make the government more stable, the framers made the Senate more removed from the will of the people. To do this, they had Senators chosen by state legislatures. (They are now elected directly by the voters in each state [Amendment 17]). Senators are elected for longer terms than House members, six-years.

Only one-third of the Senate is elected every two years. That also adds stability. Each state, regardless of population, has two Senators. This equal representation

gives small states more power in the Senate than they have in the House.

Section 2.5 of Article 1 gives the House the power of impeachment. It can bring charges of misbehavior in office against officials in other branches of government, including the president. When the House impeaches a federal official, the Senate tries the case. It takes a two-thirds vote of the Senate to convict the impeached person.

The power of impeachment means that the legislative and judicial branches can make sure that a president does not take too much power. It is part of the system of **checks and balances,** in which the Constitution prevents any branch from dominating the others.

2. What are two important differences between the House and the Senate?

_____

_____

SECTIONS 8–10: POWERS OF THE LEGISLATURE (Pages 86–90)
What power does Congress have?

Section 7 of Article 1 explains how new laws are passed. A bill may be introduced in either the House or the Senate. But it must be approved by a majority vote in both houses. To become a law, a bill needs the approval of the president. That is part of the system of checks and balances. It gives the president, who is elected by all of the people, a say in what becomes the law of the land. If the president does not sign, or approve, the bill, he is said to veto it. The bill can still become law if two-thirds of both houses vote to override the veto. This procedure ensures that the president does not have too much power.

Section 7 also states that all bills for raising money—such as taxes—must

Guided Reading Workbook

begin in the House of Representatives. That is the house most responsive to the people. The Senate may propose changes to the bill.

Section 8 lists particular powers of the Congress. They are often called the federal government's **enumerated powers.** They include the power to tax, to borrow money, and to set up courts. Clauses 11–16 in Section 8 make sure that the civilians control the military. This is designed to prevent the armed forces from staging a coup, or seizing control of the government.

The 18th clause is different. It gives Congress the power to do what is "necessary and proper" to carry out its other powers. This is the basis of the **implied powers** of the federal

government. It is called the **elastic clause** because it can be used to stretch, or expand, the government's power.

Section 9 tells what powers the federal government does not have. Clauses 2 and 3 say the government cannot take away a citizen's right to a fair trial. Section 10 tells what powers the states do not have. It emphasizes that they cannot make treaties or war. Only a sovereign nation can do that.

3. How does Congress limit the power of the president and the military?

_____

_____

As you read the Preamble and Article 1 of the Constitution, answer the questions below. Circle **Yes** or **No** for each question and provide the location of the information that supports your answer. All information is in Article 1, so you need to supply only the section and clause information. Section 4, Clause 2 would be written 4.2.

Example: Do states have varying numbers of Senators? _____ Location _____   Yes 3.1 (No)

1. Lois Deevers, a Texan for two years, is 26 years old and has been a U.S. citizen for ten years. Could she serve as a congresswoman from Texas? _____ Location _____   Yes   No

2. Ky Pham is 32 years old and became a U.S. citizen at the age of 24. Could he serve as a senator from Maine, where he has lived his entire life? _____ Location _____   Yes   No

3. If the Senate votes 49 to 49 on a bill, does the President of the Senate cast the tie-breaking vote? _____ Location _____   Yes   No

4. Can a senator be sued for slander because of things he or she said in a speech on the floor of the Senate? ___._____ Location _____   Yes   No

5. If Congress creates a new government agency, can a senator or representative resign from office to become the head of that agency? _____ Location _____   Yes   No

6. Can the Senate expel one of its members? _____ Location _____   Yes   No

7. If the House unanimously votes to override a presidential veto, and the Senate votes to override by a vote of 64 to 34, does the bill become law? _____ Location _____   Yes   No

8. Can Congress pass an *ex post facto* law if both houses favor it by a two-thirds majority? _____ Location _____   Yes   No

9. Can a state impose an import tax on goods entering from another state? _____ Location _____   Yes   No

10. Could a bill pass the Senate by a vote of 26 to 27? _____ Location _____   Yes   No

11. If a bill is sent to the president one week before Congress adjourns, and the president neither signs it nor returns it, does it become law? _____ Location _____   Yes   No

12. Can a state legally engage in war with a foreign nation if the state is invaded by troops of that nation? _____ Location _____   Yes   No

Articles 2 and 3: The Executive and the Judiciary

Terms and Names

chief executive President of the United States

electoral college Electors chosen by the states to elect the president and vice president

succession Order in which the office of president is filled if it becomes vacant before an election

State of the Union Address Message delivered by the president once a year

Supreme Court Highest federal court in the United States

judicial power Authority to decide cases involving disputes over the law or behavior of people

judicial review Authority to decide whether a law is constitutional

Before You Read

In the last section, you saw that the Preamble introduced the Constitution and that Article 1 dealt with the powers of Congress. In this section, you will see that Article 2 covers the powers of the president and Article 3 lists the powers of the judiciary.

As You Read

Continue your outline of the Constitution, and take notes on the powers of the executive and the judicial branches of government.

ARTICLE 2. THE EXECUTIVE
(Pages 90–92)
What are the powers of the president?

The president is the **chief executive,** or administrator of the nation. It is his or her responsibility to "take care that laws be faithfully executed," or carried out.

Section 1.2 sets up the **electoral college.** The president and vice-president are elected by electors chosen by the states. At first, this clause did not work well in practice. In 1800, when only one ballot was used to elect both president and vice-president, two candidates received the same number of votes. The election had to be settled by the House of Representatives. To prevent this from happening again, the Twelfth Amendment was passed in 1804. It calls for separate ballots for president and vice-president.

However, the electoral college is still important. Each state has as many electors as it has senators and representatives in Congress. That is why presidential candidates work hard to "carry," or get the majority of the popular vote in, the largest states. The candidate that gets the majority of votes in a state gets all the electoral votes of that state.

Section 1.6 explains **succession:** what happens if a president dies in office or leaves office for another reason. It is important that everyone understands who will assume the power of the president. That prevents a struggle for power or a time when no one is in charge. It also makes sure that power will be transferred in a peaceful and orderly manner.

The president's salary cannot be changed during his or her term of office. In other words, the president cannot be punished or rewarded by payment for particular policies or official acts.

Section 2.1 makes the president commander-in-chief of the armed forces. This authority is another way to ensure civilian control of the military. It is also another example of checks and balances, because only Congress has the power to declare war. In practice, this authority has caused some problems. Since the president has the power to give orders to American military forces, some presidents have taken military action against the wishes of Congress and without a declaration of war.

Presidential appointments are another example of the separation of powers. The president can appoint ambassadors, justices of the Supreme Court, and other officials only "with the advice and consent of the Senate." In other words, the Senate must approve these appointments. The president can also make treaties, but these must also be approved by the Senate.

"Heads of departments" are mentioned in Section 2.1. These departments actually carry out the functions of the executive branch of government under the direction of the president. The heads of important departments make up the president's Cabinet.

The framers included reporting to the Congress as one of the president's

duties. This requirement has led to the president making a **State of the Union Address** once a year. It is a report to the other branches of government and to the people. Its subject is the condition, or state, of the nation. The address includes the president's plans and policies for the year.

1. What are two examples of checks and balances found in Article 2?

_____

_____

ARTICLE 3. THE JUDICIARY
(**Pages** 92–93)
What are the powers of the federal courts?

Article 3 sets up the judicial branch of the federal government. It establishes one **Supreme Court** but leaves the rest of the "inferior," or lower, federal courts to be set up by Congress. District courts and federal courts of appeal are now part of the regular federal court system. (States have their own court systems that deal with state laws.) Federal judges are appointed by the president with the approval of the Senate.

Judges serve "during good behavior." In other words, they are appointed for life, unless they are found guilty of misbehavior, or inappropriate conduct. The salary of a judge cannot be lowered while the judge is in office.

The federal courts have jurisdiction, or authority, only in certain kinds of cases. These are listed in Section 2. The Constitution gives the courts **judicial power**—the authority to decide cases involving disputes over the law or behavior of people. It does not specifically grant the Supreme Court the power of **judicial review**—the authority to decide

Guided Reading Workbook

whether a law is constitutional. The Supreme Court claimed this authority in the famous case of *Marbury* v. *Madison* in 1803.

Clause 3 again protects citizens' rights to a trial by jury. (See Article 1, Section 9.) The framers' concern for this right is a result of the American colonists' experiences under British rule.

2. What does the federal judiciary do?

_____

_____

As you read Articles 2 and 3, answer each of the following questions by writing **Yes** or **No** on the blank line. Each question is specifically answered by the Constitution.

Article 2

_____ 1. Is the length of a president's term set by the Constitution?

_____ 2. Does the number of electors that each state has in the Electoral College vary from state to state?

_____ 3. Must national elections be held in November?

_____ 4. Can a 30-year-old, natural-born citizen hold the office of president?

_____ 5. Can an 80-year-old person who became a U.S. citizen at the age of 21 hold the office of president?

_____ 6. Does a president's salary always remain the same while in office?

_____ 7. Must someone elected to the presidency take an oath before taking office?

_____ 8. Can the president pardon someone convicted of treason?

_____ 9. Must the president report to Congress about how the nation is doing?

_____ 10. Can a president convicted of bribery remain in office?

Article 3

_____ 11. Can a president dismiss a member of the Supreme Court and replace him or her with someone more in agreement with the president?

_____ 12. Can the salary paid to a federal judge be lowered while that judge remains in office?

_____ 13. Must a case in which a resident of Nebraska sues a citizen of Louisiana be heard in a federal court?

_____ 14. Can someone who publicly urges others to overthrow the federal government be convicted of treason for that position?

_____ 15. Can a person who gives secret information about U.S. military plans to a foreign government be convicted of treason?

_____ 16. Can a person who denies having committed treason be convicted on the testimony of a single person who witnessed the treasonous act?

Articles 4–7: The States and the Federal Government; Amendments and Ratification

Terms and Names

extradition Procedure for returning a person charged with a crime to the state where the crime was committed

ratify Officially approve the Constitution or an Amendment to it

Before You Read

In the last section, you saw how Articles 2 and 3 set forth the powers of the executive and judicial branches. In this section, you will see how Articles 4–7 grant specific powers to the national and state governments. You will also learn how the Constitution assures the unity of the nation and the supremacy of the national government.

As You Read

Continue your outline of the Constitution, and take notes on the relations among the states and between the states and the national government.

ARTICLE 4. RELATIONS AMONG STATES (Page 94)
Who has more power—the states or the national government?

Article 4 sets out many principles of the federal system. It describes the relations among the states. It also describes the relations between the national government and the states.

Sections 1 and 2 make it clear that the United States is one nation. The separate states must accept decisions, such as criminal convictions, that occur in other states. Section 2.2 allows for **extradition.** This means that if a person charged with a crime in one state flees to another state, he or she must be returned to the state where the crime was committed.

Section 2 also makes it clear that citizens of the United States are citizens of the whole nation. They have the same rights and privileges of citizenship no matter which state they are in. However, slaves were not considered to be citizens and so did not have the rights of citizens.

Clause 3 provides for the return of runaway slaves to their masters, even if the slave escapes to another state. This shows that the Constitution recognized slavery as legitimate, even though the word "slave" is not used. When the Thirteenth Amendment abolished slavery in 1865, it effectively canceled this clause.

Section 3 describes the process for forming new states. It says that new states cannot be formed within any existing state without that state's approval. However, there is a case where something very close to that happened. During the Civil War, Virginia seceded, or separated, from the Union. However, the people of the western part of Virginia did not want to secede. They asked Congress for permission to form the new state of West Virginia. They wanted West Virginia to be part of the Union. Congress agreed. After the Civil War, the legislature of Virginia gave its formal approval to the creation of West Virginia.

1. List two ways the framers made it clear that the United States is one nation, not a loose confederation of semi-independent states.

_____

_____

ARTICLES 5–7. AMENDING THE CONSTITUTION; THE SUPREMACY OF THE NATIONAL GOVERNMENT; RATIFICATION (Pages 94–95)
How can the Constitution be amended?

Article 5 sets up two ways of amending, or changing, the Constitution. In both cases, it takes more votes to **ratify,** or officially approve, than to propose an amendment. To propose an amendment takes two-thirds of Congress or two-thirds of state legislatures. To ratify takes three-fourths of state legislatures or state conventions.

The framers wanted it to be relatively easy to consider changes to the Constitution. Yet they wanted proposed changes to be carefully considered. They also wanted to be sure that Amendments had the full support of the nation.

Therefore, it is more difficult to ratify an Amendment and make it into law than it is to propose, or suggest, it.

Article 6 makes the laws of the federal government, or national laws, the supreme law of the land. If a state law is in conflict with a national law, it is the national law which must be obeyed. States must then change their laws to agree with the national law. This article strengthens the national government. It again makes sure that the United States is one nation, not just a loose confederation of states.

Finally, Article 7 says that the Constitution was to go into effect as soon as nine states voted to accept it. It did not require agreement of all 13 states. The framers felt that it would be difficult to get all 13 states to agree right away. But they also felt that if nine states ratified, the others would follow. The Constitution was ratified on June 21, 1788, when the ninth state, New Hampshire, agreed. The last state, Rhode Island, finally ratified the Constitution in May of 1790. The first presidential election under the Constitution was to be in 1792.

2. Why is it harder to ratify an amendment than to propose it?

_____

_____

As you read Articles 4–7, answer the following questions and note the
article (with section and clause, when necessary) that is the source for the
relevant information. Article 4, Section 3, Clause 2 would be written 4.3.2.

Example: Could Utah refuse to allow a U.S. citizen from Ohio
to buy a home in Utah? _____ Location ___4.2___

Article 4

1. Must one state honor the ruling of a state court in another
   state? _____ Location _____

2. If a woman commits a crime in Kentucky and is captured
   in New York, can New York refuse to return her to
   Kentucky? _____ Location _____

3. Would it be possible for North and South Dakota to become
   one state if both state legislatures, and Congress, approved of
   such a merger? _____ Location _____

4. Can one state establish a dictatorship within that state as long
   as it does not interfere with the lives of citizens in other
   states? _____ Location _____

Article 5

5. What institution decides when an amendment to the Constitution
   should be proposed and considered? _____ Location _____

6. How many states must approve an amendment for it to take
   effect? _____ Location _____

Article 6

7. Can one state enforce a law within its own borders that conflicts
   with a national law? _____ Location _____

8. If a man refused to support the Constitution, could he serve
   as a member of his state's legislature? _____ Location _____

9. Can an atheist be denied the right to hold federal office? _____ Location _____

Article 7

10. How many states had to ratify the Constitution for it to become
    the law of the land? _____ Location _____

11. In what year was the Constitution signed by delegates to the
    Constitutional Convention? _____ Location _____

The Living Constitution

The Bill of Rights and the Other Amendments

Terms and Names

Bill of Rights First ten Amendments

double jeopardy Being tried more than once for the same crime

due process of law All the procedures for fair treatment must be carried out whenever a citizen is accused of a crime

reserved powers Powers not specifically granted to the federal government or denied to the states belong to the states and the people

suffrage Right to vote

Before You Read

In the last section, you saw the process of amending the Constitution. In this section, you will learn about the Bill of Rights and the other Amendments.

As You Read

Continue your outline of the Constitution, and take notes on how amendments added to or changed the U.S. government.

THE BILL OF RIGHTS (Pages 96–97)
What liberties are protected by the Bill of Rights?

The first ten Amendments are called the **Bill of Rights.** They were added to the Constitution in 1791. The supporters of the Constitution had to promise to include these protections of citizens' rights in order to get the states to ratify the Constitution. Some of these rights are the ones that the colonists had under British rule. The framers wanted to be sure the people still had these rights under the new government. Some are the rights that the colonists felt Britain had taken away from them. That was one reason why they fought the Revolutionary War.

Amendment 1 protects basic civil liberties. It prevents the government from interfering with citizens' freedom of religion, speech, and press. It says that citizens can gather together, or assemble, freely. Citizens also have the right to ask the government to redress, or correct, injustices. Because of this amendment, citizens can protest government action without fear of punishment.

Amendment 2 says the federal government cannot prevent states from having an armed militia. This was designed to make sure that states and citizens could protect themselves from the military power of a tyrannical government—as they did during the Revolution. The right of individual citizens to carry weapons has become controversial in modern times.

Amendment 3 says that citizens cannot be forced to let soldiers stay in their homes during peacetime. Amendment 4 extends the people's right to privacy. It is why a search warrant is required to look through a citizen's home or belongings. Such a warrant can be issued only if a judge decides that it is likely that evidence of a crime will be found. The warrant must state exactly what evidence the government is looking for.

Amendments 5 through 8 deal with the rights of citizens accused of crimes. Amendment 5 prevents **double jeopardy,** or being tried more than once for the same crime. In other words, if a citizen is found not guilty in a trial, the government cannot keep bringing the case to trial until it gets a conviction. (Citizens found guilty do have the right of appeal, however.)

This amendment is also the basis for "pleading the Fifth." That is the slang term for a citizen's right to refuse to testify when that testimony might incriminate him/her. It also guarantees **due process of law.** That means that all of the procedures for fair treatment (including the rights mentioned here) must be carried out whenever a citizen is accused of a crime.

Amendment 6 guarantees the right to a "speedy and public trial." It is intended to protect citizens from being kept in jail (in a sense, punished) for long periods of time before they are even brought to trail. The right to know the charges and to have legal counsel also prevents citizens from having to defend themselves in court. This amendment also makes sure the public is informed of what is going on in their courts.

Amendment 9 guarantees that rights are not denied simply because they have not been mentioned in the Constitution. And

Amendment 10 establishes the so-called **reserved powers.** It states that the powers that are not specifically given to the federal government—as long as they are not specifically denied to the states—belong to the states and to the people.

1. Name two ways the Bill of Rights protects citizens accused of crimes.

   _____

   _____

AMENDMENTS 11–27 (Pages 98–103)
How have Amendments changed American society?

The amendments ratified after 1791 have had a variety of purposes. Some are quite technical, such as the legal question decided in Amendment 11. This amendment said that citizens of another state or a foreign country cannot sue a state in federal court unless the state agrees to it. Other amendments changed American society.

Amendments 13, 14, and 15 were a result of the Union victory in the Civil War. Amendment 13 (ratified in 1865) abolishes slavery. Amendment 14 (1868) grants citizenship to African Americans by saying that all persons born or naturalized in the United States are citizens. Amendment 15 (1870) protects the voting rights of citizens, particularly former enslaved persons.

However, it was not until 1964 that Amendment 24 made the poll tax illegal. Some Southern states used this tax to keep African Americans from voting. Because many blacks could not afford to pay the tax required at the polls, they could not exercise their right to vote.

Voting is the subject of several other Amendments. Amendment 17 provides for direct election of Senators by the people (rather than by state legislatures as described in Article 1). Amendment 19 grants **suffrage,** or the right to vote, to women. And Amendment 26 lowers the age at which citizens can vote to 18.

Amendment 18 is known as Prohibition. It prohibited, or banned, the manufacture, sale, or shipment of alcoholic beverages. It was an attempt to change American society that failed. It was repealed by Amendment 21.

Amendment 22 sets limits on the number of terms a president may serve. No person may be elected president more than twice. Franklin Roosevelt was the first and only president to be elected to more than two terms. He was elected to four. Many people felt that was too long to be president. Today, the idea of term limits for other federal offices has some supporters.

2. How did Amendments 15, 19, 24, and 26 change American society?

_____

_____

Guided Reading Workbook

As you read the amendments to the Constitution, circle the correct choice
from each parenthetical pair of choices in the summary below.

Amendment 1	establishes the people's right to (vote/criticize the government).
Amendment 2	maintains that states have the right to have (armed militias/legislatures).
Amendment 4	requires police to provide a (good reason/written accusation) to obtain a search warrant.
Amendment 5	guarantees that the government cannot take private property for its own use without (the owner's agreement/fair payment).
Amendment 6	protects the rights of (crime victims/people accused of crimes).
Amendment 8	says that bails, fines, and punishments for crimes cannot be (delayed/unfair or cruel).
Amendment 9	states that people's rights (are/are not) limited to those listed in the Constitution.
Amendment 10	says that government powers not mentioned in the Constitution belong to (the states or the people/the House of Representatives).
Amendment 11	prohibits a citizen of one state from suing another (state/citizen) in a federal court.
Amendment 13	forbids slavery in the (South/United States).
Amendment 14	requires that states give all people (the right to vote/equal protection under the law).
Amendment 15	prohibits denying voting rights because of (sex/race).
Amendment 17	changes the way in which (the president/U.S. senators) are elected.
Amendment 18	establishes (prohibition/civil rights).
Amendment 19	prohibits denying the right to vote based on (age/sex).
Amendment 21	repeals Amendment (17/18).
Amendment 22	limits the (years/number) of presidential terms.
Amendment 24	forbids a tax on (voting/property).
Amendment 25	establishes when and how the (Speaker of the House/vice-president) can take over presidential powers.
Amendment 26	extends suffrage to (residents/citizens) who are 18 years of age.
Amendment 27	deals with pay raises for (members of Congress/the president).

Section 1

The Jeffersonian Era

Terms and Names

Democratic-Republicans Political party led by Thomas Jefferson

Jeffersonian republicanism The belief that a simple government, controlled by people, is best

Marbury* v. *Madison Court case that established the power of judicial review

John Marshall Chief Justice of the Supreme Court

judicial review The power of judges to declare a law unconstitutional

Louisiana Purchase Land bought from France in 1803

impressment Act of seizing sailors to work on ships

James Monroe Fifth president

Monroe Doctrine Warning to European nations not to interfere in the Americas

Before You Read

In the last section, you saw how Washington and Adams led the young country. In this section, you will learn about the presidencies of Jefferson, Madison, and Monroe.

As You Read

Use a chart to list significant events from the Jefferson, Madison, and Monroe administrations.

JEFFERSON'S PRESIDENCY
(Pages 112-114)
What kind of president was Jefferson?

The presidential election of 1800 was close and bitter. Thomas Jefferson, a leader of the **Democratic-Republicans,** and his followers accused President Adams of making the federal government too powerful. They said he put the people's liberties in danger.

Jefferson won the most popular votes. But a tie in the electoral college showed a problem. Jefferson tied with Aaron Burr in the Electoral College. Alexander Hamilton helped break the deadlock and Jefferson was elected president. The 12th

Amendment was passed to change the way presidents would be chosen.

As president, Jefferson got a chance to put his theory of **Jeffersonian republicanism** into practice. This was a belief that the people should control the government and that government should be simple and small. Jefferson reduced the size of the military and lowered government expenses.

He was the first president to take office in the new federal capital, Washington, D.C. He also was the first of three consecutive presidents from Virginia, showing the rise in importance of the South in American politics.

In the court case *Marbury* v. *Madison,* Chief Justice **John Marshall** strengthened the power of the Court. The Supreme Court ruled a law passed by Congress to be unconstitutional. This power is called **judicial review**.

In 1803, Jefferson got the chance to buy land from France. He was not sure he had the constitutional power to do so, but he bought it anyway. The **Louisiana Purchase** stretched from the Mississippi River to the Rocky Mountains.

Jefferson sent Meriwether Lewis and William Clark to explore the new territory. The Lewis and Clark expedition showed that people could travel across the continent. It paved the way for settlement of the West.

1. What are two ways in which Jefferson's presidency was important?

_____

_____

MADISON AND THE WAR OF 1812
(**Page** 114)
What brought the country to war?

Britain and France went to war. Both nations threatened American ships. The British also engaged in **impressment:** they seized American sailors and forced them to serve in the British navy. American anger at Britain grew.

James Madison had become president in 1808. In 1812, he asked Congress to declare war on Britain. During the War of 1812, the British attacked Washington, D.C. President Madison had to flee the city. But General Andrew Jackson scored a victory for the Americans in the Battle of New Orleans. The Treaty of Ghent ended the war.

The War of 1812 had three important results:

- The anti-war Federalist Party died out.
- Americans began to develop their own industries.
- It showed that the United States was truly independent.

2. What were the two reasons United States went to war with Great Britain?

_____

_____

NATIONALISM SHAPES FOREIGN POLICY (**Pages** 116-117)
What was the basis of Monroe's foreign policy?

National pride grew after the War of 1812. **James Monroe** was elected president in 1816. His Secretary of State was John Quincy Adams.

Foreign policy under Adams was based on nationalism: a belief that national interests as a whole should be more important than what one region wants. Adams settled some issues with Britain. He also convinced Spain to give Florida to the United States.

In 1823, President Monroe warned European nations not to interfere with any nation in the Americas. He said the United States would stay out of European affairs. This statement is called the **Monroe Doctrine**.

3. Name three things that marked Monroe's foreign policy.

_____

_____

As you read about Jefferson's presidency, write answers to the questions below.

Key Trends in the Jeffersonian Era
1. How did Jefferson simplify the federal government?
2. How did the election of 1800 change all presidential elections to come?
3. How did the Federalists lose power during the Jefferson administration?

Key Events in the Jeffersonian Era
4. What was the long-term importance of the Supreme Court's decision in *Marbury* v. *Madison?*
5. How did the Louisiana Purchase affect the United States and its government?
6. What were the important results of the Lewis and Clark expedition?

Section 2

The Age of Jackson

Terms and Names

Henry Clay Speaker of the House of Representatives and political leader from Kentucky

American System Clay's plan for economic development

John C. Calhoun Vice-president and congressional leader from South Carolina

Missouri Compromise Agreement that temporarily settled the issue of slavery in the territories

Andrew Jackson Military hero and seventh president

John Quincy Adams Sixth president of the United States

Jacksonian democracy Political philosophy that puts its faith in the common people

Trail of Tears Path the Cherokee were forced to travel from Georgia to Indian Territory

John Tyler Tenth president

Before You Read

In the last section, you learned about the presidencies of Jefferson, Madison, and Monroe. In this section, you will learn about politics in the 1820s and 1830s.

As You Read

Use a chart to write newspaper headlines for important dates.

REGIONAL ECONOMIES CREATE DIFFERENCES (Pages 120-122)
What was the Industrial Revolution?

Manufacturing increased in the North. Production of goods moved from small workshops to large factories that used machines. This was the Industrial Revolution.

Farmers in the North began to grow crops for sale. They bought goods made in Northern factories. In this market economy, farming and manufacturing supported each other.

In the South, the invention of the cotton gin increased cotton production and made large cotton plantations more profitable.

More and more slaves were used to work on cotton plantations.

1. How did the Industrial Revolution affect each region?

_____

_____

BALANCING NATIONALISM AND SECTIONALISM (Page 122)
What held the nation together?

Speaker of the House **Henry Clay** created the **American System** to unify the nation. It included a protective tariff, a national bank, and internal improvements.

Most Northerners supported the tariff because it would help industry. Southerners did not want to pay the higher prices for goods. But Clay and **John C. Calhoun,** a Southerner, convinced Southern Congressmen to approve the tariff.

The nation built roads and canals. The Erie Canal linked the Great Lakes to the Atlantic Ocean.

In 1819, Missouri asked to enter the union. A crisis developed over whether the new state would have slavery or not. In the **Missouri Compromise** of 1820, Missouri was admitted as a slave state, and Maine was admitted as a free state. Also, slavery would be legal only south of a certain line.

2. What government actions helped to unify the nation?

_____

_____

THE ELECTION OF ANDREW JACKSON (Pages 122-123)
How did Jackson become president?

Andrew Jackson lost the 1824 presidential election to **John Quincy Adams**. Jackson's followers accused Adams of stealing the election.

Between 1824 and 1828, most states eased property requirements for voting. This allowed many more common people to vote. In the election of 1828, Jackson, the champion of the common man, won in a landslide.

3. What change in voting laws helped Jackson win the election of 1828?

_____

_____

JACKSONIAN DEMOCRACY
(**Pages** 123-124)
What kind of president was Andrew Jackson?

Jackson's philosophy, called **Jacksonian democracy,** was based on faith in the common people. Jackson used the spoils system to fill many federal jobs. He gave jobs to friends and supporters.

In 1830, Congress passed the Indian Removal Act. It said that Native Americans must move west of the Mississippi River.

The Cherokee fought the act in court. The Supreme Court struck it down. Jackson refused to obey the court's ruling. In 1838, the Cherokee were forced to walk from Georgia to the new Indian Territory. A quarter of the Cherokee died on this **Trail of Tears**.

4. What is the spoils system?

_____

_____

NULLIFICATION AND THE BANK WAR (**Pages** 124-126)

Southerners continued to object to tariffs. John C. Calhoun fought for states' rights. He argued that states could nullify federal laws that they felt were unconstitutional. In 1832, South Carolina tried to nullify a federal tariff. They also threatened to secede, or leave the union.

The Senate debated the issue. Daniel Webster of Massachusetts opposed efforts to nullify federal law. Later, Senator Robert Hayne of South Carolina defended nullification. Henry Clay worked out a compromise that kept South Carolina in the union.

President Jackson was against the second national bank. He took federal money out of the national bank and put it in other banks. The national bank went out of existence. Some people felt Jackson had too much power. They formed the Whig Party.

5. Name three major issues of Jackson's presidency.

_____

_____

SUCCESSORS DEAL WITH JACKSON'S LEGACY (Page 127)
What was the Panic of 1837?

Martin Van Buren was elected president in 1836. By 1837, many of the banks Jackson had put money in during the bank

war had failed. This helped cause the Panic of 1837 and a depression.

In 1840, Van Buren lost to Whig candidate William Henry Harrison. Harrison died soon after, and his vice-president, **John Tyler,** became president.

6. How did Jackson's actions cause economic problems during Van Buren's presidency?

_____

_____

As you read about the Jacksonian era, write answers to the questions about
events that appear on the time line.

1824	**John Quincy Adams wins the presidency.** ⟶	1. Why did the House of Representatives support John Quincy Adams over Andrew Jackson?
1830	**Congress passes the Indian Removal Act. Jackson forces the Cherokee and Choctaw from their lands.** ⟶	2. What did the Indian Removal Act call for?
1832	**The nullification crisis comes to a head.** ⟶	3. What was John C. Calhoun's theory of nullification?
1834	**National Republicans form the Whig Party.** ⟶	4. How did the style of politics change during the Age of Jackson?
1836	**Martin Van Buren wins the presidency.**	
1837	**The Panic of 1837 bankrupts many businesses and causes deep unemployment.** ⟶	5. How did Jackson's policies contribute to the Panic of 1837?

Section 3

Manifest Destiny

Terms and Names

manifest destiny Belief that the United States would expand across the continent

Santa Fe Trail Trail from Missouri to Santa Fe, New Mexico

Oregon Trail Trail from Missouri to Oregon

Stephen F. Austin Most successful land agent in Texas

Texas Revolution Texas's war for independence from Mexico

the Alamo Site of a key battle in the Texas Revolution

Sam Houston First president of the Republic of Texas

James K. Polk 11th president

Republic of California Proclaimed by American settlers who rebelled against Mexico

Treaty of Guadalupe Hidalgo Treaty ending the War with Mexico

---

Before You Read

In the last section, you learned about politics in the 1820s and 1830s. In this section, you will see how Americans continued to move westward and gained new territory through diplomacy and war.

As You Read

Use a chart to take notes on boundary changes of the United States.

SETTLING THE FRONTIER
(Pages 130-133)
Why did Americans move west?

Many Americans believed that God wanted the United States to expand across the continent. They felt that Americans were meant to control the West. This belief was called **manifest destiny.**

People went west for economic reasons. Many went in order to get cheap land. After the Panic of 1837, many Americans wanted a fresh start on the frontier.

Americans took several trails to the West. The **Santa Fe Trail** was a trade route between Independence, Missouri, and Santa Fe, New Mexico. The **Oregon Trail** stretched from Independence to Portland, Oregon.

The Mormons followed the Oregon Trail to Utah. This religious group had been persecuted in the East. They settled on the edge of the Great Salt Lake.

1. Give two reasons why Americans moved west.

_____

_____

TEXAN INDEPENDENCE
(Pages 133-135)
What caused the revolution in Texas?

In the 1820s Mexico encouraged Americans to settle in Texas. They offered land to settlers. They hoped these settlers would make the area more stable.

Stephen F. Austin, a land agent, set up a colony of American settlers in Texas. Soon Anglos, or English-speaking settlers, outnumbered Spanish-speaking Texans. There was conflict over cultural issues.

First, the Anglo settlers spoke English instead of Spanish. Second, the Anglos tended to be Protestant instead of Catholic. Third, many of the settlers were Southerners who brought their slaves with them. Mexico had outlawed slavery in 1829. They unsuccessfully tried to get the Texans to free their slaves.

Mexico tried to prevent more American settlers from coming to Texas, but the settlers came anyway. Austin asked Mexico for more self-government for Texas.

In 1836 a war broke out that became known as the **Texas Revolution.**

A small Texan force tried to defend **the Alamo,** a mission in San Antonio. When the Mexicans captured it, they killed all 187 of the Americans. "Remember the Alamo" became a rallying cry for Texas rebels. Under their commander **Sam Houston,** the Texans captured Mexican leader Santa Anna and won their independence.

James K. Polk was elected president in 1844. He was a slaveholder and favored westward expansion. In 1845, Texas was admitted to the union.

2. Name three conflicts between Anglo settlers and Mexico.

   _____

   _____

THE WAR WITH MEXICO
(**Pages** 135-137)
What did the United States gain in the Mexican War?

The United States and Mexico had a dispute over the northern region of Mexico. President Polk sent the U.S. army to blockade the Rio Grande River.

War broke out between the United States and Mexico. New Mexico immediately asked to join the United States. American settlers in California declared their independence from Mexico. They set up the **Republic of California.** American troops won victory after victory.

The **Treaty of Guadalupe Hidalgo** gave almost half of Mexico's land to the United States. The United States bought more land from Mexico with the Gadsden Purchase in 1853. This set the current borders of the lower 48 states.

3. Identify two states that became part of the United States as a result of the Mexican War.

   _____

   _____

THE CALIFORNIA GOLD RUSH
(**Pages** 137-138)
How did the Gold Rush change California?

In 1848 gold was discovered in California. People streamed into California in the rush for gold. These "forty-niners" came from all over the United States as well as from foreign countries. California's population exploded. San Francisco became a boom town.

The Gold Rush brought thousands of people to California and spurred the development of farming, manufacturing, shipping, and banking.

4. How did the Gold Rush affect California?

   _____

   _____

As you read about expansion to areas of the West, fill out the charts.

Despite the hardships of the journey and the difficult living conditions at journey's end, the West drew increasing numbers of Americans during the mid-19th century.

	Texas	Oregon	Utah
1. Who went?			
2. Why did they go?			
3. How did they get there?			
4. What did they find when they got there?			

Discuss the causes and effects of the treaty that ended the war with Mexico.

5. Treaty of Guadalupe Hidalgo
Causes:
Results:

The Market Revolution

Terms and Names

market revolution Economic changes where people buy and sell goods rather than make them themselves

free enterprise Economic system in which individuals and businesses control the means of production

entrepreneurs Businessmen

Samuel F. B. Morse Inventor of the telegraph

Lowell textile mills Early factories in Lowell, Massachusetts, where cloth was made

strike Work stoppages by workers

immigration Migration of people into the United States

National Trades' Union Early national workers' organization

Commonwealth* v. *Hunt Court case supporting labor unions

Before You Read

In the last section, you read about American expansion to the West. In this section, you will learn about changes in the American economy.

As You Read

Use a time line to record important developments in manufacturing during the early 19th century.

THE MARKET REVOLUTION
(Pages 139-141)
***What* was the market revolution?**

There were great economic changes in the United States during the first half of the 19th century. In this **market revolution,** people began to buy and sell goods rather than making them for themselves. **Free enterprise,** an economic system in which private businesses and individuals control production, also expanded at this time.

Entrepreneurs, or businessmen, invested in new industries. New industries produced goods that made life more comfortable for ordinary people. New inventions improved manufacturing, transportation, and communication.

Samuel F. B. Morse invented the telegraph. It could send messages by wire in a few seconds. Steamboats, canals, and railroads helped improve transportation. Improved transportation linked North to South and East to West.

The different regions became dependent on each other because each region needed goods produced by other regions. The North became a center of commerce and manufacturing. Many people who wanted to farm moved to the Midwest. New inventions, such as the steel plow and the reaper, made farming easier. Midwestern crops were carried by canal and trains to markets in the East.

The South remained an agricultural, or farming, region. It still relied on cotton, tobacco, and rice. And it relied on slave labor to raise those crops.

1. How did new inventions create a market revolution in the United States?

_____

_____

CHANGING WORKPLACES
(Pages 141-142)
How **did workplaces change?**

The new market economy changed the way Americans worked. Work that had been done in the home or in small, local shops moved to factories. New machines allowed unskilled workers to make goods that skilled artisans once made. But these new workers had to work in the factory.

Thousands of people worked in the **Lowell textile mills.** These Massachusetts factories made cloth. The mills hired mostly young women because they could be paid less than men. These "mill girls" lived in boarding houses owned by the factory. At first, they felt lucky to have these jobs. Factory work paid better than other jobs for women—teaching, sewing, and being a servant.

Working conditions in the textile mills became worse in the 1830s. The workday was more than 12 hours. Factories were hot, noisy, and dirty. Many workers became ill.

2. How did the new factories change how Americans worked?

_____

_____

WORKERS SEEK BETTER CONDITIONS **(Pages** 142-143)
What **did workers want?**

Bad working conditions in factories led workers to organize. In 1834, the Lowell textile mills cut the wages of workers by 15 percent. The mill girls went on **strike**—they refused to work until they got their old rate of pay back. Public opinion was against the workers.

There were dozens of strikes for shorter hours or higher pay in the 1830s and 1840s. Employers won most of them because they could hire strikebreakers, new workers to replace strikers. Many strikebreakers were European immigrants.

European **immigration,** people moving into the United States, increased between 1830 and 1860. Irish immigrants fled the Great Potato Famine. In the 1840s, a disease killed most of the potato crop in Ireland. About 1 million Irish people starved. Over 1 million came to America. The Irish met prejudice in the United States.

Small trade unions began to band together in the 1830s. The **National Trades' Union** was formed in 1834. It represented a variety of trades. At first, the courts had declared strikes illegal. But in 1842, the Massachusetts Supreme Court supported the right of workers to strike in *Commonwealth* v. *Hunt.*

3. Why did workers begin to organize into unions?

_____

_____

As you read about the formation of the national market economy, fill out the charts.

How did these innovations and inventions help expand the national market economy?	
1. Entrepreneurial activity	
2. Telegraph	
3. Steamboat	
4. Railroad	
5. Canals	
6. Steel Plow	

How did these developments affect the lives of workers?	
7. Textile mills	
8. National Trades' Union	
9. *Commonwealth* v. *Hunt*	
10. Industrialization	

Section 5

Reforming American Society

Terms and Names

Unitarians Religious group that emphasized reason

Ralph Waldo Emerson Leading philosopher of the era

transcendentalism Philosophy that emphasized the truth to be found in nature and intuition

abolition The movement to do away with slavery

William Lloyd Garrison Abolitionist leader

Frederick Douglass Escaped slave who became a noted abolitionist leader

Nat Turner Leader of a violent slave rebellion

Elizabeth Cady Stanton Leader in the abolitionist and women's rights movements

Seneca Falls convention Convention held in 1848 to argue for women's rights

Sojourner Truth Former slave who became an abolitionist and women's rights activist

Before You Read

In the last section, you learned about changes in the American economy. In this section, you will read about reform movements in 19th-century America.

As You Read

Use a diagram to take notes on historical events or key figures related to reforming American society in the 19th century.

A SPIRITUAL AWAKENING INSPIRES REFORM (Pages 144-145)
***What* changes in religion took place in America in the first half of the 1800s?**

The Second Great Awakening was a wide-spread religious movement. In revival meetings that lasted for days, people studied the Bible and listened to impassioned preaching. Many Americans joined churches as a result of the movement.

Unitarians were a religious group that appealed to reason instead of emotion. **Ralph Waldo Emerson,** a New England minister, writer, and philosopher, founded **transcendentalism.** It was a philosophy that

emphasized the interconnection between nature, human emotions, and the imagination.

Enslaved African Americans also experienced the urge to reform. Many in the South heard the sermons and hymns as a promise of freedom. In the North, free African Americans formed their own churches. These churches became political, cultural, and social centers for African Americans.

1. Name three religious movements that took place in America in the first half of the 1800s.

_____

_____

SLAVERY AND ABOLITION
(Pages 145-147)
Why did abolitionists oppose slavery?

By the 1820s, many people began to speak out against slavery in a movement called **abolition.** One extreme abolitionist was **William Lloyd Garrison.** In his newspaper, *The Liberator,* Garrison called for immediate emancipation, or freeing of the slaves. Many people in both the North and the South thought that Garrison's ideas were too extreme.

Another important abolitionist was **Frederick Douglass.** Douglass was an escaped slave who had learned to read and write. Garrison was impressed with Douglas and sponsored his speeches. Later Douglas broke with Garrison. Douglas believed slavery could be ended without violence. He published his own newspaper, *The North Star.*

By 1830 there were two constants in the lives of slaves—hard work and oppression. Most slaves worked as field hands or house servants. Some slaves were manumitted or freed, but most lived lives filled with suffering.

In 1831, a Virginia slave named **Nat Turner** led a violent slave rebellion. The rebels were captured and executed. The Turner rebellion frightened white Southerners. They made restrictions on slaves even tighter. Some Southerners also began to defend slavery as a good thing.

2. Describe how three people fought against slavery in the 1830s.

_____

_____

WOMEN AND REFORM
(Pages 147-149)
What did women reformers do?

Women were active in the 19th-century reform movements. Many women worked for abolition. Women also played key roles in the temperance movement, the effort to ban the drinking of alcohol.

Until 1820, American girls had little chance for education. Some female reformers opened schools of higher learning for girls. In 1821, Emma Willard opened one of the nation's first academically oriented schools for girls. In 1833, Oberlin College in Ohio became the first co-educational college in the nation. Four years later, in 1837, Mary Lyon started a school that became Mount Holyoke College.

Health reform for women was another important issue. Elizabeth Blackwell was the first woman to graduate from medical college. Catherine Beecher, the sister of Harriet Beecher Stowe undertook a survey of women's health that showed that three out of every four women had serious health problems.

Some women addressed the issue of women's rights. **Elizabeth Cady Stanton** and Lucretia Mott had been abolitionists. In 1848, they organized a women's rights convention. The **Seneca Falls convention** supported many reforms. The most controversial one was women's suffrage, or the right to vote.

For the most part, African American women did not have a voice at that time. **Sojourner Truth,** however, made her voice heard. A former slave, Truth became famous for speaking out for both abolition and women's rights.

3. How did women work for reform in the 19th century?

_____

_____

As you read about reform movements, answer the questions below.

What ideas and practices did each of the following promote?
1. African-American church
2. *The Liberator*
3. Seneca Falls convention
4. Transcendentalism

5. What people and events shaped the aboltion movement the most?
6. How did the African-American church interpret the message of Christianity?
7. How effective were efforts to reform education for women?

Section 1

The Divisive Politics of Slavery

Terms and Names

secession Decision by a state to leave the Union

popular sovereignty The right to vote for or against slavery

Underground Railroad Secret network of people who hid fugitive slaves who went north to freedom

Harriet Tubman Famous "conductor" on the Underground Railroad

Harriet Beecher Stowe Author of the antislavery novel *Uncle Tom's Cabin*

Franklin Pierce 14th president

Dred Scott Slave who was briefly taken by his owner into free territory

Abraham Lincoln President during the Civil War

Confederacy The Confederate States of America

Jefferson Davis President of the Confederate States of America

Before You Read

In the last section, you saw how some people began a movement to abolish slavery. In this section, you will see how slavery divided the nation.

As You Read

Create a time line showing events that heightened tensions between the North and the South.

DIFFERENCES BETWEEN NORTH AND SOUTH; SLAVERY IN THE TERRITORIES (Pages 156-158)
How was a temporary slavery compromise reached?

The North and the South had developed into very separate regions. The plantation economy in the South depended on slavery. Northern industry did not need slavery and opposition to slavery grew in the region.

In 1849, California asked to enter the Union as a free state. Southerners were angry because much of California was south of the Missouri Compromise line. Southerners thought that any move to ban slavery was an attack on their way of life. They threatened **secession,** the decision by a state to leave the Union.

Henry Clay presented the Compromise of 1850. To please the North, it said that California would be admitted as a free state. For the South, it included the Fugitive Slave Act. This law required Northerners to return fugitive, or escaped, slaves to their masters. The Compromise called for **popular sovereignty** in New Mexico and Utah territories.

Congress turned down the Compromise. But Senator Stephen Douglas took up the leadership and managed to get the Compromise passed.

Guided Reading Workbook

1. What were two features of the Compromise of 1850?

_____

_____

PROTEST, RESISTANCE, AND VIOLENCE (Pages 159-161)
How did people oppose slavery?

The Fugitive Slave Act provided harsh punishment for escaped slaves—and for anyone who helped them. Many Northerners were angry. Free African Americans and white abolitionists organized the **Underground Railroad.** This was a secret network of volunteers who hid fugitive slaves on their dangerous journey north to freedom. **Harriet Tubman,** an escaped slave, was a famous "conductor," or worker, on the Underground Railroad.

Meanwhile, a popular book helped many in the North see the fight to ban slavery as a moral struggle. **Harriet Beecher Stowe's** novel *Uncle Tom's Cabin* (1852) showed slavery's horrors. Southerners saw the book as an attack on their way of life.

In 1854, slavery in the territories became an issue again. The Kansas-Nebraska Act of 1854 split Nebraska into the territories of Nebraska and Kansas. Both could decide whether to allow slavery. Proslavery and antislavery people rushed into Kansas. Each side wanted to have enough people to decide the vote on slavery. After violence on both sides, the territory was nicknamed "Bleeding Kansas."

2. What were two ways in which people took actions against slavery?

_____

_____

NEW POLITICAL PARTIES EMERGE (Pages 161-162)
How did the slavery issue affect political parties?

The Whig Party split over the issue of slavery. That split left an easy victory for Democratic presidential candidate **Franklin Pierce** in 1852. Several new parties appeared in the North, including the Free Soil Party and the Know-Nothing Party. The Know-Nothing Party supported nativism and was against immigration. The Free-Soil Party was against the extension of slavery into the territories but was not abolitionist. Free-Soilers feared slavery competing with the wage labor system of the North.

The Republican Party formed in 1854 bringing together Free-Soilers, anti-slavery Whigs, Democrats and nativists. In the election of 1856, the Republican candidate, John C. Frémont lost to the Democrat, James Buchanan.

3. What major political party was born out of the slavery issue?

_____

_____

CONFLICTS LEAD TO SECESSION (Pages 162-165)
What events widened the split between North and South?

Dred Scott was a slave who had been taken by his master into the free states of Illinois and Wisconsin for a time. Scott claimed that being in free states had made him a free man. In 1857, the Supreme Court ruled in the *Dred Scott* case that slaves were property protected by the Constitution. Southerners felt that this decision allowed slavery to be extended into the territories.

In 1858, Stephen Douglas ran for re-election to the Senate in Illinois. Republican **Abraham Lincoln** ran against him. They held a series of debates about slavery in the territories. Douglas was against slavery but favored popular sovereignty. This meant that the voters in each territory should decide whether to allow slavery. Lincoln called slavery "a vast moral evil." Douglas won the election, but the Lincoln-Douglas debates made Lincoln famous.

In 1859, a Northern white abolitionist tried to start a slave rebellion. John Brown and a few followers attacked a federal arsenal in Harpers Ferry, Virginia. They were captured and executed. Brown was praised in the North. Southerners were furious.

Republicans nominated Lincoln for president in 1860. The Democratic Party split into Northern and Southern branches.

Lincoln won—without any electoral votes from the South. Southern reaction to Lincoln's election was dramatic. South Carolina seceded in December of 1860.

Southerners felt they had lost their political power in the United States. They feared an end to their whole way of life. By February 1861, seven Southern states had seceded. They formed the Confederate States of America, or **Confederacy.** They elected **Jefferson Davis** president.

4. What major event led to the secession of Southern states from the Union?

_____

_____

Name _____ Class _____ Date _____

Section 1, *continued*

As you read about the events and decisions that led to the South's secession, fill out the chart below.

	Supporters	Reasons for their Support
1. Compromise of 1850	❑ Proslavery forces ❑ Antislavery forces	
2. Fugitive Slave Act	❑ Proslavery forces ❑ Antislavery forces	
3. Underground Railroad	❑ Proslavery forces ❑ Antislavery forces	
4. Kansas-Nebraska Act	❑ Proslavery forces ❑ Antislavery forces	
5. Republican Party	❑ Proslavery forces ❑ Antislavery forces	
6. *Dred Scott* decision	❑ Proslavery forces ❑ Antislavery forces	
7. The raid on Harpers Ferry	❑ Proslavery forces ❑ Antislavery forces	
8. The election of Lincoln to the presidency	❑ Proslavery forces ❑ Antislavery forces	

Guided Reading Workbook

Section 2

The Civil War Begins

Terms and Names

Fort Sumter Union fort in Charleston, South Carolina

Bull Run Battle won by the Confederates

Stonewall Jackson Confederate general

Ulysses S. Grant Union general

Robert E. Lee Confederate general

Antietam Union victory

Emancipation Proclamation Order issued by Lincoln freeing slaves behind Confederate lines

conscription Drafting of civilians to serve in the army

Clara Barton Union nurse

income tax Tax that takes a percentage of an individual's income

Before You Read

In the last section, you saw how North and South came to war over slavery. In this section, you will see that the Civil War became a long, bloody conflict.

As You Read

Use a chart to take notes on the military actions and social and economic changes of the first two years of the Civil War.

UNION AND CONFEDERATE FORCES CLASH (Pages 168-171)
What were the advantages of the North and of the South?

Lincoln called for troops to fight to restore the Union. The Confederates attacked and took **Fort Sumter.** The fall of Fort Sumter united the North. Lincoln's call for troops was met with an overwhelming response. The response in the South was that four more Southern states seceded. Only four slave states remained in the Union. These were Maryland, Kentucky, Delaware, and Missouri.

The North had many advantages over the South. It had more people, more factories, more food production, and better railroads. The South's advantages were the demand for its cotton, better generals, and soldiers eager to defend their way of life. The North would have to conquer Southern territory to win.

The North had a three-part plan: 1) to blockade Southern ports to keep out supplies; 2) to split the Confederacy in two at the Mississippi; 3) to capture the Confederate capital of Richmond, Virginia.

The Confederates won the first battle of the war, **Bull Run,** just 25 miles from Washington, D.C. The Southern general who stood firm and inspired his

Guided Reading Workbook

troops was nicknamed **Stonewall Jackson.**

In 1862, a Union army led by General **Ulysses S. Grant** captured Confederate forts in Tennessee. Both sides suffered terrible losses in the Union victory at Shiloh. Then the Union navy captured the port of New Orleans.

Also in 1862, the Union army marched toward Richmond. General **Robert E. Lee** successfully defended the Confederate capital. Then he marched toward Washington. He was defeated by Union forces at **Antietam,** Maryland, in the bloodiest clash of the war. Union troops did not chase Lee back into Virginia. If they had, they might have won the war then and there.

1. What four advantages did the North have over the South?

_____

_____

THE POLITICS OF WAR
(Pages 171-173)
What led Lincoln to issue the Emancipation Proclamation?

The South hoped that Britain would support them in the war. But Britain had a large supply of cotton. It needed to buy wheat and corn from the North. So the British remained neutral.

More and more people in the North felt that slavery should be abolished. At first, Lincoln did not feel he had the constitutional right to end slavery where it already existed. But pressure to free the slaves increased. On January 1, 1863, Lincoln issued the **Emancipation Proclamation,** freeing all slaves behind Confederate lines. Lincoln's reasoning was that the slaves were enemy resources that contributed to the war effort. The

Proclamation did not apply to slave states still in the Union.

In the North, the Emancipation Proclamation gave the war a high moral purpose. In the South, people became even more determined to fight to preserve their way of life. But there was dissent in both the North and South. Both presidents Davis and Lincoln expanded their presidential power to keep order and to put down dissent in time of war.

2. What were two effects of the Emancipation Proclamation?

_____

_____

LIFE DURING WARTIME
(Pages 173-174)
How did the war affect Northerners and Southerners?

The high number of casualties forced both sides to impose **conscription,** a draft that forced men to serve in the army. In the North this led to draft riots, the most violent of which took place in New York City.

The Civil War caused many changes in both North and South. In 1862, Congress allowed African Americans to serve in the Union Army. After the Emancipation Proclamation of 1863, many African Americans enlisted. By the end of the war, they were 10 percent of Union forces. African-American soldiers served in separate regiments. They were usually paid less than whites and suffered other kinds of discrimination.

Soldiers suffered and died not only from wounds they got in battles. They also suffered from poor army food, filthy conditions, and disease. Conditions in war prisons were even worse.

Early in the war, some Northern women and doctors founded a commission to improve sanitary conditions for soldiers. They set up hospital trains and ships. Over 3,000 women served as nurses. Some, like **Clara Barton,** went to the front lines. The Confederacy had many volunteer nurses, too.

In the North, the war caused the economy to grow rapidly. Factories produced supplies needed by the army. But wages for factory workers did not keep up with prices. Some workers went on strike for higher wages.

To help pay for the war, Congress decided to collect the nation's first **income tax.** This tax takes a part of an individual's earned income.

3. How did the war affect the economies of both North and South?

_____

_____

As you read about wartime politics, briefly note the causes or effects
(depending on which is missing) of each situation.

Causes	Effects
1. Confederate troops fire on Union troops in Fort Sumter.	→
2.	→ Lincoln issues the Emancipation Proclamation.
3. The Union accepts African Americans as soldiers.	→
4. The Confederacy faces a food shortage due to the drain of manpower into the army.	→

Section 3

The North Takes Charge

Terms and Names

Gettysburg Most decisive battle of the war

Gettysburg Address Important speech by President Lincoln

Vicksburg Union victory in Mississippi

William Tecumseh Sherman Commander of Union troops in Georgia and South Carolina

Appomattox Court House Site of the Confederate surrender

Thirteenth Amendment Abolished slavery everywhere in the United States

John Wilkes Booth Assassin of President Lincoln

Before You Read

In the last section, you saw the Civil War begin and the early battles fought. In this section, you will see the South lose important battles and surrender. You will also see how the Civil War changed the nation in many ways.

As You Read

Use a diagram to take notes on the consequences of the Civil War.

THE TIDE TURNS (Pages 175-179)
What battle turned the tide?

The South won several battles in 1863, but their famous general Stonewall Jackson died when he was shot accidentally by his own troops. That year General Robert E. Lee decided to invade the North. The Battle of **Gettysburg,** in Pennsylvania, turned the tide of the war. After three days of fierce fighting, Lee retreated to Virginia. He gave up any hope of invading the North.

In November of 1863, a cemetery was dedicated at Gettysburg. More than 50,000 soldiers had been lost on both sides at that battlefield. President Lincoln delivered a short speech. The **Gettysburg Address** honored the dead and asked Americans to rededicate themselves to preserving the Union. Lincoln promised that "this government of the people, by the people, for the people" would survive.

The day after Gettysburg, General Grant captured **Vicksburg,** Mississippi, for the Union. When one more Mississippi River city fell, the Union controlled the river. The Confederacy was split in two.

1. How did Gettysburg change the war?

_____

_____

THE CONFEDERACY WEARS DOWN (Pages 180-181)
How did Union forces wear down the South?

The losses at Gettysburg and Vicksburg caused Southern morale to drop. Many men had been lost in battle. The Confederate army was low on food, ammunition, and supplies. Soldiers began to desert. The

South was exhausted and had few resources left. Some people called for peace.

Meanwhile, Lincoln made U.S. Grant commander of all Union armies. Grant gave **William Tecumseh Sherman** command of the military division of the Mississippi. Both generals believed in waging total war. Not only did they fight the Confederate army; their goal was to destroy the Southern population's will to fight.

Grant fought Lee's army in Virginia. At the same time, Sherman's army invaded Georgia and marched across the state to the sea, destroying cities and farms as they went.

Lincoln feared he would not be re-elected in 1864. Many Northerners felt the war had gone on too long and had caused too much destruction. But news of Sherman's victories helped Lincoln win a second term.

On April 3, 1865 Union troops conquered Richmond. On April 9, Generals Lee and Grant met in **Appomattox Court House,** Virginia, and arranged the Confederate surrender. Lincoln insisted the terms be generous. Confederate soldiers were allowed to go home, not taken prisoner. The Civil War was over.

2. Why did Lincoln fear he might not be reelected?

_____

_____

THE WAR CHANGES THE NATION
(**Pages** 181-182)
How did the Civil War change the nation?

The Civil War changed the nation in many ways. It exacted a high price in terms of human life. Approximately 360,000 Union soldiers and 260,000 Confederates died. The war also brought political change in the ways the federal government increased its power through such measures as conscription and the income tax.

The war widened the economic gap between North and South. The Northern economy boomed as the region produced goods of many kinds. The Southern economy collapsed. The labor system of slavery was gone. Southern industry and railroads were destroyed. Many farms were also in ruins.

The Civil War was also one of the first modern wars. It saw such deadly technological advances as the rifle and minié ball. The development of the ironclad ship led to the end of wooden war ships, and changed the nature of war forever.

3. What were two ways in which the Civil War changed the nation?

_____

_____

THE WAR CHANGES LIVES
(**Pages** 182-183)
How was the life of African Americans changed?

The situation of African Americans changed dramatically after the war. In 1865, the **Thirteenth Amendment** to the Constitution abolished slavery everywhere in the United States.

Only five days after Lee surrendered at Appomattox, President Lincoln was shot by a Southern sympathizer. Lincoln was at a play in Ford's Theater in Washington, D.C., when **John Wilkes Booth** shot him. He died the next day. Lincoln's body was carried by train from Washington to his hometown of Springfield, Illinois. Seven million people, or almost one-third of the Union population, turned out to pay their respects.

4. How was slavery finally abolished in the United States?

_____

_____

Name _____ Class _____ Date _____

Section 3, *continued*

As you read about the final years of the Civil War and its consequences, make notes to answer the questions.

1863	**Gettysburg** →	1. Why is the battle of Gettysburg considered a turning point in the war?
	Gettysburg Address →	2. What did the Gettysburg Address help Americans to realize?
1864	**Grant appointed commander of all Union armies** →	3. What was Grant's overall strategy for defeating Lee's army? What tactics did he use?
	Sherman's march from Atlanta to the sea →	4. What was Sherman's goal in his march to the sea? What tactics did he use to accomplish that goal?
	Lincoln reelected	
1865	**John Wilkes Booth** →	5. After the war ended, why didn't Lincoln implement his plans for reunifying the nation?
	Impact of the war →	6. What were some of the political and economic changes brought about by the war?
	Thirteenth Amendment ratified →	7. What was the purpose of the Thirteenth Amendment?

Guided Reading Workbook

Section 4

Reconstruction and Its Effects

Terms and Names

Freedmen's Bureau Agency established by Congress to help former slaves in the South

Reconstruction The period of rebuilding the nation after the Civil War

Radicals Republicans who wanted to destroy the political power of former slaveholders

Andrew Johnson President after Lincoln's assassination

Fourteenth Amendment Gave African Americans citizenship

Fifteenth Amendment Banned states from denying African Americans the right to vote

scalawag White Southerners who joined the Republican Party

carpetbagger Northerners who moved to the South after the war

Hiram Revels First African-American senator

sharecropping System in which landowners gave a few acres of land to farm workers in return for a portion of their crops

Ku Klux Klan (KKK) A secret group of white Southerners who used violence to keep blacks from voting

Before You Read

In the last section, you saw how the Union won the Civil War. In this section, you will see that the federal government's efforts to rebuild Southern society after the war collapsed.

As You Read

Use a table to list problems facing the South after the Civil War and their proposed solutions.

THE POLITICS OF RECONSTRUCTION (Pages 184-186)
What was Reconstruction?

The **Freedmen's Bureau** was an agency established by Congress to help former slaves in the South. It was part of **Reconstruction,** the period during which the United States began to rebuild after the Civil War. It also refers to the process of bringing the Southern states back into the nation. It lasted from 1865 to 1877.

During the war, Lincoln made a plan for Reconstruction that was lenient, or easy,

on the South. It included pardoning Confederates if they would swear allegiance to the Union. Lincoln's plan angered the **Radicals,** a group of Republicans who wanted to destroy the political power of former slaveholders. After Lincoln died, his vice-president, **Andrew Johnson,** became president. Johnson's plan was similar to Lincoln's.

However, Radical Republicans thought both plans were too easy on the South. They wanted to destroy the political power of former slave owners. They also wanted

African Americans to be citizens with the right to vote.

Republicans in Congress won a struggle with the president to control Reconstruction. They had enough votes to pass a law creating the Freedman's Bureau. It gave food and clothing to former slaves and set up hospitals and schools. Congress also passed the Civil Rights Act of 1866. It said that states could not enact laws that discriminated against African Americans.

Congress then passed the **Fourteenth Amendment.** It gave African Americans citizenship. Johnson urged Southern states not to ratify it because they had no say in creating it. Congress responded with the Reconstruction Act of 1867. It said no state could re-enter the Union until it approved the Fourteenth Amendment and gave the vote to African-American men.

The fight between Congress and Johnson led Congress to look for a way to impeach the president. Johnson had removed a cabinet member. Congress said he did it illegally. Johnson was impeached, but he avoided conviction and removal from office by just one Senate vote.

In 1868, war hero Ulysses S. Grant was elected president. African-American votes in the South helped him win. Then, in 1870, the **Fifteenth Amendment** was ratified. It banned states from denying the vote to African Americans.

1. How did the Fourteenth and Fifteenth Amendments improve the lives of African Americans?

_____

_____

RECONSTRUCTING SOCIETY
(Pages 186-188)
How did the economy in the South change after the war?

By 1870, all former Confederate states were back in the Union. Their governments were run by Republicans. The South faced terrible economic conditions. Many men had died in the war. People had lost their investments. Farms were ruined. The state governments began public works programs to repair the physical damage. They also provided social services. They raised taxes to pay for these programs.

Three groups of Republicans had different goals. **Scalawags** were white Southerners. They were small farmers who did not want wealthy planters to regain power. **Carpetbaggers** were Northerners who had moved South. African Americans had voting rights for the first time and voted Republican. But many white Southerners resisted equality for African Americans.

During Reconstruction, many former slaves moved to the cities. With help, they organized schools and churches. Many African Americans voted, and some were elected to office. **Hiram Revels** was the first African-American senator.

African Americans wanted to farm their own land. They had been promised "forty acres and a mule" by General Sherman. Congress, though, did not honor this promise.

Meanwhile, Southern planters wanted to return to the plantation system. They tried to make sure African Americans could not own land. To survive, many former slaves became sharecroppers. **Sharecropping** is a system in which landowners give a few acres of land to

Guided Reading Workbook

their farm workers. The "croppers" keep a small portion of their crops and give the rest to the landowner.

Another system that allowed whites to control the labor of African Americans was tenant farming. Tenant farmers rented land from the landowners for cash.

2. Who had control of land and labor in the South?

_____

_____

THE COLLAPSE OF RECONSTRUCTION (Pages 188-189)
What gains of Reconstruction were undone?

Many Southern whites did not like African Americans voting. Some formed secret groups such as the **Ku Klux Klan (KKK)** that used violence to keep blacks from voting. Other whites refused to hire blacks who voted. Congress passed the Enforcement Acts to stop the violence. However, Congress also gave the vote to many former Confederates. As a result, Democrats began to regain power.

Support for Reconstruction was weakened by division in the Republican Party and a series of bank failures known as the Panic of 1873, which led to a five-year depression.

The disputed election of 1876 resulted in the end of Reconstruction. Southern Democrats agreed to accept the Republican Rutherford B. Hayes as president in return for the withdrawal of federal troops from the South. Without federal troops, Southern democrats took control and Reconstruction was over.

3. How was Reconstruction undone?

_____

_____

Name _____ Class _____ Date _____

Section 4, *continued*

As you read this section, make notes that summarize the changes that took place as a result of Reconstruction. List the postwar problems, classifying each problem as political, economic, or social. Then indicate how individuals and the government responded to each difficulty or crisis.

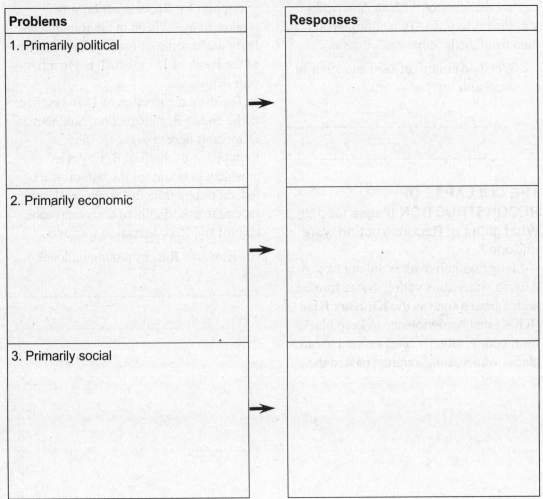

Problems		Responses
1. Primarily political	→	
2. Primarily economic	→	
3. Primarily social	→	

Guided Reading Workbook

Changes on the Western Frontier

Section 1

Cultures Clash on the Prairie

Terms and Names

Great Plains The grassland region of the United States

Treaty of Fort Laramie 1868 treaty in which the Sioux agreed to live on a reservation

Sitting Bull Leader of Hunkpapa Sioux

George A. Custer Colonel in U.S. Cavalry

assimilation Name of plan to make Native Americans part of white culture

Dawes Act Law that broke up Native American reservations

Battle of Wounded Knee U.S. massacre of Sioux at Wounded Knee Creek, South Dakota

longhorn Sturdy cattle accustomed to dry grasslands

Chisholm Trail Major cattle route from San Antonio, Texas, through Oklahoma to Kansas

long drive Three-month long overland transport of cattle

Before You Read

In the last section, you read about Reconstruction and its effects on the nation. In this section, you will read how Americans began settling the West in the years following Reconstruction. This spelled disaster for Native Americans.

As You Read

Use a diagram to take notes about the culture of the Plains Indians.

THE CULTURE OF THE PLAINS INDIANS; SETTLERS PUSH WESTWARD (Pages 202–204)
How did the Plains Indians live?

Native Americans lived on the **Great Plains,** the grasslands in the west-central portion of the United States. They followed a way of life that centered on the horse and buffalo. The horse allowed them to hunt more easily and to travel farther. The buffalo provided food, clothing, shelter, and other important items.

The Indians of the Great Plains lived in small extended family groups. The men hunted for food. The women helped butcher the game and prepare the buffalo

hides that the men brought back to camp. Children learned the skills they would need as adults.

After the Civil War, thousands of white settlers moved to the Great Plains. Some travelled there searching for gold. Others wanted to own land. They argued that because Native Americans had not settled down to "improve" the land, white settlers could stake their claim.

1. What were the responsibilities of the different members of Indian families?

_____

_____

THE GOVERNMENT RESTRICTS NATIVE AMERICANS; BLOODY BATTLES CONTINUE (Pages 204–206)
Why did Indians and settlers fight each other?

Along the Great Plains, Native Americans and white settlers often clashed—mainly over land and resources. One of the more tragic clashes occurred in 1864. The army was on the side of the settlers. The Cheyenne, living in an area of the Colorado Territory known as Sand Creek, had attacked settlers. In response, the army attacked and killed about 200 Cheyenne in an incident known as the Sand Creek Massacre.

In the **Treaty of Fort Laramie,** most Sioux agreed to live on a reservation. But **Sitting Bull,** an important Sioux leader, never signed the treaty. In 1876, he defeated army troops led by **George A. Custer,** at the Little Bighorn River. The Sioux won decisively, killing Custer and all his soldiers. The army recovered, however. Within months it defeated the Sioux.

2. What were the reasons for the clashes between the U.S. government and the Sioux?

_____

_____

THE GOVERNMENT SUPPORTS ASSIMILATION; THE BATTLE OF WOUNDED KNEE (Pages 206–208)
Why did assimilation fail?

To deal with the Native American problem, the U.S. government adopted a plan of **assimilation.** In this plan, Native Americans would give up their beliefs and culture and become part of white culture.

To push assimilation, Congress passed the **Dawes Act** in 1887. The act broke up reservations and gave some of the land to each Native American family for farming. The plan, however, failed. Native Americans were cheated out of the best land. As a result, they had little success farming. Worse yet, by 1900, whites had killed nearly all the buffalo. Native Americans depended on the buffalo for their food, clothing, and shelter.

The Sioux adopted a ritual called the Ghost Dance which they hoped would bring the buffalo back. This made the Army nervous. In 1890 they rounded up a group of Sioux including Sitting Bull. When they tried to take the Sioux's weapons a fight broke out. Army troops killed 300 unarmed Sioux in the **Battle of Wounded Knee.**

3. What were two reasons why assimilation failed?

_____

_____

CATTLE BECOMES BIG BUSINESS; A DAY IN THE LIFE OF A COWBOY; THE END OF THE OPEN RANGE (Pages 208–211)
What caused the cattle business to grow?

Cattle ranching became a big business after the Civil War. Ranchers raised **longhorns,** a sturdy breed first brought to the Americas by the Spanish. American cowboys learned from *vaqueros*, the first cowboys who worked on Spanish ranches in Mexico.

Growing cities spurred the demand for beef. Cattle ranchers drove their cattle over the **Chisholm Trail** from San Antonio, Texas, to Kansas where they were shipped by rail to Chicago.

Between 1866 and 1885, about 55,000 cowboys worked the plains. About 12 percent of these cowboys were Mexican. About 25 percent were African American.

A cowboy's life was difficult. Cowboys worked between 10 and 14 hours a day in all kinds of weather. They worked hard all spring and summer. In the winter, they lived off their savings or went from ranch to ranch and looked for odd jobs. In the spring, cowboys rounded up their cattle and headed them out on the **long drive.** This was the journey from the plains to the shipping yards in Abilene, Kansas. The days of the open range and cattle drive did not last long. Bad weather in the 1880s wiped out many ranchers. Others started using barbed wire to fence in their ranches.

4. What two factors helped the cattle business to grow?

_____

_____

Section 1, *continued*

As you read about the conflicts that occurred during the settlement of the
Western frontier, answer questions about the time line below.

1858	**Discovery of Gold in Colorado**	1. How did the discovery of gold affect the settlement of the West?
1864	**Sand Creek Massacre**	2. What happened at Sand Creek?
1868	**Treaty of Fort Laramie**	3. What were the terms of the Treaty of Fort Laramie? Why did it fail?
1874	**Invasion by gold miners of the Sioux's sacred Black Hills**	
1876	**George A. Custer's Last Stand**	4. What happened at the Battle of Little Bighorn?
1887	**The policy of assimilation formalized in the Dawes Act**	5. What was the purpose of the Dawes Act?
1890	**The Spread of the Ghost Dance movement; the death of Sitting Bull; the Battle of Wounded Knee**	6. What happened at Wounded Knee Creek?

Changes on the Western Frontier

Settling on the Great Plains

Terms and Names

Homestead Act Act that offered free land to western settlers

exodusters African-American settlers in the West

soddy A frontier home, usually dug into a hill or made from sod

Morrill Act Act that helped establish agricultural colleges

bonanza farm Large, single-crop farms

Before You Read

In the last section you read about how Native Americans and white settlers clashed over the land in the American West, and the growth of the cattle industry and the life of cowboys. In this section, you will read about life on the Great Plains for the men and women who settled there in search of land and prosperity.

As You Read

Use a time line to make notes of the important events that shaped the settling of the Great Plains.

SETTLERS MOVE WESTWARD TO FARM (Pages 214–216)
How did the U.S. get people to go west?

More and more people migrated to the Great Plains with the building of the transcontinental railroads. From 1850 to 1871, the federal government gave huge tracts of land to companies ready to lay tracks through the West.

In 1867, the Central Pacific company began laying tracks east from Sacramento, California. Another railroad company, the Union Pacific, began laying tracks west from Omaha, Nebraska. Much of the work was done by Irish and Chinese immigrants. African Americans and Mexican Americans also did the back-breaking work. In 1869, the two routes met at Promontory, Utah. America's first transcontinental railroad was finished.

The railroad companies sold some of their land at low prices to settlers willing to farm it. Some companies even recruited people from Europe to settle on the land.

In addition, a growing number of people were responding to the **Homestead Act** of 1862. Under this law, the government offered 160 acres of free land to anyone who would farm it for five years. By 1900, the Great Plains was filled with more than 400,000 homesteaders, or settlers on this free land.

Several thousand settlers were **exodusters**—African Americans who moved from the post-Reconstruction South to Kansas.

But the law did not always work as the government had planned. Only about 10 percent of the land was settled by the families for whom it was intended. Cattlemen and miners claimed much of the rest.

Guided Reading Workbook

The government continued to pass other laws to encourage people to settle the West. In 1889, Oklahoma offered a major land giveaway. This led thousands of settlers to claim 2 million acres in less than 24 hours.

As more and more settlers gobbled up land in the West, the government took action to preserve some wilderness. In 1872, the government set aside land in Wyoming to create Yellowstone National Park. Millions of acres more were set aside later.

1. How did the government and the railroads encourage settlement of the West?

_____

_____

SETTLERS MEET THE CHALLENGES OF THE PLAINS
(Pages 216–218)
What **was life like for settlers of the West?**

From 1850 to 1900, the number of people living west of the Mississippi River grew from 1 percent of the nation's population to almost 30 percent. These new settlers had to endure many hardships.

The Great Plains did not have many trees. As a result, people built what became known as **soddys.** These homes were dug into the side of hills or made from sod. A soddy was warm in winter and cool in summer. However, it offered little light or air.

Homesteaders were largely isolated from one another. They had to make

nearly everything they needed. Women worked in the fields alongside men. They also took care of the children, ran the house, and did the cooking and laundry.

Farming the Great Plains was difficult work. But several inventions helped make the task easier. The steel plow helped break up the prairie's tough soil. A new reaper cut wheat even faster.

The government also helped in the effort to improve farming techniques. The **Morrill Act** of 1862 and 1890 helped establish agricultural colleges. The government also established experiment stations on the Great Plains. Researchers there developed new types of crops as well as new growing techniques.

To buy much of the new farming machinery, farmers often went into debt. When crop prices fell, farmers ended up losing money. As a result, they had trouble repaying their loans. To make more money, they often had to raise more crops. This in turn led to the growth of **bonanza farms.** These were huge single-crop farms.

By 1900, the average farmer had nearly 150 acres under cultivation. However, when a drought hit the Plains between 1885 and 1890, many bonanza farms folded. They could not compete with the smaller farmers, who were more flexible in the crops they grew. The high price of shipping their crops also added to farmers' debt.

2. Name at least one social and economic hardship settlers faced.

_____

_____

Guided Reading Workbook

As you read this section, note how each of the factors listed below
(Causes) helped to settle the West and turned the eastern Great Plains
into the nation's "breadbasket" (Effects).

Causes	Effects
1. Land grants given to the railroads	
2. The Homestead Act and related laws passed in the 1870s	
3. Inventions and improvements in farm technology	
4. The Morrill Land Grant Acts and Hatch Act	

What were some hardships faced by frontier farmers? (Note: one hardship per box)

Changes on the Western Frontier

Farmers and the Populist Movement

Terms and Names

Oliver Hudson Kelley Farmer who founded the Grange

Grange Organization that fought for farmers' rights

Farmers' Alliances Groups of farm organizations

Populism Political movement that sought advancement for farmers and laborers

bimetallism backing money with silver and gold

gold standard Backing dollars solely with gold

William McKinley 1896 Republican presidential nominee

William Jennings Bryan 1896 Populist/Democratic presidential nominee

Before You Read

In the last section, you read about life for thousands of farmers trying to make a living on the Great Plains. In this section, you will read how these farmers organized and fought to improve their conditions.

As You Read

Use a chart to take notes about the causes of the rise of the Populist Party and the effects the party had.

FARMERS UNITE TO ADDRESS COMMON PROBLEMS (Pages 219–221)
How did farmers fight back?

Farmers faced serious problems after the Civil War. The prices they could sell their crops for kept going down. This was because the United States was withdrawing greenbacks—money printed for the Civil War—from circulation. The decline in prices also meant that farmers had to pay back their loans in money that was worth more than when they borrowed it. Farmers urged the government to increase the the money supply. But the government refused.

Meanwhile, farmers continued to pay high prices to transport grain. Often they paid as much to ship their crops as they received for them. Many farmers were on the brink of ruin. The time, it seemed, had come for reform.

Many farmers joined together to push for reform. In 1867, a farmer named **Oliver Hudson Kelley** started an organization that became known as the **Grange.** Its original purpose was to provide a place for farm families to discuss social and educational issues. By the 1870s, however, Grange members spent most of their time and energy fighting the railroads.

The Grange gave rise to other organizations. They included the **Farmers' Alliances**. These organizations included teachers, preachers, and newspaper editors who sympathized with farmers. Alliance members traveled throughout the Great Plains. They educated farmers about a variety of issues, including how to obtain lower interest rates and ways to protest the railroads.

1. What steps did farmers take to address their concerns?

_____

_____

THE RISE AND FALL OF POPULISM
(Pages 221–223)
What **did the Populist movement hope to achieve?**

Alliance leaders realized that to make far-reaching changes, they needed political power. So in 1892, they created the Populist Party, or People's Party. This party was the beginning of **Populism.** This was a movement to gain more political and economic power for common people.

The Populist Party pushed for reforms to help farmers. It also called for reforms to make government more democratic. These reforms included direct election of senators and a secret ballot to stop cheating in voting.

Most Americans thought the populists' beliefs too radical. However, the party appealed to many struggling farmers and laborers. In 1892, the Populist presidential candidate won more than a million votes. That was almost 10 percent of the total vote. In the West, Populist candidates won numerous local elections. While not as strong as the two major parties, the Populist Party had become a political force.

Then, in 1893, the nation faced an economic crisis called the Panic of 1893. The causes of the panic started in the 1880s. During that decade, many companies and individuals had borrowed too much money. But starting in 1893, many of these companies went bankrupt because they were not making enough money to pay back their loans. Many people lost their jobs.

The panic continued into 1895. Then political parties began to choose candidates for the 1896 presidential election. One important issue was whether the country's paper money should be backed with both gold and silver.

The central issue of the campaign was which metal would be the basis of the nation's monetary system. On one side were the "silverites" who favored **bimetallism,** a monetary system in which the government would give people either gold or silver in exchange for paper currency or checks. On the other side were the "gold bugs" who favored the **gold standard**—backing dollars solely with gold.

"Gold bugs" favored gold because using the gold standard would keep prices from rising. Silverites favored bimetallism because it would make more dollars available and therefore prices and wages would rise.

Republicans were "gold bugs." They elected **William McKinley** for president. The Democrats and the Populists both favored bimetallism. Both parties nominated **William Jennings Bryan.** At the Democratic convention, Bryan delivered an emotional speech, known as the "Cross of Gold" speech, in support of bimetallism.

But on election day McKinley won. McKinley's election brought an end to Populism. The movement left two powerful legacies: a message that poor people and less powerful groups in society could organize and have a political impact, and an agenda of reforms many of which would be enacted in the 20th century.

2. Which groups did the Populists appeal to most?

_____

_____

As you read this section, take notes to answer questions about the pressures
that made farming increasingly unprofitable.

In the late 1800s, farmers faced increasing costs and decreasing crop prices.

1. Why had farming become unprofitable during this period?	2. Why did farmers support bimetallism or "free silver"?

In 1892, farmers and farm organizations, such as the Grange, found support in Populism and the People's Party.

3. What economic reforms did the People's Party call for?	4. What political reforms did the party call for?

In 1896, the Populists supported presidential candidate William Jennings Bryan.

5. What factions did Bryan and the Populists see as opposing forces in the presidential election of 1896?	6. In what ways did the results of the 1896 election confirm this view?

A New Industrial Age

Section 1

The Expansion of Industry

Terms and Names

Edwin L. Drake First person to use steam engine to drill for oil

Bessemer process Technique used to make steel from iron

Thomas Alva Edison Inventor of the light bulb

Christopher Sholes Inventor of the typewriter

Alexander Graham Bell Inventor of the telephone

Before You Read

In the last section, you read about the growth of the Populist movement. In this section, you will read how Americans used their natural resources and technological breakthroughs to begin building an industrialized society.

As You Read

Use a chart to list the resources and ideas that affected the industrial boom and how each contributed to industrialization.

NATURAL RESOURCES FUEL INDUSTRIALIZATION (Pages 230–232)
***What* were America's important natural resources?**

In the years after the Civil War, advances in technology began to change the nation. There were three causes of these advances: a large supply of natural resources, an explosion of inventions, and a growing city population that wanted the new products.

One of the more important natural resources was oil. In 1840 a Canadian geologist discovered that kerosene could be used to light lamps. Kerosene was produced from oil. This increased Americans' demand for oil.

In 1859, **Edwin L. Drake** used a steam engine to drill for oil. This technological breakthrough helped start an oil boom. Oil-refining industries started in Cleveland

and Pittsburgh. There, workers turned oil into kerosene.

Oil produced yet another product—gasoline. At first, gasoline was thrown away. However, when the automobile became popular, gasoline was in great demand.

In addition to oil, Americans discovered that their nation was rich in coal and iron. In 1887, explorers found large amounts of iron in Minnesota. At the same time, coal production increased from 33 million tons in 1870 to more than 250 million tons in 1900.

Iron is a strong metal. However, it is heavy and tends to break and rust. Researchers eventually removed the element carbon from iron. This produced a lighter, more flexible metal that does not rust. It became known as steel. The **Bessemer process,** named after British

Guided Reading Workbook

manufacturer Henry Bessemer, provided a useful way to turn iron into steel.

Americans quickly found many uses for steel. The railroads, with their thousands of miles of track, bought large amounts of the new metal. Steel was also used to improve farm tools such as the plow and reaper. It also was used to make cans for preserving food. Engineers used steel to build bridges. One of the most remarkable bridges was the Brooklyn Bridge. It connected New York City and Brooklyn. Steel also was used to build skyscrapers, such as the Home Insurance Building in Chicago.

1. Name two ways Americans used steel.

_____

_____

INVENTIONS PROMOTE CHANGE
(**Pages** 232–233)
How did the new inventions change Americans' way of life?

Beginning in the late 1800s, inventors produced items that changed the way people lived and worked. In 1876, **Thomas Alva Edison** established the world's first research laboratory in Menlo Park, New Jersey. He used the lab to develop new inventions. Edison perfected an early light bulb there. He then worked to establish power plants to generate electricity.

Another inventor, George Westinghouse, developed ways to make electricity safer and less expensive.

The use of electricity changed America. By 1890, electricity ran machines such as fans and printing presses. Electricity soon became available in homes. This led to the invention of many appliances. Cities built electric streetcars. They made travel cheaper and easier.

In 1867, **Christopher Sholes** invented the typewriter. This led to dramatic changes in the workplace. Almost ten years later, in 1876, **Alexander Graham Bell** and Thomas Watson invented the telephone.

The wave of inventions during the late 1800s helped change Americans' daily life. More women began to work in offices. By 1910, women made up about 40 percent of the nation's office work force. In addition, work that had been done at home—such as sewing clothes—was now done in factories. Unfortunately, many factory employees worked long hours in unhealthy conditions.

Inventions had several positive effects. Machines allowed employees to work faster. This led to a shorter work week. As a result, people had more leisure time. In addition, citizens enjoyed new products such as phonographs, bicycles, and cameras.

2. Name two ways in which electricity changed people's life.

_____

_____

After the Civil War, the United States was still a mostly rural nation. By the 1920s, it had become the leading industrial nation of the world. This immense change was caused by three major factors. Answer the questions for two of the factors.

Factor 1: Abundant Natural Resources

1. Which resources played crucial roles in industrialization?	2. How did Edwin L. Drake help industry to acquire larger quantities of oil?	3. How did the Bessemer process allow better use of iron ore?	4. What new uses for steel were developed at this time?

Factor 2: Increasing Number of Inventions

5. How did Thomas Alva Edison contribute to this development?	6. How did George Westinghouse contribute to it?	7. How did Christopher Sholes contribute?	8. How did Alexander Graham Bell contribute?

Factor 3: Expanding Urban Population

Provided markets for new inventions and industrial goods	Provided a ready supply of labor for industry

Section 2

The Age of the Railroads

Terms and Names

transcontinental railroad A railroad that crosses the entire country

George M. Pullman Inventor of the sleeping car

Crédit Mobilier Name of company involved in stealing of railroad money

Munn* v. *Illinois Court case that gave government right to regulate private industry

Interstate Commerce Act Law granting Congress authority to regulate railroad activities

Before You Read

In the last section, you read about how Americans used their natural resources and numerous inventions to begin transforming society. In this section, you will read about the growth of the nation's railroad industry and its effect on the nation.

As You Read

Use a diagram to take notes on the effects of the rapid growth of railroads.

RAILROADS SPAN TIME AND SPACE (Pages 236–237)

How did the railroads change the way Americans told time?

Before and after the Civil War, railroads were built to span the entire United States. In 1869, the nation completed work on its first **transcontinental railroad**—a railroad that crossed the entire continent. In the years that followed, railroad tracks spread throughout the country. By 1890, more than 200,000 miles of rail lines zigzagged across the United States.

Railroads made long-distance travel a possibility for many Americans. However, building and running the railroads was difficult and dangerous work. Those who did most of the work were Chinese and Irish immigrants and desperate out-of-work Civil War veterans. Accidents and diseases affected thousands of railroad

builders each year. By 1888, more than 2,000 workers had died. Another 20,000 workers had been injured.

Railroads eventually linked the many different regions of the United States. However, railroad schedules proved hard to keep. This was because each community set its own times—based mainly on the movement of the sun. The time in Boston, for example, was almost 12 minutes later than the time in New York.

To fix this problem, officials devised a plan in 1870 to divide the earth into 24 time zones, one for each hour of the day. Under this plan, the United States would contain four time zones: Eastern, Central, Mountain, and Pacific. Everyone living in a particular zone would follow the same time. The railroad companies supported this plan. Many communities also supported it.

1. How did times zones first come about?

_____

_____

OPPORTUNITIES AND OPPORTUNISTS (Pages 237–238)
How did the growth of the railroads affect the nation?

Railroads made it easier for people to travel long distances. They also helped many industries grow. The iron, steel, coal, lumber, and glass industries all grew partly because the railroads needed their products. Railroads also increased trade among cities, towns, and settlements. This allowed many communities to grow and prosper.

Railroads led to the creation of new towns. In 1880, **George M. Pullman** built a factory on the prairie outside Chicago. There, workers made the sleeping cars he invented for trains. As demand for his sleeping cars rose, Pullman built a large town to house the workers he needed. Pullman created quality housing for his workers. But he tried to control many aspects of their lives. Eventually, his workers rebelled.

The railroad industry offered people the chance to become rich. The industry attracted many corrupt individuals. One of the most well-known cases of corruption was the Crédit Mobilier scandal. In 1868, some officers of the Union Pacific railroad formed a construction company called **Crédit Mobilier.** They gave their company contracts to lay railroad track at two to three times the actual cost. They kept all profits. To prevent the government from interfering, they paid off members of Congress. Eventually, authorities uncovered the scheme.

2. What was one positive and negative effect of the growth of railroads?

_____

_____

THE GRANGE AND THE RAILROADS (Pages 238–240)
Why did the farmers fight the railroads?

One group angered by corruption in the railroad industry were farmers. Farmers were upset for a number of reasons. First, they claimed that railroads sold government land grants to businesses rather than to families. They also accused the railroad industry of setting high shipping prices to keep farmers in debt.

In response to these abuses, the Grangers took political action. They convinced some states to pass laws regulating railroad activity. Members of the railroad companies challenged the states' rights to regulate them.

The battle reached the Supreme Court in 1877. In the case of *Munn v. Illinois,* the Court declared that government could regulate private industries in order to protect the public interest. The railroads had lost their fight.

A decade later, Congress passed the **Interstate Commerce Act.** The act gave the federal government even more power over the railroads. The railroad companies, however, continued to resist all government intervention.

Beginning in 1893, an economic depression struck the country. It affected numerous institutions—including the railroads. Many railroad companies failed. As a result, they were taken over by financial firms. By 1900, seven companies owned most of the nation s railways.

3. Give two reasons why farmers were upset with the railroad companies.

_____

_____

Name _____ Class _____ Date _____

Section 2, *continued*

As you read, take notes to answer questions about the growth of the railroads.

Realizing that railroads were critical to the settlement of the West and the development of the nation, the federal government made huge land grants and loans to the railroad companies.

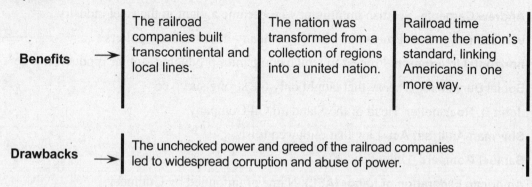

Benefits →

| The railroad companies built transcontinental and local lines. | The nation was transformed from a collection of regions into a united nation. | Railroad time became the nation's standard, linking Americans in one more way. |

Drawbacks → The unchecked power and greed of the railroad companies led to widespread corruption and abuse of power.

1. What problems did employees of the railroad companies face?	2. What was it like to live as a Pullman employee in the town of Pullman?
3. Who was involved in Crédit Mobilier, and what was the purpose of this company?	4. In what ways did the railroad companies use their power to hurt farmers?
5. Why didn't the decision in the *Munn v. Illinois* case succeed in checking the power of the railroads?	6. Why didn't the Interstate Commerce Act immediately limit the power of the railroads?

Guided Reading Workbook

Big Business and Labor

Terms and Names

Andrew Carnegie Scottish immigrant who became a giant in the steel industry

vertical integration Process in which a company buys out its suppliers

horizontal integration Process in which companies producing similar products merge

Social Darwinism Theory that taught only the strong survived

John D. Rockefeller Head of the Standard Oil Company

Sherman Antitrust Act Law that outlawed trusts

Samuel Gompers Union leader

American Federation of Labor (AFL) Name of union led by Gompers

Eugene V. Debs Leader of the American Railway Union

Industrial Workers of the World (IWW) Union of radicals and socialists nicknamed the Wobblies

Mary Harris Jones Organizer for United Mine Workers

Before You Read

In the last section, you read about the growth of the railroad industry in the United States. In this section, you will read about the growth and power of big business in America and how workers united to improve conditions in the nation's growing industries.

As You Read

Use a time line to take notes on the achievements and setbacks of the labor movement between 1876 and 1911.

CARNEGIE'S INNOVATIONS; SOCIAL DARWINISM AND BUSINESS (Pages 241–243)
How did Carnegie take control of the steel industry?

Andrew Carnegie attempted to control the entire steel industry. Through **vertical integration** he bought companies that supplied his raw materials such as iron and coal, and railroads needed to transport the steel. He used **horizontal integration** by buying out or merging with other steel companies.

Carnegie's success helped popularize the theory of **Social Darwinism.** This theory, based on the ideas of biologist Charles Darwin, said that "*natural selection*" enabled the best-suited people to survive and succeed. Social Darwinism supported the ideas of competition, hard work, and responsibility.

1. Describe two ways in which Carnegie tried to control the steel industry.

_____

_____

_____

FEWER CONTROL MORE; LABOR UNIONS EMERGE (Pages 243–245)
How did entrepreneurs try to control competition?

Most entrepreneurs tried to control competition. Their goal was to form a monopoly by buying out competitors or driving them out of business. **John D. Rockefeller** used the Standard Oil trust to almost completely control the oil industry. Rockefeller's ruthless business practices earned him huge profits, but caused people to label him a robber baron. In 1890, the **Sherman Antitrust Act** made it illegal to form a trust, but many companies were able to avoid prosecution under the law. The business boom in the United States bypassed the South which continued to suffer economic stagnation.

Workers responded to business consolidation by forming labor unions. Many workers worked long hours under dangerous conditions for low wages. Women, children, and workers in sweatshops worked under especially harsh conditions. The National Labor Union (NLU) was an early labor union that persuaded Congress to legalize an eight-hour day for government workers in 1868. The NLU excluded African-American workers who formed the Colored National Labor Union (CNLU). The Knights of Labor also enjoyed success but declined after the failure of a series of strikes.

2. Why did entrepreneurs form trusts?

_____

_____

UNION MOVEMENTS DIVERGE; STRIKES TURN VIOLENT
(Pages 245–249)
What were the two major types of unions?

Two major types of unions made great gains. One was craft unions. **Samuel Gompers** formed the **American Federation of Labor (AFL)** in 1886. Gompers used strikes and collective bargaining— negotiations between labor and management to win higher wages and shorter workweeks. **Eugene V. Debs** believed in industrial unionism—a union of all workers, both skilled and unskilled in a single industry. He formed the American Railway Union (ARU). Debs and other workers turned to socialism. In 1905, a union of radicals and socialists was formed called the **Industrial Workers of the World (IWW)** or the Wobblies. In the West, Japanese and Mexican farm workers formed a union to improve conditions.

Unions used strikes to improve conditions. In 1877, workers for the Baltimore and Ohio railroad went out on strike. The strike was broken up when the railroad president persuaded President Rutherford B. Hayes to bring in federal troops to end the strike.

Later strikes turned violent. The Haymarket Affair took place in 1886. A bomb exploded at a demonstration in Chicago's Haymarket Square in support of striking workers. Several people were killed. Labor leaders were charged with inciting a riot and four were hanged although no one knows who actually set off the bomb. In 1892, steel workers and Pinkerton Guards fought a battle at Homestead, Pennsylvania, near Pittsburgh, that left dead on both sides. Two years later a strike against the Pullman Company led by Eugene Debs and his American Railway Union turned violent when federal troops were called out to break the strike.

Mary Harris Jones, known as Mother Jones, gained fame as an organizer for the United Mine Workers. The unions' struggle for better conditions was hurt by government intervening on the side of management. Courts used the Sherman Antitrust Act against the workers. Despite the pressures of government action, unions continued to grow.

3. What were the two types of unions?

_____

_____

As you read this section, answer the questions below about government's
attempts to regulate big business.

a. What is it?

**b. How did it help businesses such as the Carnegie Company and tycoons like Andrew
Carnegie?**

1. Vertical integration	a.
	b.
2. Horizontal integration	a.
	b.
3. Social Darwinism	a.
	b.
4. Monopoly	a.
	b.
5. Holding company	a.
	b.
6. Trust	a.
	b.

**c. How did it harm businesses such as Standard Oil and tycoons like
John D. Rockefeller?**

| 7. The perception of tycoons as "robber barons" | |
| 8. Sherman Antitrust Act | |

Immigrants and Urbanization

Section 1

The New Immigrants

Terms and Names

Ellis Island Inspection station for immigrants arriving on the East Coast

Angel Island Inspection station for immigrants arriving on the West Coast

melting pot A mixture of different cultures living together

nativism Overt favoritism toward native-born Americans

Chinese Exclusion Act Act that limited Chinese immigration

Gentlemen's Agreement Agreement that limited Japanese emigration to U.S.

Before You Read

In the last section, you read about the nation's labor union movement. In this section, you will read how millions of immigrants entered the United States, where they faced culture shock, prejudice, and opportunity.

As You Read

Use a diagram to take notes on the causes and effects of immigration to the United States.

THROUGH THE "GOLDEN DOOR"
(Pages 254–256)
Where did the immigrants come from?

Between 1870 and 1920, about 20 million Europeans immigrated to the United States. Many of them came from eastern and southern Europe.

Some immigrants came to escape religious persecution. Many others were poor and looking to improve their economic situation. Still others came to experience greater freedom in the United States. Most European immigrants arrived on the East Coast.

A smaller number of immigrants came from Asia. They arrived on the West Coast. About 200,000 Chinese immigrants came between 1851 to 1883. Many Chinese immigrants helped build the nation's first transcontinental railroad. When the United States annexed Hawaii in

1898, several thousand Japanese immigrants came to the United States.

From 1880 to 1920, about 260,000 immigrants arrived from various islands in the Caribbean Sea. They came from Jamaica, Cuba, Puerto Rico, and other islands. Many left their homelands because jobs were scarce.

Many Mexicans came to the United States as well. Some became U.S. citizens when the nation acquired Mexican territory in 1848 as a result of the Mexican War. About a million Mexicans arrived between 1910 to 1930 to escape turmoil in their country.

1. Name two regions of the world where immigrants to the U.S. came from.

_____

_____

LIFE IN THE NEW LAND
(Pages 256–258)
How did immigrants cope in America?

Many immigrants traveled to the United States by steamship. On board the ship they shared a cramped, unsanitary space. Under these harsh conditions, disease spread quickly. As a result, some immigrants died before they reached America.

Most European immigrants to the United States arrived in New York. There, they had to pass through an immigration station located on **Ellis Island** in New York Harbor. Officials at the station decided whether the immigrants could enter the country or had to return. Any immigrant with serious health problems or a contagious disease was sent home. Inspectors also made sure that immigrants met the legal requirements for entering the United States.

Asian immigrants arriving on the West Coast went through **Angel Island** in San Francisco. The inspection process on Angel Island was more difficult than on Ellis Island.

Getting along in a new country with a different language and culture was a great challenge for new immigrants. Many immigrants settled in communities with other immigrants from the same country. This made them feel more at home. They also formed organizations to help each other.

2. Name two ways immigrants dealt with adjusting to life in the United States.

_____

_____

IMMIGRATION RESTRICTIONS
(Pages 258–259)
How did some Americans react to immigration?

By the turn of the century, some observers called America a **melting pot.** This term referred to the fact that many different cultures and races had blended in the United States.

However, this was not always the case. Many new immigrants refused to give up their culture to become part of American society.

Some Americans also preferred not to live in a melting pot. They did not like the idea of so many immigrants living in their country. The arrival of so many immigrants led to the growth of **nativism.** Nativism is an obvious preference for native-born Americans. Nativism gave rise to anti-immigrant groups. It also led to a demand for immigration restrictions.

On the West Coast, prejudice against Asians was first directed at the Chinese. During the depression of the 1870s, many Chinese immigrants agreed to work for low wages. Many American workers feared they would lose their jobs to the Chinese. As a result, labor groups pressured politicians to restrict Asian immigration. In 1882, Congress passed the **Chinese Exclusion Act.** This law banned all but a few Chinese immigrants. The ban was not lifted until 1943.

Americans showed prejudice against Japanese immigrants as well. In San Francisco, the local school board put all Chinese, Japanese, and Korean children in special Asian schools. This led to anti-American riots in Japan. President Theodore Roosevelt persuaded San Francisco officials to stop their separation policy. In exchange, Japan agreed to limit emigration to the United States under the **Gentlemen's Agreement** of 1907–1908.

3. Give two examples of anti-immigration measures in the U.S.

_____

_____

Guided Reading Workbook

As you read about people who immigrated to the United States in the late 19th and early 20th centuries, write notes to answer the questions below.

Immigrants from . . .	What were some of the countries they came from?	What reasons did they often have for coming to the U.S.?	Where did they often enter the U.S.?
1. Southern and Eastern Europe			☐ Ellis Island ☐ Angel Island ☐ Southeastern U.S. ☐ Southwestern U.S.
2. Asia			☐ Ellis Island ☐ Angel Island ☐ Southeastern U.S. ☐ Southwestern U.S.
3. Caribbean Islands and Central America			☐ Ellis Island ☐ Angel Island ☐ Southeastern U.S. ☐ Southwestern U.S.

In each box below, identify an important difference that tended to exist between native-born Americans and some or all of the new immigrants around the turn of the century.

Native-Born	New Immigrants

Section 2

The Challenges of Urbanization

Terms and Names

urbanization The growth of cities

Americanization movement Program to teach American culture to immigrants

tenement Multifamily urban dwellings

mass transit Transportation system designed to move large numbers of people along fixed routes

Social Gospel movement Movement that urged people to help the poor

settlement house Community center that addressed problems in slum neighborhoods

Jane Addams Social reformer who helped the poor

Before You Read

In the last section, you read about the arrival of millions of immigrants to America's shores. In this section, you will read how the arrival of so many immigrants caused cities' populations to swell—and their problems to increase.

As You Read

Use a diagram to take notes on the problems of urbanization and the attempts made to solve the problems.

URBAN OPPORTUNITIES
(Pages 262–263)
Why did people move to the cities?

Many of the nation's new immigrants settled in the cities in the early 1900s. They came there to find jobs in the cities' growing factories and businesses. Immigrants settled mainly in cities in the Northeast and Midwest. The result was rapid **urbanization,** or growth of cities, in those regions.

By 1910, immigrants made up more than half of the populations of 18 major American cities. Many immigrants settled in neighborhoods with others from the same country or even from the same village.

Newcomers to the United States learned about their new country through an education program known as the **Americanization movement.** Under this program, schools taught immigrants English, and American history and government. These subjects helped immigrants become citizens.

Immigrants were not the only people who settled in the cities around the turn of the century. On the nation's farms, new machines replaced workers. As a result, many workers in the rural areas lost their jobs. Unemployed farm workers soon moved to cities to find jobs.

Many of the Southern farmers who lost their jobs were African Americans. Between 1890 and 1910 about 200,000 African Americans moved from the South to cities in the North. They hoped to escape economic hardship and racial violence. However, many found prejudice and low wages in the North.

1. Name two groups that settled in the cities.

_____

_____

tenements and lack of water made fire especially dangerous.

2. Name two problems that city residents faced.

_____

_____

URBAN PROBLEMS (Pages 264–265)
What problems did city dwellers face?

City populations grew rapidly. This created many problems. One major problem was a shortage in housing. New types of housing allowed many people to live in a small amount of space. One type was the row house. This was a single-family dwelling that shared side walls with other similar houses.

Another type was **tenements,** multifamily urban houses that were often overcrowded and unsanitary. The growing population of cities created transportation challenges. Cities developed **mass transit**—transportation systems designed to move large number of people along fixed routes.

Cities also faced problems supplying safe drinking water. New York and Cleveland built public waterworks but many city residents were still left without convenient water and had to get their water from taps on the street. Sanitation was also a problem. People threw garbage out their windows. Sewage flowed in the streets. By 1900, many cities had built sewers and created sanitation departments.

Crime and fire were also ongoing problems. Overcrowded and poorly built

REFORMERS MOBILIZE (Page 266)
How did reformers help the poor?

A number of social reformers worked to improve life in the cities. One early reform program was the **Social Gospel movement.** Leaders of this movement preached that people reached salvation by helping the poor. Many reformers responded to the movement's call. They established **settlement houses.** These were community centers located in slum neighborhoods. Workers there provided help and friendship to immigrants and the poor.

Many of these houses were run by middle-class, college-educated women. The settlement houses also offered schooling, nursing, and other kinds of help to those in need.

One of the more well-known social reformers of this time was **Jane Addams.** She helped establish Hull House. This was a settlement house that helped the poor of Chicago.

3. Name two things a settlement house provided for the poor.

_____

_____

Name _____ Class _____ Date _____

Section 2, *continued*

As you read about the rapid growth of American cities in the late 19th and early 20th centuries, take notes to answer the questions below.

The People	Why was each group drawn to cities in the Northeast and Midwest?
1. Immigrants	
2. Farmers	
3. African Americans	

The Problems	What was done in response to each problem?
4. Lack of safe and efficient transportation	
5. Unsafe drinking water	
6. Lack of sanitation	
7. Fire hazards	
8. Crime	

Guided Reading Workbook

Section 3

Politics in the Gilded Age

Terms and Names

political machine A group that controlled a political party

graft Illegal use of political influence for personal gain

Boss Tweed Head of New York City's powerful Democratic political machine

patronage The giving of government jobs to people who had helped a candidate get elected

civil service Government administration

Rutherford B. Hayes 19th president of the United States

James A. Garfield 20th president of the United States

Chester A. Arthur 21st president of the United States

Pendleton Civil Service Act That implemented merit system in civil service hiring

Grover Cleveland 22nd and 24th president of the United States

Benjamin Harrison 23rd president of the United States

Before You Read

In the last section, you read about the problems that residents faced in America's growing cities. In this section, you will read about the people and organizations that controlled the nation's major cities and how reformers tried to end corruption.

As You Read

Use a diagram to list examples of corruption in politics in the Gilded Age.

THE EMERGENCE OF POLITICAL MACHINES (Pages 267–268)
How did political machines control the cities?

During the late 1800s, many cities were run by a **political machine.** This was an organized group, headed by a city boss, that controlled the activities of a political party in a city. The machine offered services to voters and businesses in exchange for political or financial support.

The boss controlled city government, as well as jobs in the police, fire, and sanitation departments. Bosses also controlled city agencies that granted licenses to businesses, and funded construction projects. By controlling the cities' finances, and by solving problems for voters, bosses won loyalty and influence. Furthermore, many bosses were immigrants who had worked their way up in politics. They could speak to the immigrants in their own language, helping them to find jobs and housing. In return, the immigrants pledged their votes.

1. Name two ways in which political machines held power.

_____

_____

MUNICIPAL GRAFT AND SCANDAL
(Page 269)
How were political bosses corrupt?

Political machines provided city dwellers with vital services. But as they gained power, many bosses became corrupt. They became rich through **graft,** or the illegal use of political influence for personal gain. To win elections, some bosses filled the list of eligible voters with the names of dogs, children, and people who had died. They then used those names to cast votes for themselves.

Another illegal practice was the kickback. Workers on city construction projects would charge a higher price for their service and then "kick back" part of the fee to the bosses, who were also taking bribes from businesses in return for allowing illegal or unsafe activities.

One of the most powerful political bosses was William Marcy Tweed, known as **Boss Tweed.** He became the head of Tammany Hall, New York City's most powerful Democratic political machine. The Tweed Ring was a group of corrupt politicians led by Boss Tweed.

Thomas Nast, a political cartoonist, made fun of Tweed in newspapers. Eventually, the public grew outraged by Tweed's corrupt practices. Authorities broke up the Tweed Ring in 1871. Tweed and many of his followers were sentenced to prison.

2. Describe two forms of corruption practiced by political bosses.

_____

_____

CIVIL SERVICE REPLACES PATRONAGE (Pages 270–271)
How was civil service reformed?

For many decades, presidents had complained about the problem of **patronage.** This is the giving of government jobs to people of the same party who had helped a candidate get elected. As a result, many unqualified and corrupt workers were hired.

Reformers wanted to end the patronage system. They called for a merit system, in which jobs in **civil service**—government administration—would go to the most qualified people, regardless of their political views.

President **Rutherford B. Hayes** attempted to reform civil service, but when some members of the Republican party objected, Hayes decided not to run for reelection in 1880.

The party quickly divided over the issue of patronage hiring. The Stalwarts opposed changes in the patronage system. The reformers supported changing the system. The party eventually settled on an independent candidate, **James A. Garfield,** who won the presidential election but turned out to have ties to the reformers. Shortly after being elected he was assassinated by a Stalwart.

Garfield's vice-president, **Chester A. Arthur,** succeeded him. Despite being a Stalwart, Arthur turned reformer when he became president. He pushed through a civil service reform bill known as the **Pendleton Civil Service Act** of 1883. This act created a civil service commission to give government

Guided Reading Workbook

jobs based on merit, not politics. It helped reform the civil service.

However, the Pendleton Act had mixed results. More qualified workers did fill government positions. But because politicians had no jobs to offer, they had trouble seeking money from supporters. As a result, some politicians turned to wealthy leaders for financial support. This strengthened the ties between government and business.

3. Describe two effects of the Pendleton Act.

_____

_____

BUSINESS BUYS INFLUENCE
(Page 271)
What happened to tariffs?

Political reformers in the late 1800s also addressed the issue of tariffs. A tariff is a

tax placed on goods coming into or going out of a country. Most Americans believed that tariffs were necessary to protect U.S. industries from foreign competition. But tariffs did cause prices to rise.

For 12 years tariffs were a key issue in presidential elections. President **Grover Cleveland,** a Democrat, tried, but failed to reduce tariffs. In 1890, Republican President **Benjamin Harrison,** who was supported by big business, signed the McKinley Tariff Act into law, raising tariffs to their highest level ever. Cleveland defeated Harrison in 1892 but was unsuccessful in reducing tariffs.

4. Which two presidents raised tariffs?

_____

_____

Name _____ Class _____ Date _____

As you read this section, fill out the chart below by writing answers to
questions about the Gilded Age.

1876	**Rutherford B. Hayes elected president**	1. What was Hayes's position on civil service reform? What did he do to promote it?
1880	**James A. Garfield elected president**	2. In the debate over civil service reform, did Garfield seem to favor the Stalwarts or the reformers?
1881	**Garfield assassinated; Chester A. Arthur assumes the presidency**	3. What position did Arthur take on civil service reform, and what did he do to support it?
1883	**Pendleton Act passed**	4. What did the Pendleton Act do?
1884	**Grover Cleveland elected president**	5. What was Cleveland's position on tariffs, and what did he do to promote this position?
1888	**Benjamin Harrison elected president**	6. What was Harrison's position on tariffs, and what did he do to support that stand?
1892	**Cleveland reelected president**	7. What happened to tariffs during Cleveland's second presidency?
1897	**William McKinley elected president**	8. What happened to tariffs during McKinley's presidency?

Guided Reading Workbook

Life at the Turn of the 20th Century

Section 1

Science and Urban Life

Terms and Names

Louis Sullivan Early leader of architecture

Daniel Burnham Chicago architect

Frederick Law Olmsted Developer of Central Park

Orville and Wilbur Wright Brothers who flew the first airplane

George Eastman Inventor of the camera

Before You Read

In the last section, you read about the people and organizations that controlled the nation's major cities and how reformers tried to end corruption. In this section, you will read about how technology improved life in the cities and dramatically changed the world of communications.

As You Read

Use a chart to take notes on important changes in city design, communications, and transportation.

TECHNOLOGY AND CITY LIFE
(Pages 276–279)
How did cities cope with their growing populations?

By 1900, millions of Americans had settled in the nation's cities. To accommodate their growing populations, cities had to rely on technology. One example of this was the development of the skyscraper. Skyscrapers are tall buildings that allow people to live many floors above ground. As a result, skyscrapers save space.

Two factors allowed architects to design taller buildings: the invention of elevators, and the development of steel. One of the early skyscraper architects was **Louis Sullivan.** In 1890, he designed the ten-story Wainwright building in St. Louis. In 1902, **Daniel Burnham** designed the Flatiron Building, a

skyscraper at one of New York's busiest intersections.

Skyscrapers allowed cities to grow upward. Changes in transportation helped cities spread outward. In 1888, Richmond, Virginia, became the first American city to use electric-powered streetcars. Soon other cities installed electric streetcars. By the turn of the century, electric streetcars carried people from their homes in outlying neighborhoods to downtown stores, offices, and factories. People could now live in one part of a city and work in another.

To avoid overcrowding on streets, a few large cities moved their streetcars above street level. This created elevated or "el" trains. Other cities built subways by moving rail lines underground. Steel bridges joined sections of cities across rivers.

Guided Reading Workbook

City planners also tried to make cities more livable by creating parks and recreational areas. Journalist and farmer **Frederick Law Olmsted** led the movement for planned city parks. In 1858, he and an architect drew up plans for Central Park in New York. The finished park included boating and tennis facilities, a zoo, and bicycle paths. All of these were placed in a natural setting.

In Chicago, Daniel Burnham designed a plan that would change a swampy region near Lake Michigan into a recreational area. His plan resulted in elegant parks and sandy beaches along Chicago's Lake Michigan shores.

1. Name two technological advances that helped make cities more livable.

_____

_____

NEW TECHNOLOGIES
(Pages 279–281)
How did technology transform communications?

Technology also improved the field of communications. There were several technological advances in printing. American mills began to produce huge amounts of cheap paper from wood pulp. A new kind of high-speed printing press was able to print on both sides of the paper, making magazines and newspapers more affordable. Two brothers, **Orville and Wilbur Wright,** built the first airplane. Their first successful flight occurred in 1903 at Kitty Hawk, North Carolina. It covered 120 feet and lasted 12 seconds.

People paid little attention to the Wright brothers' achievement. Many newspapers didn't even bother to print the story. Within two years, though, the Wright brothers were making distant flights of 24 miles. By 1908, however, the government took an interest in the new technology and by 1920, the United States had established the first transcontinental airmail service.

In 1888, **George Eastman** invented his Kodak camera. This provided millions of Americans with an easy way to take pictures. The camera also changed news reporting. Reporters could now photograph events as they occurred, and this helped create the field of photojournalism. When the Wright brothers made their first successful flight at Kitty Hawk, an amateur photographer caught the event on film.

2. Name two inventions that helped change the world of communications.

_____

_____

Guided Reading Workbook

As you read about how technological changes at the turn of the 20th century affected American life, write notes in the appropriate boxes. Leave the shaded boxes blank.

	1. Who was involved in its development?	2. What other inventions helped make this one possible?	3. How did this invention or development affect Americans' lives?
Skyscraper			
Electric transit			
Suspension bridge			
Urban planning			
Airmail			
Web-perfecting press			
Kodak camera			

Guided Reading Workbook

Life at the Turn of the 20th Century

Section 2

Expanding Public Education

Terms and Names

Booker T. Washington Prominent African-American educator

Tuskegee Normal and Industrial Institute School headed by Booker T. Washington

W.E.B. Du Bois First African American to receive Ph.D from Harvard

Niagara Movement Insisted that blacks should seek a liberal arts education

Before You Read

In the last section, you read about how technology transformed cities and the world of communications. In this section, you will read about the growth of public education in America.

As You Read

Use a chart to take notes on developments in education at the turn of the 20th century and their major results.

EXPANDING PUBLIC EDUCATION
(Pages 282–284)

How did education change in the late 1800s?

During the late 1800s, reformers tried to improve public education. At that time, most children in the United States received little education. Many children did not even attend school. Those who did left after only four years.

Eventually, the situation began to improve. Between 1865 and 1895, 31 states passed laws requiring children from 8 to 14 years-old to attend school for at least three months out of every year. By 1900, almost three-quarters of American children between those ages attended school. Schools taught reading, writing, and arithmetic.

By the turn of the century, the number of schools had increased greatly. The number of kindergartens grew from 200 in 1880 to 3,000 in 1900. The number of high schools increased even more. In 1878

there were 800 high schools in the United States. By 1898, that number had grown to 5,500.

The high-school curriculum also expanded. It included courses in science, civics, home economics, history, and literature. Many people realized that the new industrial age needed people who had technical and managerial skills. As a result, high schools also included courses such as drafting and bookkeeping. This prepared students for industrial and office jobs.

The growth of public education mainly affected the nation's white communities. During the late 1880s, only 34 percent of African-American children attended elementary school. Fewer than one percent attended high school.

Unlike African Americans, immigrants attended schools in large numbers. Some immigrant parents hoped that school would "Americanize" their children.

Many adult immigrants also went to school. They attended night classes to learn American culture and English. Some employers offered daytime programs to Americanize their workers.

1. Provide two examples of how public education changed in the late 1800s.

_____

_____

EXPANDING HIGHER EDUCATION
(**Pages** 284–285)
What changes did colleges make?

At the turn of the century, only about 2 percent of Americans attended college. Most college students came from middle-class or wealthy families. Colleges prepared well-to-do young men for successful careers in business.

Between 1880 and 1900, more than 150 new colleges were founded in the United States. From 1880 to 1920, the number of students enrolled in college quadrupled.

During this time, colleges added more subjects. Before, many universities had taught only classical subjects such as Greek and Latin. Now they began teaching more modern subjects. In response to the needs of expanding big business, the research university emerged offering courses in modern languages, physical sciences, and the new disciplines of psychology and sociology. Professional schools in law and medicine were established. Many private colleges and universities began requiring entrance

exams, while some state universities required only a high school diploma for admission.

Thousands of freed African Americans began attending college in greater numbers after the Civil War. With the help of the Freedmen's Bureau and other groups, blacks founded Howard, Atlanta, and Fisk Universities between 1865 and 1868. Still, blacks were excluded from many private institutions. Financially, it was difficult for private donors to support or educate enough black college graduates to meet the needs of their communities. In 1900, only about 4 percent of all African Americans were in attendance at colleges or professional schools.

Booker T. Washington founded the **Tuskegee Normal and Industrial Institute.** Washington believed that racism would end when blacks acquired useful labor skills and were valuable to society. Washington taught those skills at Tuskegee. **W. E. B. Du Bois** was a black educator who disagreed with Washington. Du Bois had been the first black to get a doctorate from Harvard. Du Bois founded the **Niagara Movement** which insisted that blacks should seek a liberal arts education.

2. Name two ways in which colleges changed during the late 1800s.

_____

_____

As you read this section, write notes to describe the chief characteristics of
each type of educational institution and the developments that took place at
the turn of the 20th century.

	Chief Characteristics and Important Developments
1. Elementary schools	
2. High schools	
3. Colleges and universities	
4. Education for immigrant adults	

Life at the Turn of the 20th Century

Segregation and Discrimination

Terms and Names

Ida B. Wells African-American reformer who tried to end lynching

poll tax Money one had to pay in order to vote

grandfather clause Clause that allowed poor, uneducated whites to vote

segregation The word used to describe racial separation

Jim Crow laws Laws that helped keep whites and blacks separate

Plessy* v. *Ferguson Court case that upheld the Jim Crow laws

debt peonage A system in which a person is forced to work to pay off debts

Before You Read

In the last section, you read about improvements made to public education around the turn of the century. In this section, you will read about how life for African Americans and other nonwhites remained one of hardship and discrimination.

As You Read

Use a time line to take notes on important events in race relations at the turn of the 20th century.

AFRICAN AMERICANS FIGHT LEGAL DISCRIMINATION
(Pages 286–287)
How were African Americans kept from voting?

Ida B. Wells was a leader in the fight against discrimination. Wells crusaded against racial violence. After Reconstruction, African Americans were kept from voting in the South. By 1900, however, all Southern states had set up new voting restrictions meant to keep blacks from voting.

For example, some states required voters to be able to read. To determine this, officials gave each voter a literacy test. They often gave African Americans more difficult tests. The officials giving the test could pass or fail people as they wished.

Another voting requirement was the **poll tax.** This was a tax that one had to be pay to enter a voting booth. African Americans and poor whites often did not have the money to pay the tax. So they were unable to vote.

Several Southern states wanted to make sure that whites who could not read or pay a poll tax still could vote. So they added a **grandfather clause** to their constitutions. This clause stated that any person could vote if their father or grandfather was qualified to vote before January 1, 1867. This date was important because before that time, freed slaves did not have the right to vote. Therefore, the grandfather clause did not allow African Americans to vote. Some Americans challenged the literacy test

Guided Reading Workbook

and poll tax laws. But the Supreme Court allowed the laws to stand.

Separating people on the basis of race became known as **segregation.** Racial segregation developed in such places as schools, hospitals, and transportation systems throughout the South. The Southern states also passed **Jim Crow laws.** These laws separated whites and blacks in private and public places.

Eventually a legal challenge to segregation reached the U.S. Supreme Court. However, in the case *Plessy* v. *Ferguson,* the Supreme Court ruled that separating the races in public places was legal.

1. Name two ways that Southern states restricted the voting rights of African Americans.

_____

_____

TURN-OF-THE-CENTURY RACE RELATIONS (Pages 287–288)
How did social customs restrict African Americans?

In addition to laws, customs also restricted the rights of African Americans. African Americans had to show respect to whites, including children. These customs often belittled and humiliated African Americans. For example, blacks had to yield the sidewalk to whites. Black men always had to remove their hats for whites.

African-American reformers debated over how to address racial discrimination. Booker T. Washington argued that blacks should not insist on full legal equality—which whites would never allow. Instead, he argued, blacks should concentrate on gaining economic power. Other African Americans, like W. E. B. Du Bois and Ida B. Wells, demanded legal equality right away.

African Americans who did not follow the customs could face severe punishment. Often, African Americans accused of failing to perform the customs were lynched—hanged without trial.

African Americans in the North also faced discrimination. They lived in segregated neighborhoods. They faced discrimination in the workplace, some of which turned violent.

2. Name two ways blacks had to show respect to whites.

_____

_____

DISCRIMINATION IN THE WEST
(Pages 288–289)
What other groups faced discrimination in America?

African Americans were not the only ones who faced discrimination at the turn of the century. Mexican Americans faced similar treatment. In the 1880s and 1890s, railroad companies hired many Mexicans to build new rail lines in the Southwest. Railroad managers hired Mexicans because they were used to the Southwest's hot, dry climate. Managers also felt they could pay Mexicans less than members of other ethnic groups.

Mexicans also played an important role in the Southwest's mining and farming industries. Raising crops such as grapes, lettuce, and citrus fruits required large amounts of labor. Mexicans provided much of this farm work.

Landowners often forced Mexicans to work to repay debts. This system was called **debt peonage.** The Supreme Court ruled against this system in 1911. The Court called it a violation of the Thirteenth Amendment.

The Chinese also faced discrimination in America. Whites feared losing their jobs to Chinese workers. Chinese workers lived in segregated neighborhoods and their children attended segregated schools.

3. Name two groups that faced discrimination in the West.

_____

_____

As you read about racial tensions at the turn of the 20th century, write
notes to answer the questions.

	In what region or regions did it exist?	Who were its targets?	How did it affect the lives of these people?
1. Literacy test			
2. Poll tax			
3. Grandfather clause			
4. Jim Crow laws			
5. Racial etiquette			
6. Debt peonage			
7. Chinese Exclusion Act			

Life at the Turn of the 20th Century

Section 4

The Dawn of Mass Culture

Terms and Names

Joseph Pulitzer Owner of the *New York World* newspaper

William Randolph Hearst Owner of the New York *Morning Journal San Francisco Examiner*

Ashcan school A school of painting that featured urban life and working people with gritty realism

Mark Twain Pen name of the novelist and humorist Samuel Langhorne Clemens

rural free delivery (RFD) System that brought packages directly to homes

Before You Read

In the last section, you read about how African Americans and other nonwhites continued to suffer racial discrimination at the turn of the century. In this section, you will read about how Americans developed new forms of entertainment and ways to spend their money.

As You Read

Use a diagram to take notes on the development of leisure activities and mass culture.

AMERICAN LEISURE (Pages 292–294)
How **did Americans spend their free time?**

The use of machines allowed workers at the turn of the century to do their jobs faster. This led to a shorter workweek. As a result, Americans had more leisure time.

Americans found new ways to use that time. Many city dwellers enjoyed trips to amusement parks. There, rides such as the roller coaster and the Ferris wheel thrilled people.

Another recreational activity that became popular at the turn of the century was bicycling. This activity entertained both men and women. Many Americans also grew fond of playing tennis.

Several kinds of snack foods also became popular. Americans turned to brand-name

snacks such as a Hershey chocolate bar and drinks such as a Coca-Cola.

Those Americans who did not wish to exercise watched professional sports. Boxing became popular in the late 1800s. Baseball also became a well-loved spectator sport. The National League was formed in 1876 and the American League in 1901. African-American baseball players were not allowed to play in either league. As a result, they formed their own clubs—the Negro National League and the Negro American League.

1. Name two activities that were popular in the United States at the turn of the century.

_____

_____

THE SPREAD OF MASS CULTURE
(**Pages** 294–296)
How did newspapers attract more readers?

Newspapers also entertained Americans. Many publishers changed their newspapers in order to attract more readers. They filled their pages with sensational headlines. They also devised promotional stunts. In 1889, for example, one newspaper introduced its story about the horrors of a flood in Johnstown, Pennsylvania with the headline "THE VALLEY OF DEATH."

Some publishers used other techniques. **Joseph Pulitzer,** the owner of the *New York World,* introduced a large Sunday edition. It included comics, sports coverage, and women's news. Pulitzer presented news in a sensational way to beat his main competitor, **William Randolph Hearst.** Hearst owned the New York *Morning Journal* and the San Francisco *Examiner.* Hearst tried to outdo Pulitzer by publishing exaggerated and even made-up stories. By 1898, both publishers were selling more than one million copies each day.

By 1900, at least one art gallery could be found in every large city. American artists like Thomas Eakins of Philadelphia used realism to portray life as it was really lived. Eakins was a leader of the **Ashcan School** which painted urban life and working people with gritty realism and no frills.

Light fiction such as "dime novels" was popular as more people read books. **Mark Twain,** the pen name of the humorist and novelist Samuel Langhorne Clemens, wrote realistic portrayals of American life that became popular. His novel *The Adventures of Huckleberry Finn* became a classic of American literature. The efforts of American libraries and art galleries to raise public taste were not always

successful. Many Americans had no interest in high culture. African Americans and others were denied access to most white-controlled cultural institutions.

2. Name two ways in which publishers tried to sell more newspapers.

_____

_____

NEW WAYS TO SELL GOODS
(**Pages** 296–297)
How did Americans shop?

Americans at the turn of the century also began to change the way they shopped. As cities grew, shopping centers emerged. These structures made many kinds of stores available in one area.

Another new development was the department store. This type of store offered consumers a wide range of goods to buy. Marshall Field of Chicago was the first department store in America. Chain stores—groups of stores owned by the same person—also started in the late 1800s. F. W. Woolworth's "five-and-dime store" and other chain grocery stores became popular. These types of stores offered consumers brand names and low-cost sales.

As shopping became more popular, so too did advertising. Companies filled magazines and newspapers with ads for their products. Advertisers also placed their products on barns, houses, and billboards.

In the late 1800s, Montgomery Ward and Sears Roebuck introduced mail-order catalogs. These books brought department store items to those who lived outside of the cities. Each company's catalog contained a description of its goods. The company mailed its catalog to farmers and small town residents. These people then could order goods from the catalog. By

1910, about 10 million Americans shopped by mail.

The United States Post Office increased mail-order business by starting a **rural free delivery (RFD)** system. This brought packages directly to every home.

3. Name two developments in the ways goods were sold.

_____

_____

As you read about the emergence of modern mass culture, give *either* an example of each item *or* mention one of the people who invented or popularized it. Then note one reason why the item became so popular around the turn of the 20th century.

	1. Amusement parks	2. Bicycling	3. Boxing	4. Baseball
Example				
Reason				

	5. Shopping centers	6. Department stores	7. Chain stores	8. Mail-order catalogs
Example				
Reason				

The Origins of Progressivism

Terms and Names

progressive movement Social reform movement in the early 20th century

Florence Kelley Social reformer

prohibition Making the sale or use of alcohol illegal

muckraker Writer who exposes wrongdoing

scientific management Using scientific ideas to make work more efficient

Robert M. LaFollette Progressive Wisconsin governor and senator

initiative A way for people to propose laws directly

referendum A way for people to approve changes in laws by a vote

recall A vote on whether to remove a public official from office

Seventeenth Amendment Amendment providing for senators to be elected directly

Before You Read

In the last section, you read about popular culture at the turn of the century. In this section, you will learn about the social reforms that made up the progressive movement.

As You Read

Use a web diagram to list the organizations and people who worked for social, political, moral, and economic reform.

FOUR GOALS OF PROGRESSIVISM
(Pages 306–309)
What did reformers want?

As the 1900s opened, reformers pushed for a number of changes. Together their efforts built the **progressive movement.** The progressive movement had four major goals: (1) to protect social welfare, (2) to promote moral improvement, (3) to create economic reform, and (4) to foster efficiency.

Reformers tried to promote social welfare by easing the problems of city life. The YMCA built libraries and exercise rooms. The Salvation Army fed poor people in the cities and cared for children in nurseries. Settlement houses helped families. One reformer, **Florence Kelley,** helped to win the passage of the Illinois Factory Act in 1893. The law prohibited child labor and limited women's working hours. The law became a model for other states.

Reformers promoted moral reform by working for **prohibition**—the banning of alcoholic drinks. Many of these reformers, called prohibitionists, were members of the Woman's Christian Temperance Union (WCTU). The well-organized union became the largest women's group the country had ever seen.

Reformers tried to make economic changes by pointing out the great inequality between the rich and the poor.

They pushed for better treatment of workers. Journalists called **muckrakers** wrote stories about corruption and unfair practices in business.

To help make businesses more efficient and profitable, some reformers promoted the idea of **scientific management.** The idea was to apply scientific ideas to make each task simpler. One outcome was the assembly line.

1. How did reformers try to make businesses more efficient and profitable?

_____

_____

CLEANING UP LOCAL GOVERNMENT (Pages 309–310)
How did progressives change city governments?

Progressives also reformed politics. City governments were sometimes corrupt. For instance, they might be run by party bosses who gave jobs to their friends and bribed people to vote for them. One answer to this problem was a new system of city government called the commission system.

In the commission system a group of experts runs the city. Each expert takes charge of a different city department. By 1917, about 500 cities had commission forms of city government.

Another reform idea was the council-manager form of government. By 1925, nearly 250 cities had managers. These managers were appointed by councils elected by the people.

Some cities had progressive mayors. They improved cities without changing their system of government. They put in such reforms as fairer tax systems and lower public transportation fares.

2. How did the commission system help clean up city government?

_____

_____

REFORM AT THE STATE LEVEL
(Pages 310–312)
How did state laws change?

Reformers also worked at the state level. Many states had progressive governors. These states passed laws to regulate railroads, mines, telephone companies, and other large businesses.

Robert M. La Follette, as governor of Wisconsin, led the way in regulating big business. His reforms of the railway industry taxed railroad property at the same rate as other business property. He set up a commission to regulate rates and forbade railroads to issue free passes to state officials.

Progressives also worked to improve conditions in the workplace and to end the employment of children. Factories hired children because children could do the same unskilled work as adults for less money. Often wages were so low that every member of the family needed to work.

Progressive reformers did not get a federal law to ban child labor. They did, however, get state legislatures to ban child labor. States also set maximum hours for all workers.

Progressives also won some reforms from the Supreme Court. In the case of *Muller* v. *Oregon,* the Court decided that a state could legally limit the working hours of women. In 1917, the Supreme Court upheld a ten-hour workday for men.

Electoral reforms at the state level gave voters more power. Oregon was the first to adopt the secret ballot, giving voters privacy. Three other reforms were important: (1) **initiative** gives voters themselves the right to propose a law, (2) voters could accept or reject the initiative by a direct vote on the initiative, called a **referendum,** and (3) voters got the right of **recall,** which meant they could force a government official to face another election.

Minnesota became the first state to use a mandatory statewide direct primary system. This meant that voters, instead of political machines, would choose candidates for public office through a special popular election. The direct

primary led to the passage of the **Seventeenth Amendment** to the Constitution. This amendment called for senators to be elected directly by the people instead of by state lawmakers.

3. What are three ways progressive reforms helped ordinary people?

_____

_____

As you read about the era of reform, take notes about the goals, reformers, and successes of the reform movements.

Social Reforms	People and Groups Involved	Successes (laws, legal decisions, etc.)
1. Social welfare reform movement		
2. Moral reform movement		
3. Economic reform movement		
4. Movement for industrial efficiency		
5. Movement to protect workers		

Political Reforms	People and Groups Involved	Successes (laws, legal decisions, etc.)
6. Movement to reform local government		
7. State reform of big business		
8. Movement for election reform		

Women in Public Life

Terms and Names

NACW National Association of Colored Women; founded in 1896 to improve living and working conditions for African-American women

suffrage The right to vote; a major goal of women reformers

Susan B. Anthony Leader of the woman suffrage movement, who helped to define the movement's goals and beliefs and to lead its actions

NAWSA National American Woman Suffrage Association; founded in 1890 to help women win the right to vote

Before You Read

In the last section, you read about the progressive movement. In this section, you will learn about the new, active roles women were taking in the workplace and in politics.

As You Read

Use a diagram to take notes about working women in the late 1800s.

WOMEN IN THE WORK FORCE
(Pages 313–314)
What jobs did women do?

Before the Civil War, most married women worked at home. They cared for their families and did not have paid jobs. By the end of the 19th century, however, many women had to work outside the home in order to earn money.

Farm women continued to work as they always had. They did the cooking, cleaning, sewing, and child rearing. They helped with the crops and animals.

As better-paying opportunities in towns and cities became available, more women began working outside the home. By 1900, one in five American women held jobs; 25 percent of them worked in manufacturing. About half of the women working in manufacturing were employed in the garment trades. They typically held the least skilled positions and were paid

only half as much as men. Women also began filling new jobs in offices, stores, and classrooms. Women went to new business schools to learn to become stenographers and typists. These jobs required a high school education. Women without a formal education took jobs as domestic workers, cleaning, and taking care of children of other families. Almost two million African-American workers— forced by economic necessity—worked on farms and in cities as domestic workers, laundresses, scrubwomen, and maids. Unmarried immigrant women did domestic labor, took in piecework, or cared for boarders at home.

1. What are three jobs that women without a formal education often held?

_____

_____

WOMEN LEAD REFORM
(Pages 314–316)
What reforms did women want?

Dangerous conditions, long hours, and low wages caused working women to fight for reforms. The Triangle Shirtwaist fire in New York City in 1911 killed 146 young workers, mostly women, and spurred the cause for reform.

Women who became active in public life attended college. New women's colleges such as Vassar, Smith, and Wellesley opened. By the late 19th century, marriage was no longer a woman's only alternative.

In 1896, African-American women founded the National Association of Colored Women **(NACW).**

This organization created nurseries, reading rooms, and kindergartens.

Women's crusade for **suffrage,** or the right to vote, began at the Seneca Falls Convention in 1848. The women's movement split over whether or not to support the Fourteenth and Fifteenth Amendments which granted the vote to African-American men, but not to women of any race. **Susan B. Anthony** led the opposition. By 1890, suffragists had united in the National American Woman Suffrage Association **(NAWSA).**

Women tried three approaches to win the vote: (1) they tried to convince state legislatures; (2) they went to court to clarify whether the provisions of the Fourteenth Amendment meant women should be allowed to vote, and (3) they pushed for a national constitutional amendment. This was voted down several times.

2. What are three ways in which women tried to win the vote?

_____

_____

Guided Reading Workbook

As you read this section, take notes to answer the questions.

1. What types of jobs were women in each group likely to hold?			
Lower Class	Middle and Upper Class	African American	Immigrant

2. How did educational opportunities for middle- and upper-class women change?

3. How did these new opportunities affect the lives of middle- and upper-class women?

4. What three strategies were adopted by the suffragists to win the vote?		
a.	b.	c.

5. What results did each strategy produce?		
a.	b.	c.

Section 3

Teddy Roosevelt's Square Deal

Terms and Names

Theodore Roosevelt President from 1901 to 1909

Square Deal President Roosevelt's program of progressive reforms

Upton Sinclair Novelist who exposed social problems

The Jungle Novel by Upton Sinclair describing meatpacking

Meat Inspection Act Law reforming meatpacking conditions, 1906

Pure Food and Drug Act Law to stop the sale of unclean food and drugs, 1906

conservation The planned management of natural resources

NAACP National Association for the Advancement of Colored People, founded in 1909 to work for racial equality

Before You Read

In the last section, you read about women who worked for reforms in their communities and for the right to vote. In this section, you will learn about President Theodore Roosevelt's success in promoting reforms at the national level.

As You Read

Use a diagram to take notes on how the problems during Roosevelt's presidency were addressed.

A ROUGH-RIDING PRESIDENT
(Pages 317–319)
What was Roosevelt like?

Theodore Roosevelt became president in 1901. He was bold, ambitious, and full of energy. He had been active in sports and politics. In the Spanish–American War he led a fighting unit called the Rough Riders. His personality made him a popular president.

Roosevelt used his popularity to get his programs passed. He wanted to see that the common people received what he called a **Square Deal.** This term referred to a program of progressive reforms sponsored by his administration.

1. How did Roosevelt's personality shape his presidency?

_____

_____

USING FEDERAL POWER
(Pages 319–320)
How did Roosevelt handle big business?

President Roosevelt used the power of the government to help solve the nation's problems.

Roosevelt also used the power of his government to deal with the problem of trusts. Trusts were large companies that had control over their markets. Trusts, or monopolies, first drove smaller companies out by lowering their own prices. Then when the smaller companies were gone, the trusts could raise their prices. They no longer had any competition.

By 1900, trusts controlled about 80 percent of U.S. industries. Roosevelt supported big business, but he also wanted to stop trusts that harmed people. He had the government sue harmful trusts under the Sherman Antitrust Act of 1890. In all, Roosevelt filed 44 antitrust suits. He was called a trustbuster.

In 1902, about 140,000 coal miners in Pennsylvania went on strike. The mine owners refused to negotiate with them. President Roosevelt called both sides to the White House to talk. He threatened to have the government take over the mines. The two sides agreed to have an arbitration commission help settle their differences. The commission succeeded in reaching a compromise. From then on, the federal government would often step in to help settle a strike.

In 1887, the Interstate Commerce Commission (ICC) had been set up to regulate the railroad industry. It had not been effective. Roosevelt pushed through laws such as the Hepburn Act of 1906, which strictly limited the distribution of free railroad passes, a common form of bribery. Roosevelt's efforts resulted in fairer shipping rates and less corruption in the railroad industry.

2. How did Roosevelt use the power of the federal government to change business practices?

_____

_____

_____

HEALTH AND THE ENVIRONMENT
(**Pages** 320–324)
What did Roosevelt do for public health and the environment?

After reading *The Jungle* by **Upton Sinclair** which described filthy conditions in the meatpacking industry, Roosevelt pushed for passage of the **Meat Inspection Act.** This law, passed in 1906, called for strict cleanliness requirements for meatpackers. It created a program of federal meat inspection.

Also in 1906, Congress passed the **Pure Food and Drug Act** which halted the sale of contaminated foods and medicines and called for truth in labeling.

Before Roosevelt became president, the federal government had paid little attention to the nation's natural resources. John Muir, a naturalist and writer, persuaded Roosevelt to set aside 148 million acres of forest reserves and other land for waterpower sites and mineral and water resources. Roosevelt appointed Gifford Pinchot as head of the U.S. Forest Service. Roosevelt and Pinchot believed in the **conservation** of land, meaning some land should be preserved as wilderness while other areas would be developed for the common good. Roosevelt and Pinchot were opposed by Muir, who believed in complete preservation of the wilderness. Indeed, Roosevelt signed the Newlands Act which funded irrigation projects that transformed dry wilderness into land suitable for agriculture.

3. What are two ways that Roosevelt helped to make people's lives safer and healthier?

_____

_____

_____

ROOSEVELT AND CIVIL RIGHTS
(Pages 324–325)
What did Roosevelt do for African Americans?

Roosevelt supported individual African Americans like Booker T. Washington. But he did not help African Americans in general. In 1909, black leaders, including W. E. B. Du Bois, founded the National Association for the Advancement of Colored People **(NAACP).** The organization pushed for civil rights and racial equality. The progressive movement, however, continued to focus on the needs of middle-class whites.

4. What action did the NAACP take?

_____

_____

As you read this section, write notes to answer questions about President
Theodore Roosevelt. If Roosevelt took no steps to solve the problem or if
no legislation was involved in solving the problem, write "none."

Problem	What steps did Roosevelt take to solve each problem?	Which legislation helped solve the problem?
1. 1902 coal strike		
2. Trusts		
3. Unregulated big business		
4. Dangerous foods and medicines		
5. Shrinking wilderness and natural resources		
6. Racial discrimination		

Section 4

Progressivism Under Taft

Terms and Names

William Howard Taft President from 1909 to 1913, successor to Roosevelt

Payne-Aldrich Tariff Bill meant to lower tariffs on imported goods

Gifford Pinchot Head of the U.S. Forest Service under Roosevelt, who believed that it was possible to make use of natural resources while conserving them

Bull Moose Party Nickname for the new Progressive Party, which was formed to support Roosevelt in the election of 1912

Woodrow Wilson Winner of the 1912 presidential election

Before You Read

In the last section, you read about the reforms of Teddy Roosevelt's presidency. In this section, you will learn about the reforms and political problems of the next president, William Howard Taft.

As You Read

Use a diagram to take notes about the causes of Taft's problems in office.

TAFT BECOMES PRESIDENT
(Pages 328–329)
Why did Taft have problems?

President Roosevelt promised not to run for another term. Instead, he wanted **William Howard Taft** to become president. Taft had been Roosevelt's secretary of war, and Roosevelt felt Taft would carry out his policies. Taft was elected in 1909, and he did continue many of the progressive programs. In fact, he busted more than twice as many trusts as Roosevelt had. However, Taft was not as effective as Roosevelt had been. He had many problems in office.

His first problem came over tariffs. Taft wanted to lower tariffs. He supported the Payne bill, which was passed in the House. However, the Senate passed a weakened version of the bill, the **Payne-Aldrich Tariff.** The revised bill did not lower tariffs

much at all. The progressives in Taft's own Republican Party were annoyed.

Another problem for Taft arose over conservation. Conservationists like **Gifford Pinchot,** the head of the U.S. Forest Service, believed that wilderness areas could be managed for public enjoyment as well as private development. This meant, for instance, that someone could make a profit by logging land that belonged to the federal government. This was called a multi-use land program.

Taft appointed Richard A. Ballinger as secretary of the interior. Ballinger did not want to keep so much federal land in reserve. He wanted to free up land for forestry and mining. He wanted to sell some land for private uses. When he did these things, Pinchot complained. Pinchot accused him of misusing the natural resources for commercial interests. As a result of Pinchot's criticism, Taft felt he had to fire him from the U.S. Forest Service.

1. In what two areas did Taft have problems?

_____

_____

THE REPUBLICAN PARTY SPLITS
(Pages 329–330)
Why did the Republican Party split?

The Republican Party had two wings: (1) the progressives, who wanted change and (2) the conservatives, who did not want reform. Taft was not able to hold the two wings of his party together.

The two groups disagreed over Taft's support of political boss Joseph Cannon. Cannon was Speaker of the House of Representatives, and he ran the House his own way. He appointed people to committee positions who weren't the next in line. He even made himself the head of the Committee on Rules. This gave him the power to control what bills Congress would take up. As a result, under Cannon, the House often did not even vote on progressive bills.

The Republican party split over how to handle Cannon. This gave the Democrats a chance to take over the House in the 1910 midterm elections. Democrats had control of the House for the first time in almost 20 years.

By 1912, Teddy Roosevelt had decided to run for a third term as president, after all. Taft had an advantage because he was already in office. The Republican Party nominated Taft, but Roosevelt's supporters broke off and formed the Progressive Party. This third party was also called the **Bull Moose Party.** It ran on a platform of reform. The Democrats were in a stronger position now that the

Republicans were split. They nominated the reform governor of New Jersey, **Woodrow Wilson.**

2. Who formed the Bull Moose Party?

_____

_____

DEMOCRATS WIN IN 1912
(Pages 330–331)
Who won the election of 1912?

The 1912 election offered Americans four main choices: Wilson, Taft, Roosevelt, and the socialist Eugene V. Debs.

Wilson campaigned on a progressive platform, called the New Freedom. He wanted stronger antitrust legislation, banking reform, and lower tariffs.

Both Roosevelt and Wilson wanted to give the government a stronger role in the economy. But they differed over strategies, that is, how to do that. Roosevelt supported government supervision of big business. Wilson opposed all business monopolies, or trusts. Debs went even further. He wanted the government to distribute national wealth more equally among the people.

Wilson won the 1912 election. He also brought in a Democratic majority in Congress. In all, about 75 percent of the vote went to the candidates who favored economic reform—Wilson, Roosevelt, and Debs. Because so many people supported reform, Wilson had more power to carry out his reforms once in office.

3. What did Wilson have in common with Roosevelt? With Debs?

_____

_____

As you read this section, take notes to answer questions about growing conflicts between reform and business interests.

In 1912, the Republican Party splits at its convention.

	Progressives	Conservatives
1. Why did they support or oppose Taft?		
2. What party did they form or stay with?		

In the 1912 election, four parties run candidates.

	Progressive Party	Republican Party	Democratic Party	Socialist Party
3. Who did they run for president?				
4. What was their candidate's position on big business?				

Section 5

Wilson's New Freedom

Terms and Names

Clayton Antitrust Act Law that weakened monopolies and upheld the rights of unions and farm organizations

Federal Trade Commission (FTC) A federal agency set up in 1914 to investigate businesses to help enforce the laws

Federal Reserve System National banking system begun in 1913

Carrie Chapman Catt President of NAWSA, who led the campaign for woman suffrage during Wilson's administration

Nineteenth Amendment Amendment to the Constitution giving women the right to vote

Before You Read

In the last section, you read about the problems Taft faced as president. In this section, you will learn how Woodrow Wilson managed to get some parts of his progressive platform passed but had to give up others.

As You Read

Use a time line to take notes on the key events during Wilson's first term.

WILSON WINS FINANCIAL REFORMS (Pages 332–334)
What reforms did Wilson support?

Woodrow Wilson grew up in a religious family in the South. He began his career as a lawyer and then became a college professor, university president, and finally state governor. As governor of New Jersey, he worked for many progressive causes. When he was elected president, he pushed for a reform program called the New Freedom.

Under Wilson, Congress passed two antitrust measures. The first was the **Clayton Antitrust Act** of 1914. This law had several important effects. The law (1) made it more difficult for monopolies to form, (2) said that the people who ran a company could be held personally

responsible if the company violated the law, and (3) ruled that labor unions and farm organizations were not themselves to be considered trusts. This made strikes, peaceful picketing, and boycotts legal.

The second antitrust measure was the Federal Trade Act of 1914, which set up the **Federal Trade Commission (FTC)**. This agency had the power to investigate businesses for the government. The FTC became very active during Wilson's administration. It issued nearly 400 orders telling companies to stop breaking the law.

Wilson also worked to lower tariffs. He believed that high tariffs encouraged monopolies. By raising the cost of imported goods, they cut competition against American goods. He supported the Underwood Tariff of 1913, which lowered tariffs for the first time since the Civil War.

With less money coming in from tariffs, however, the government needed another source of money. It turned to an income tax. This tax on people's earnings was created by the Sixteenth Amendment to the Constitution, which was ratified by the states in 1913. The tax gave to the federal government a small percentage of all workers' income and business profits.

After reforming tariffs, Wilson turned his attention to the banking system. It was difficult for people far from banking centers to obtain credit. The new **Federal Reserve System** solved this problem by dividing the country into 12 districts, each with a federal reserve bank. This system controlled the money supply and made credit more easily available. Setting up the federal reserve was one of Wilson's most important reforms.

1. What were three areas that Wilson reformed?

_____

_____

_____

Carrie Chapman Catt succeeded Susan B. Anthony as president of NAWSA. Catt believed in continuing the cautious tactics of the past. Lucy Burns and Alice Paul formed the National Woman's Party and adopted more radical tactics such as around-the-clock picketing of the White House.

Some of the picketers went to jail and even started a hunger strike. But it took World War I to bring women the vote. A great number of women became active in supporting the war effort. Women ran committees, rolled bandages, and sold liberty bonds in order to raise funds for the war. Once they were active in public life, women felt more strongly than ever that they should have the right to vote. At last, in 1919 Congress passed the **Nineteenth Amendment**. This amendment giving women the vote was ratified by the states the next year.

2. How did World War I help women get the right to vote?

_____

_____

_____

WOMEN WIN SUFFRAGE
(**Pages** 334–335)
How did women get the vote?
At the same time Wilson was pushing for reforms, women continued to push for voting rights. By 1912, only five states had given suffrage to women. But several things were happening that gave the suffrage movement hope.

Local suffrage organizations used door-to-door campaigns to win support. College-educated women joined in reaching out to working-class women. Women who had visited Europe adopted the more bold tactics of British suffragists such as heckling government officials.

THE LIMITS OF PROGRESSIVISM
(**Pages** 335–337)
Did Wilson support civil rights?
Like Roosevelt and Taft, Wilson backed away from civil rights. During the 1912 campaign he won the support of the NAACP by promising to treat blacks equally. He also promised to speak out against lynching, that is, mob killings of blacks. However, once he was president Wilson opposed federal laws against lynching. This was because he felt that states, rather than the federal government, had the right to make such laws.

Another blow for those who wanted integration of blacks and whites was

Guided Reading Workbook

Wilson's appointment of his cabinet. Wilson chose cabinet members who extended segregation, or separate facilities for blacks and whites. Wilson's angry meeting with an African-American delegation led by a Boston newspaper editor brought African Americans' feeling of betrayal to a head.

Even before the U.S. entered World War I, the war became a factor in dimming the reform spirit as legislators had less interest in reform.

3. Why did African Americans feel betrayed by President Wilson?

_____

_____

As you read about President Wilson's approach to reform, take notes to answer the questions.

What were the aims of each piece of legislation or constitutional amendment?	
1. Federal Trade Act	
2. Clayton Antitrust Act	
3. Underwood Tariff	
4. Sixteenth Amendment	
5. Federal Reserve Act	

6. Which three new developments finally brought the success of the woman suffrage movement within reach?
7. Which constitutional amendment recognized women's right to vote?

8. How did Wilson retreat on civil rights?

Imperialism and America

Terms and Names

Queen Liliuokalani The Hawaiian queen who was forced out of power by a revolution started by American business interests

imperialism The practice of strong countries taking economic, political, and military power over weaker countries

Alfred T. Mahan American imperialist and admiral who urged the United States to build up its navy and take colonies overseas

William Seward Secretary of state under Presidents Lincoln and Johnson

Pearl Harbor Naval port in Hawaii

Sanford B. Dole American businessman who became president of the new government of Hawaii after the queen was pushed out

Before You Read

In the last section, you read about Woodrow Wilson. In this section, you will learn how economic activity led to political and military involvement overseas.

As You Read

Use a diagram to take notes on the causes of U.S. imperialism.

AMERICAN EXPANSIONISM
(Pages 342–344)
Why did Americans support imperialism?

In 1893, **Queen Liliuokalani** of Hawaii gave up her throne. Hawaii was about to be taken over by the United States.

By the 1880s, many American leaders thought the United States should establish colonies overseas. This idea was called **imperialism**—the policy in which stronger nations extend economic, political or military control over weaker territories. European countries had competed for territory all over the world. Most Americans gradually accepted the idea of overseas expansion.

Three factors fueled American imperialism: desire for military strength, thirst for new markets, and a belief in the superiority of American culture.

Admiral **Alfred T. Mahan** of the U.S. Navy supported growing American naval power so the U.S. could compete with other nations. The U.S. built such modern battleships as the *Maine* and the *Oregon*. The new ships made the U.S. the world's largest naval power.

By the late 1800s, technology had changed American farms and factories. They produced more than Americans could consume. So the U.S. needed foreign trade. American businesses needed markets for their products and raw materials for their factories.

The third root of American imperialism was a belief that the people of the United States were better than the people of other countries. This racist belief came from people's pride in their Anglo-Saxon (Northern European) heritage. People sometimes felt they had a duty to spread their culture and Christian religion among other people.

1. What were three reasons Americans supported imperialism?

_____

_____

THE UNITED STATES ACQUIRES ALASKA; THE UNITED STATES TAKES HAWAII (Pages 344–345)
How **did the Hawaiian Islands become a U.S. territory?**

William Seward was Secretary of State for presidents Lincoln and Andrew Johnson. In 1867 he purchased Alaska from Russia for $7.2 million. Some opponents in Congress made fun of the deal calling it "Seward's Icebox" or "Seward's Folly."

The Hawaiian Islands, in the Pacific Ocean, had been important to the United States since the 1790s. Merchants had stopped there on their way to China and India. In the 1820s, American missionaries founded Christian schools and churches on the islands.

A number of Americans had established sugar plantations in Hawaii. In the mid-1800s, these large farms accounted for about three-quarters of the wealth in the islands. Plantation owners brought thousands of laborers to Hawaii from Japan, Portugal, and China. This weakened the influence of the native Hawaiians. By 1900, the foreign laborers outnumbered the Hawaiians three to one.

In 1875, the United States agreed to import Hawaiian sugar duty-free. Over the next 15 years, Hawaiian sugar production increased nine times. Then the McKinley Tariff caused a crisis for Hawaiian sugar growers. With the duty on their sugar, Hawaiian growers faced stiff competition from other growers. The powerful Hawaiian sugar growers called for the U.S. to annex Hawaii. The U.S. military had already understood the value of Hawaii. In 1887, the U.S. forced Hawaii to let it build a naval base at **Pearl Harbor**, Hawaii's best port.

When the Hawaiian king died in 1891, his sister became queen. Queen Liliuokalani wanted a new constitution that would give voting power back to ordinary Hawaiians. American business interests did not want this to happen.

American business groups organized a revolt against the queen. The U.S. ambassador John L. Stevens helped them. The planters took control of the island. They established a temporary government and made American businessman **Sanford B. Dole** the president.

Stevens urged the U.S. government to annex the Hawaiian Islands. President Grover Cleveland refused to take over the islands unless a majority of Hawaiians favored that. In 1897, however, William McKinley became president. He favored annexation. In 1898, Hawaii became a U.S. territory.

2. How did Hawaiians lose control of their islands?

_____

_____

As you read this section, fill out the chart below by summarizing reasons
why the United States became an imperial power.

The Roots of American Imperialism		
1. Economic roots	2. Political and military roots	3. Racist roots

↓

4. What did Admiral Mahan urge the United States to do to protect its interests?

For each year on the time line below, identify one important event in the history of
U.S. involvement in Hawaii.

U.S. Imperialism in Hawaii	
1875	
1887	
1890	
1891	
1897	
1898	

America Claims an Empire

The Spanish–American War

Terms and Names

José Martí Political activist who worked for Cuban independence

Valeriano Weyler General sent from Spain to Cuba to restore order in 1896

yellow journalism Reporting in newspapers and magazines that exaggerates the news in order to make it more exciting

U.S.S. Maine U.S. warship that exploded in a Cuban harbor in 1898

George Dewey U.S. naval commander who led the American attack on the Philippines

Rough Riders Fighting unit led by Theodore Roosevelt in Cuba

San Juan Hill Location of an important American land victory in Cuba

Treaty of Paris The treaty that ended the Spanish-American War

Before You Read

In the last section, you learned how the United States became an imperialist power and took over the Hawaiian Islands. In this section, you will learn how the United States became involved in Cuba and fought a war with Spain.

As You Read

Use a web diagram to take notes on the pros and cons of annexing the Philippines.

CUBANS REBEL AGAINST SPAIN
(**Pages** 346–347)
***What* happened when Cuba rebelled against Spain?**

Between 1868 and 1878, Cubans fought their first war for independence from Spain. The rebels did not win, but they did force Spain to abolish slavery in 1886. After that, United States capitalists invested heavily in sugar cane plantations in Cuba.

Sugar was the most important product of Cuba. The United States was the main market for the sugar. As long as the United States did not charge a tariff on Cuban sugar, the Cuban economy thrived. But the Cuban economy collapsed in 1894 when a tariff on sugar was imposed.

In 1895, Cubans began a second war for independence. The rebellion was led by **José Martí.** He was a Cuban poet and journalist who had been living in exile in New York. The rebels wanted the United States to join their cause.

American opinion was mixed. Some wanted to support Spain in order to keep their investments safe. Others wanted to help the Cuban people win their freedom from Spain just as the United States had won its independence from England.

Guided Reading Workbook

1. How did Cuba's two wars for independence affect American business interests?

_____

_____

WAR FEVER ESCALATES
 (Pages 347–348)
Why did Americans become angry with Spain?

In 1896, Spain sent an army to Cuba to restore order. The army was led by General **Valeriano Weyler.** Weyler rounded up the entire rural population of central and western Cuba. He kept 300,000 people as prisoners in concentration camps. That way they could not help the rebels. Many of them died of hunger and disease.

This story was widely reported in the United States. Rival newspapers in New York made the terrible events sound even worse. They exaggerated the brutality of the story in order to attract readers. These sensational stories became known as **yellow journalism**—reporting that exaggerates the news in order to make it more exciting.

William McKinley became president in 1897. At that time, many Americans wanted the United States to help the rebels against Spain. McKinley tried to find a peaceful solution to the crisis. His efforts had several positive results. Spain sent General Weyler home, changed the concentration camp policy, and gave Cuba limited self-government.

Then two events made Americans very angry at Spain. The first was the publication of a letter that insulted the American president. The de Lôme letter was written by a Spanish diplomat. It criticized McKinley for being weak.

Although some Americans agreed that the president was weak, they did not want to hear this criticism from a Spanish official.

Only a few days after the letter was published, something worse happened. The battleship *U.S.S. Maine* was stationed in Cuba to protect American lives and property. On February 15, 1898, the ship exploded. The ship sank, and 260 officers and crew on board died. The cause of the explosion was not known. However, newspapers blamed Spain. Americans cried for war.

2. What two events led Americans to call for war against Spain?

_____

_____

WAR WITH SPAIN ERUPTS
 (Pages 348–351)
Where and when did the fighting take place?

On April 20, 1898, the United States went to war with Spain. The first battle took place in the Philippines. The Philippines had been a Spanish colony for 300 years. They had rebelled many times. In 1896, they began another rebellion.

On May 1, 1898, the American naval commander **George Dewey** sailed into Manila Bay in the Philippines. His ships destroyed the Spanish fleet there. In the next two months, U.S. soldiers fought on the side of the Filipino rebels. The Spanish surrendered to the United States in August.

In Cuba, the American navy blocked off the harbor of Santiago de Cuba. Spanish ships could not leave. Then American troops landed on the island in June 1898.

One unit of volunteer soldiers was called the **Rough Riders.** Theodore Roosevelt was one of their leaders. They helped win the important battle of **San Juan Hill.** American newspapers made Roosevelt a hero.

When the Spanish ships tried to leave the harbor, their fleet was destroyed. This led the Spanish to surrender on July 25.

Spain quickly agreed to a peace treaty. The **Treaty of Paris** granted Cuba its independence. Spain gave Puerto Rico and the Pacific island of Guam to the United States. The United States paid Spain $20 million for the annexation of the Philippine Islands. The Treaty of Paris touched off a great debate in the United States about imperialism. President

McKinley was in favor of it. But some Americans said annexing territories violated the spirit of the Declaration of Independence by denying self-government to the new territories. Booker T. Washington and Samuel Gompers also opposed the treaty. The Senate approved the treaty on February 6, 1899.

3. What three territories did the United States get from the war with Spain?

_____

_____

As you read about the Spanish-American War, write notes in the
appropriate boxes to answer the questions about its causes and effects.

Causes: How did each of the following help to cause the outbreak of the Spanish-American War?
1. American business owners
2. José Martí
3. Valeriano Weyler
4. Yellow journalism
5. De Lôme letter
6. *U.S.S. Maine*

Effects: What happened to each of the following territories as a result of the Spanish-American War?
7. Cuba
8. Puerto Rico
9. Guam
10. Philippine Islands

Section 3

Acquiring New Lands

Terms and Names

Foraker Act Law which ended military rule in Puerto Rico

Platt Amendment Provisions in the Cuban constitution that gave the United States broad rights in that country

protectorate A country that is partly controlled by another, stronger country

Emilio Aguinaldo Filipino rebel leader

John Hay U.S. secretary of state

Open Door notes Message sent by John Hay to other countries to protect U.S. trading rights in China

Boxer Rebellion Chinese rebellion against Western influence, 1900

Before You Read

In the last section, you learned how the United States and Spain fought over Cuba and the Philippines. In this section, you will read how the United States continued its imperialism.

As You Read

Use a time line to take notes on the key events relating to the relationships between the United States and Puerto Rico, Cuba, the Philippines, and China.

RULING PUERTO RICO
(Pages 352–353)
How did Puerto Ricans feel about U.S. control?

Puerto Rico had become an American territory as a result of the Spanish–American War. American forces landed in Puerto Rico in July 1898. The commanding officer declared that the Americans were there to protect the Puerto Ricans. But other U.S. military officials insulted the Puerto Ricans. They spoke of them as children and set limits on their personal freedom. Many Puerto Ricans began to resent the military government. In 1900, Congress passed the **Foraker Act** which ended military rule and set up a civil government.

The United States kept strict control over the people and their government. In 1917, however, Congress made Puerto Ricans U.S. citizens.

1. Why did some Puerto Ricans resent U.S. control of their government?

_____

_____

CUBA AND THE UNITED STATES
(**Pages** 353–355)
How did the United States keep control over Cuba?

Cuba was officially independent after the war. The U.S. army, however, remained in Cuba for four years. It punished Cubans who did not like this American occupation.

In 1900, the new Cuban government wrote a constitution. The United States insisted they add the **Platt Amendment**. The amendment limited Cuba's rights in dealing with other countries. It gave the United States special privileges, including the right to intervene to preserve order.

Cuba became a U.S. **protectorate**—a country whose affairs are partially controlled by a stronger power. The United States insisted on these rights because of its economic interests in Cuba.

2. What did the United States do to protect business interests in Cuba?

_____

_____

FILIPINOS REBEL (**Page** 355)
Why did the Filipinos rebel against the United States?

Filipinos had been fighting for independence for years. They were angry that the United States had annexed their islands. Rebel leader **Emilio Aguinaldo** believed that the United States had promised independence. He felt that the United States had betrayed the Filipinos after helping them win independence.

In 1899, Aguinaldo started a rebellion, which lasted three years. After winning that war, the United States set up a government similar to the one it had set up in Cuba.

3. Why did Aguinaldo feel betrayed by the United States?

_____

_____

FOREIGN INFLUENCE IN CHINA
(**Pages** 356–357)
What were U.S. interests in China?

By 1899, many countries had economic interests in China. The United States wanted to be able to trade with China. The Secretary of State **John Hay** sent a statement of this policy to the other countries. His policy statements were called the **Open Door notes**. They called for China's ports to remain open and for China to remain independent. No country would have special trading rights. The other countries agreed.

In 1900, a secret society in China started a rebellion. They were protesting the influence of Western countries in China. Troops from many countries including the United States fought against the rebels, or Boxers. After the **Boxer Rebellion** was defeated, the United States issued more Open Door notes to make sure other countries did not make colonies out of China.

4. Why did Secretary of State John Hay issue the Open Door notes?

_____

_____

THE IMPACT OF U.S. TERRITORIAL GAINS (**Page** 358)
How did Americans feel about U.S. imperialism?

President William McKinley was reelected in 1900. His opponent had been an anti-imperialist, William Jennings Bryan. The outcome of the election

Guided Reading Workbook

suggests that most Americans disagreed with Bryan. Imperialism was popular.

An Anti-Imperialist League formed including some prominent Americans. Among its members were former president Grover Cleveland, Andrew Carnegie, Jane Addams, and Mark Twain. Each had their own reasons for being against imperialism. But all agreed it was wrong for the United States to rule other people without their consent.

5. What did McKinley's reelection show about American attitudes toward imperialism?

_____

_____

As you read about America's relations with lands under its influence, write
notes to answer the questions below. Some answers have already been
filled in for you.

	Puerto Rico 1898–1916	Cuba 1898–1903	The Philippines 1898–1945	China 1900
1. What was its relationship to the U.S.?	very similar to that of a colony or protectorate			
2. Why did the U.S. try to control its affairs?			to provide the U.S. with raw materials and new markets	
3. What laws and policies affected its relationship with the U.S.?				
4. What violent events affected its relationship with the U.S.?	Spanish-American War			

John Hay's "Open Door notes" paved the way for greater U.S. influence in
Asia. Note three beliefs held by Americans that were reflected by the Open
Door policy.

1.
2.
3.

America Claims an Empire

America as a World Power

Terms and Names

Panama Canal A channel across Central America, between the Atlantic and Pacific Oceans, opened in 1914

Roosevelt Corollary Roosevelt's 1904 extension of the Monroe Doctrine, stating that the United States has the right to protect its economic interests in South and Central America by using military force

dollar diplomacy The policy of intervening in other countries to protect U.S. business interests

Francisco "Pancho" Villa Mexican revolutionary

Emiliano Zapata Mexican rebel

John J. Pershing U.S. general who led troops to capture Villa

Before You Read

In the last section, you learned about the growth of American imperialism. In this section, you will learn how Roosevelt and Wilson used American military and economic power.

As You Read

Use a chart to take notes on how Teddy Roosevelt and Woodrow Wilson used American power around the world.

TEDDY ROOSEVELT AND THE WORLD (Pages 359–363)
How did Roosevelt use American power?

In 1901, President McKinley was assassinated, and Theodore Roosevelt became president. Roosevelt continued the policies of imperialism. He first used U.S. influence to help settle the Russo-Japanese War.

The war began in 1904. Both Russia and Japan wanted to control Korea. Japan captured Korea and also invaded Manchuria, which was controlled by Russia.

Then Japan wanted to stop the fighting. The Japanese asked President Roosevelt to mediate the conflict. In 1905,

representatives of Russia and Japan met. Roosevelt used his personal charm to help them negotiate a compromise. They signed a treaty, and Roosevelt received the 1906 Nobel Peace Prize for his efforts.

Roosevelt also used his influence to help build the **Panama Canal**. The idea of a canal connecting the Atlantic and Pacific Oceans had been discussed for some time. Such a canal would cut travel time for military and commercial ships. Ships would no longer have to go all the way around South America in order to get from one ocean to the other.

The narrow Isthmus of Panama was a logical place to cut a canal. Political problems stood in the way, however. Panama was a province of Colombia.

Guided Reading Workbook

When Colombia did not agree to the canal, the United States helped Panama to rebel against Colombia. Panama became independent. Then the United States got Panama's permission to build the canal.

Construction of the Panama Canal was one of the world's greatest engineering accomplishments. Work began in 1904 and took 10 years. In 1913, there were 43,400 workers on the project. The work was hard and dangerous.

On August 15, 1914, the canal opened for business. It was a success from the start. More than 1,000 ships passed through during its first year. However, relations between the United States and Latin America had been damaged by the takeover of Panama.

President Roosevelt wanted the United States to be the major power in the Caribbean and Central America. He declared his policy in a message to Congress in 1904. His statement was called the **Roosevelt Corollary**. A corollary is a logical result of another statement, in this case the Monroe Doctrine of 1823. That doctrine had said the United States would not allow European influence in the Western Hemisphere. Roosevelt now said that the United States had the right to intervene in Latin American countries to protect U.S. business interests.

In 1911, President Taft used this policy in Nicaragua. A rebellion had left the country in debt. Taft arranged for U.S. bankers to loan Nicaragua money. In exchange, American business took control of the railroads and banks in the country. They also collected Nicaragua's custom duties.

Nicaraguans did not like this arrangement. They rebelled. The United States then sent troops to Nicaragua to preserve the peace. Those who did not like

this kind of intervention called it **dollar diplomacy**.

1. What are two ways Roosevelt used U.S. power in other countries?

_____

_____

WOODROW WILSON'S MISSIONARY DIPLOMACY
(**Pages** 363–365)
Why did President Wilson send troops to Mexico?

President Woodrow Wilson took a step beyond Presidents Monroe and Roosevelt by adding a moral tone to Latin American policy. He said that the United States must act in certain circumstances.

This so-called "missionary diplomacy" meant that the United States could not officially recognize governments that were oppressive, undemocratic, or opposed to U.S. business interests. The new doctrine put pressure on countries to have democratic governments. A revolution in Mexico tested this policy

In 1910, Mexican peasants and workers rebelled against their military dictator. Two new governments followed, the second headed by General Victoriano Huerta.

Wilson refused to support the Huerta government because it came to power through violence.

Wilson sent in troops. When a new leader, Venustiano Carranza, took power in Mexico, Wilson withdrew the troops.

Mexico remained in turmoil. Under the leadership of **Francisco "Pancho" Villa** and **Emiliano Zapata**, rebels revolted against Carranza. Some of Villa's followers killed Americans. The United States wanted to capture Villa.

Finally the Mexican government gave permission to send in troops. Wilson sent General **John J. Pershing** with 15,000 soldiers. A year later, Villa was still free. Wilson then stationed 150,000 National Guardsmen along the border.

Mexicans were angered by the U.S. invasion. In 1916, U.S. troops fought with Carranza's army. In 1917, Wilson withdrew U.S. troops. At that time, he was facing possible war in Europe.

Finally, Mexico adopted a constitution. The Mexicans regained control of their own resources and put limits on foreign investment. American intervention in Mexico showed how far the United States was willing to go to protect its economic interests.

In the early 20th century, the U.S. pursued several foreign policy goals. It expanded its access to foreign markets. It built a modern navy to protect its interest abroad. It used its international police power to get its way in Latin America.

2. What were two reasons Wilson sent troops to Mexico?

_____

_____

As you read this section, write notes summarizing the effects of American military, diplomatic, and economic power around the world.

ROOSEVELT'S "BIG STICK" DIPLOMACY

American action taken	Consequences of that action
1. Treaty of Portsmouth is negotiated. →	
2. U.S. warships are used to ensure Panama's independence. →	
3. Panama Canal is built. →	
4. Roosevelt Corollary is adopted. →	

WILSON'S "MISSIONARY" DIPLOMACY

American action taken	Consequences of that action
5. Wilson uses a minor incident with Mexico as an excuse to occupy Veracruz. →	
6. Wilson recognizes the Carranza government. →	
7. Wilson refuses Carranza's demand to withdraw U.S. troops sent into Mexico to capture Villa. →	

World War I Begins

Terms and Names

nationalism A devotion to the interests and culture of one's nation

militarism Building up armed forces to prepare for war

Allies One side in World War I: Great Britain, France, and Russia, later joined by the U.S.

Central Powers One side in World War I: Germany, Austria-Hungary, and the Ottoman Empire

Archduke Franz Ferdinand Young heir whose assassination triggered the war

no man's land The space between armies fighting each other

trench warfare Fighting between fortified ditches

Lusitania British passenger ship attacked and sunk by Germans

Zimmermann note Message proposing an alliance between Germany and Mexico

Before You Read

In the last section, you learned how Presidents Roosevelt and Wilson used American power around the world. In this section, you will read how war broke out in Europe while the United States tried to remain neutral.

As You Read

Use a chart to take notes on the causes of World War I.

CAUSES OF WORLD WAR I
(Pages 372-374)
What conditions led to war?

Four main factors led to the outbreak of World War I in Europe. The first was **nationalism**—the belief that the interests of a single country were more important than cooperation among countries. This led to competition.

The second cause was imperialism. Countries tried to increase the power and influence around the world. This led to conflicts among them.

The third main cause was **militarism**. Militarism meant building up armies, navies, and other armed forces. It also

meant using them as a tool for negotiating with other countries.

The fourth cause was the alliance system. Some countries in Europe had made treaties promising to defend each other. These mutual-defense treaties placed European countries in two main groups. The **Allies** were made up of France, Great Britain, and Russia. The **Central Powers** were made up of Germany, Austria-Hungary, and the Ottoman Empire.

1. Name two causes of World War I.

_____

_____

AN ASSASSINATION LEADS TO WAR (Page 374)

What sparked the war?

In 1914, **Archduke Franz Ferdinand** was assassinated. He had been the heir to the throne of Austria-Hungary. His killer was a Serb who wanted to unite all Serbs (including those in Austria-Hungary) under one government. This touched off an action to punish Serbia.

The alliance system pulled one nation after another into the conflict. If a nation had sworn to protect another, it had to declare war on that nation's enemies. Germany and Austria-Hungary were facing France, Great Britain, and Russia.

2. Why did the assassination lead to fighting?

_____

_____

THE FIGHTING STARTS (Pages 374–376)

Where did the fighting begin?

Germany began by invading Belgium. It planned to overrun France and then to attack Russia. The British and French could not save Belgium. They did, however, manage to stop Germany's advance.

By the spring of 1915, two lines of deep trenches had developed in France. Germans occupied one line. The Allies occupied the other line. Between the two lines lay **"no man's land."** The soldiers would climb out of their trenches and try to overrun enemy lines. They did this while facing machine-gun fire and poison gas.

This bloody **trench warfare** continued for more than three years. Neither side gained territory, but more than one million soldiers died.

3. Why did the fighting take place in France?

_____

_____

AMERICANS QUESTION NEUTRALITY (Page 377)

How did Americans feel?

In the United States, public opinion about the war was strong but divided. Socialists saw the war as an imperialist struggle between German and English businessmen. Pacifists believed that all wars were bad. They urged the United States to set an example for peace. Many other Americans simply did not want to send their sons to war.

Many naturalized U.S. citizens still had ties to the countries they came from. Many immigrants from Germany, for example, sympathized with Germany.

Americans tended to sympathize with Great Britain and France. They shared a common language and heritage with Britain. They were horrified at Germany's brutal attack on Belgium. And they had strong economic ties with the Allies.

4. What were three things that influenced Americans' feelings about the war?

_____

_____

THE WAR HITS HOME (Pages 378–379)

How did the war affect Americans?

The war affected American shipping. Great Britain set up a blockade along the German coast to keep goods from getting through. American ships would not challenge Britain's blockade. German U-boats attacked ships from all nations. A U-boat sank the British ship ***Lusitania***,

Guided Reading Workbook

killing more than a thousand people, including 128 Americans.

5. In what ways did the war affect American citizens?

_____

_____

THE UNITED STATES DECLARES WAR (Pages 379–380)
***Why* did the U.S. join the war?**

Three incidents brought the United States into the war. First, in January 1917, Germany announced it would sink all ships in British waters on sight whether they were hostile or neutral. Second, British agents intercepted the

Zimmermann note, a telegram that proposed an alliance between Germany and Mexico against the United States. Third, the replacement of the Russian monarchy with a representative government allowed Americans to characterize the war as a struggle of democracies against brutal monarchies. On April 6, 1917, at President Wilson's request, Congress declared war on Germany.

6. What are the three incidents that led the United States to declare war?

_____

_____

Guided Reading Workbook

As you read this section, take notes to answer questions about the
international politics that led to war in Europe.

How did the following help to ignite the war in Europe?				
1. Nationalism	2. Imperialism	3. Militarism	4. Alliances	5. Assassination of Archduke Ferdinand

Why did the following groups of Americans tend to oppose U.S. participation in the war?			
6. Naturalized citizens	7. Socialists	8. Pacifists	9. Parents

What did the following nations do to encourage U.S. participation in the war?		
10. Britain	11. Germany	12. Russia

The First World War

American Power Tips the Balance

Terms and Names

Selective Service Act Law requiring men to register for military service

convoy system Having merchant ships travel in groups protected by warships

American Expeditionary Force The name given to the American military force that fought in World War I

General John J. Pershing The commander of the American Expeditionary force

Eddie Rickenbacker Famous American fighter pilot

Alvin York American war hero

conscientious objector A person who believes fighting is wrong and therefore does not want to serve in the military

armistice Truce agreement

Before You Read

In the last section, you learned how the United States was drawn into the war. In this section, you will read how Americans prepared to fight and how they helped the Allies win.

As You Read

Use a web diagram to take notes on how Americans responded to the war.

AMERICA MOBILIZES
(Pages 381–383)
How did the U.S. prepare for war?

The United States first needed to build up its armed forces. When war was declared, only about 200,000 men were in service. To solve this problem, Congress passed the **Selective Service Act**. It required men to register with the government so that some of them could be selected for military service. This process—called the draft—put about 3 million men in uniform.

Many African Americans served in the military. They were placed in separate units, but some blacks were trained as officers. Blacks were among the first to receive the French honor of the Croix de Guerre.

Women were not drafted. The army would not let them join. But the navy accepted women in noncombat positions. Woman served as nurses, secretaries, and telephone operators.

The U.S. built ships to transport men and supplies to Europe. Shipyard workers were exempted from the draft and the importance of their work was publicized. Prefabrication techniques were used to speed the production of ships.

Guided Reading Workbook

1. How did the United States build up its armed forces?

_____

_____

AMERICA TURNS THE TIDE
(Page 383)
How did the United States help?

To reduce the loss of ships to German submarine attacks, the United States and Britain began to use the **convoy system.** In this system, merchant ships traveled in a large group guarded by naval vessels.

American soldiers helped turn the tide of battle in Europe. The Allies had absorbed many casualties and were running out of men. Thousands of fresh American soldiers were eager for battle.

2. How did the United States help the Allies?

_____

_____

FIGHTING "OVER THERE"
(Pages 384–385)
What new weapons were used?

The **American Expeditionary Force** was led by **General John J. Pershing**. American infantrymen were called doughboys because of the white belts they wore and cleaned with pipe clay, or "dough."

New weapons played a decisive role in the war. The two most innovative weapons were the tank and the airplane. Air warfare developed rapidly during the war. Pilots went from shooting at each other with pistols to using mounted machine guns.

Eddie Rickenbacker was an American ace pilot. He fought in 34 air battles and shot down 26 enemy planes.

3. Name two new weapons used in the war.

_____

_____

THE WAR INTRODUCES NEW HAZARDS **(Page** 385)
What made World War I hard for soldiers?

New weapons and tactics made World War I very destructive. Soldiers faced miserable conditions, including filth, trench foot, trench mouth, "shell shock" from constant bombardment, vermin, poison gas, and disease.

4. What hardships did soldiers face in World War I?

_____

_____

AMERICAN TROOPS GO ON THE OFFENSIVE **(Pages** 386–387)
How did American troops help end the war?

American soldiers arrived in Europe just in time to stop a German advance on Paris. One soldier from Tennessee, **Alvin York,** became a war hero for his actions in battle. At the start, York had been a **conscientious objector** (a person who opposes war on moral grounds), but he then agreed to fight. For his actions in battle he was promoted to sergeant and became a celebrity when he returned to the U.S.

Germany, exhausted from the war, finally agreed to an **armistice** on November 11, 1918. The war took a bloody toll, killing more than 22 million and causing untold suffering.

5. How did American troops help end the war?

_____

_____

As you read this section, write notes to answer questions about the
American experience in World War I.

1. How did the United States raise an army?	2. How did U.S. soldiers help win the war?
3. How did the United States build its naval force?	4. How did the U.S. Navy help win the war?

5. What new weapons of mechanized warfare threatened those in combat?

6. What did the war cost in terms of the number of...				7. What were the estimated economic costs?
civilian deaths?	military deaths?	injuries?	refugees?	

Section 3

The War at Home

Terms and Names

War Industries Board Agency to improve efficiency in war-related industries

Bernard M. Baruch Leader of the War Industries Board

propaganda A kind of biased communication designed to influence people's thoughts and actions

George Creel Head of the Committee on Public Information (CPI), the government's propaganda agency

Espionage and Sedition Acts Laws that enacted harsh penalties against anyone opposing U.S. participation in World War I

Great Migration Movement of many African Americans to northern cities from the South in the early 1900s

---

Before You Read

In the last section, you learned how the United States fought in World War I. In this section, you will read about how the war changed American society at home.

As You Read

Use a chart to take notes on the changes the war brought about for African Americans, women, and immigrants.

CONGRESS GIVES POWER TO WILSON (Pages 388–390)
How did business and government work together?

To fight the war, the United States needed the help of industry. The economy had to change from making consumer goods to making weapons and war supplies. Congress gave President Wilson direct control over much of the economy. He had the power to fix prices and to regulate war-related industries.

Wilson created the **War Industries Board (WIB)** and named **Bernard M. Baruch** to run it. This agency helped boost industrial production by 20 percent. Other federal agencies also regulated the economy for the war effort. The Railroad Administration controlled the nation's railroads. The Fuel Administration watched over the use of coal, gasoline, and heating oil.

Wages in some industries went up. But workers in other jobs lost money because of inflation. As a result, many workers joined unions. Wilson established the National War Labor Board. This agency worked to settle disputes between management and labor. It also helped to improve working conditions.

Another new agency, the Food Administration, was established to help produce and conserve food supplies. It encouraged people to grow their own food. It taught them to eat differently.

Guided Reading Workbook

Section 3, *continued*

Americans were able to send more food to the Allies.

1. How did Wilson control the economy?

_____

_____

SELLING THE WAR (Pages 390–391)
How did the government win over public opinion?

The government needed to raise money for the war. They did this by increasing several kinds of taxes and by selling war bonds. Thousands of volunteers sold the bonds. Famous people spoke at rallies to promote the sales. Newspapers and billboards carried advertisements free of charge.

To popularize the war, the government created the Committee on Public Information (CPI). It was the nation's first **propaganda** agency. The agency was headed by **George Creel.** He had been a muckraking journalist. He used artists and advertising people to create thousands of posters, paintings, and cartoons to promote the war. He distributed pamphlets in many languages.

2. How did the U.S. government pay for the war?

_____

_____

ATTACKS ON CIVIL LIBERTIES INCREASE (Pages 391–392)
How did the war affect civil liberties?

The war brought out anti-immigrant feelings. Immigrants from Germany were often targeted for attack. Americans with German-sounding names lost their jobs. Orchestras refused to play German music.

Some towns with German names changed them.

Congress passed the **Espionage and Sedition Acts** to punish people who did not support the war effort. People could not interfere with the draft or obstruct the sale of war bonds. They could not even speak against the war effort.

These laws violated the spirit of the First Amendment, which guarantees freedom of speech. The law led to 6,000 arrests and 1,500 convictions for antiwar activities.

The chief targets of the Espionage and Sedition Acts were socialists and union leaders. Labor leader Eugene V. Debs was jailed for making a speech about the economic causes of the war. The Industrial Workers of the World urged workers to strike. This was considered an antiwar activity, and they received jail sentences.

3. How did the Espionage and Sedition Acts contradict the First Amendment?

_____

_____

THE WAR ENCOURAGES SOCIAL CHANGE (Pages 392–395)
How did the war affect women and African Americans?

The war brought many social changes for African Americans and women.

African-American leaders were divided over the war. W. E. B. Du Bois believed that helping the war effort would help the fight for equality. Others believed that blacks should not help a government that did not support equality for everyone.

The war sped up the **Great Migration.** This was the movement of thousands of African Americans from the South to cities of the North. They wanted to escape

Section 3, *continued*

racial discrimination. They also wanted to find jobs in Northern industries.

American women played new roles during the war. They did jobs that had previously been done only by men. They worked as truck drivers, cooks, dockworkers, and builders. Women volunteered in the Red Cross and sold war bonds.

Women's activities made them more visible. They were not paid the same as men. But, soon after the war, Congress finally passed an amendment giving them the right to vote.

Also during the war, a worldwide flu epidemic, probably spread by American soldiers, killed 500,000 Americans and caused disruptions in the American economy.

4. How did women's roles change during the war?

_____

_____

As you read this section, take notes to answer questions about how World War I changed American society.

What were some things accomplished by the following wartime agencies and laws?		
1. War Industries Board	2. Railroad Administration	3. Fuel Administration
4. National War Labor Board	5. Food Administration	6. Committee on Public Information
7. Espionage and Sedition Acts		

What changes did the war bring about for the following groups of Americans?		
8. Immigrants	9. African Americans	10. Women

Section 4

Wilson Fights for Peace

Terms and Names

Fourteen Points Wilson's plan for world peace following World War I

League of Nations An international peace-keeping organization proposed by Wilson and founded in 1920

Georges Clemenceau French premier

David Lloyd George British prime minister

Treaty of Versailles The 1919 treaty that ended World War I

reparations Payments made by defeated countries after a war

war-guilt clause Part of the Treaty of Versailles in which Germany took responsibility for the war

Henry Cabot Lodge Conservative senator who wanted to keep the United States out of the League of Nations

Before You Read

In the last section, you learned how the war in Europe changed life at home. In this section, you will read about the treaty that ended the war and Wilson's proposal for a League of Nations.

As You Read

Use a diagram to take notes on the provisions and weaknesses of the Treaty of Versailles and the opposition to it.

WILSON PRESENTS HIS PLAN
(Pages 398–399)
What were Wilson's peace plans?

President Wilson presented his plan for world peace to Congress in January 1918. The plan was called his **Fourteen Points**.

The first five points suggested ways that wars could be avoided. They stated that (1) countries should not make secret treaties with one another, (2) freedom of the seas should be maintained, (3) tariffs should be lowered to promote free trade, (4) countries should reduce their arms, and (5) the interests of the colonial people should be considered.

The next eight points suggested new national boundaries. Wilson believed in self-determination: different ethnic groups should be able to decide for themselves what nation they would belong to.

The fourteenth point called for a **League of Nations**. This international organization would address problems between countries before they led to war.

Wilson met with leaders of France and Great Britain, **George Clemenceau** and **David Lloyd George**, to discuss the terms of peace. These leaders had won the war, and they wanted to punish Germany. Wilson had to give up most of his

Fourteen Points. The one he insisted on was the League of Nations.

1. What did Wilson's first five points address?

_____

_____

DEBATING THE TREATY OF VERSAILLES (Pages 400–402)
What did the treaty say?

On June 28, 1919, the leaders of the Allies and the Central Powers met at the Palace of Versailles in France. They were to sign the **Treaty of Versailles.**

The treaty created new national boundaries by (1) establishing nine new nations, including Poland, Czechoslovakia, and Yugoslavia; (2) shifting the boundaries of other nations; and (3) carving out parts of the Ottoman Empire to create colonies in the Middle East for Great Britain and France.

The treaty took away Germany's army and navy. It forced Germany to pay **reparations,** or war damages, to the winners. In addition, the treaty contained a **war-guilt clause.** Germany had to admit that it was responsible for causing the war.

The Treaty of Versailles had three basic weaknesses. The first was its harsh treatment of Germany. Germany was humiliated. Germany was not the only country that had also been militaristic, yet Germany alone was punished. And, Germany would not be able to pay the huge reparations.

The second weakness was that the Soviet Union (formerly Russia) lost more territory than Germany did. Russia had been one of the Allies, and had suffered more casualties than any other country. The Soviet Union was determined to get its territories back.

The third weakness concerned colonies. The treaty did not recognize the claims of colonies for self-determination, in Southeast Asia, for instance.

Wilson brought the treaty back to the United States for approval. He found several groups opposed it. Some thought the treaty too harsh. Others thought it favored the imperialists. Some ethnic groups objected to the treaty because of the way it treated their homelands.

The main opposition to the treaty was over the League of Nations. The League was the only one of Wilson's Fourteen Points that was included in the treaty. Conservative senators, headed by **Henry Cabot Lodge**, opposed joining the League. They did not like the idea of working with other countries to take economic and military action against aggression. They wanted the treaty to include the constitutional right of Congress to declare war.

Wilson refused to compromise on the League. He would not accept amendments proposed by Republican leaders. As a result, the Senate failed to ratify the treaty. The United States never entered the League of Nations. It finally signed a separate treaty with Germany in 1921, when Wilson was no longer president.

2. Name the three weaknesses of the treaty.

_____

_____

THE LEGACY OF THE WAR (Page 403)
What was the legacy of the war?

The end of the war made Americans yearn for what Warren G. Harding called "normalcy." But the war had transformed the United States and the world. World

War I had strengthened both U.S military power and the power of government. It accelerated change for African Americans and women. However, the propaganda campaign left a legacy of mistrust and fear.

In Europe, the war left a legacy of massive destruction, loss of life, political instability, and violence. Communists ruled in Russia and soon after the war fascist organizations seized power in Italy.

Americans hoped that the war had convinced the world to never fight again. But in Europe the war settled nothing. In

Germany, Adolf Hitler exploited Germans' discontent with the Treaty of Versailles and threatened to fight again. Hitler was true to his predictions; America did have to fight again years later in a second world war.

3. What were the long-term results of the war?

_____

_____

As you read about President Wilson's plan for world peace, make notes to
answer questions related to the time line below

1918	**Wilson delivers Fourteen Points speech to Congress.** →	What were Wilson's points? 1. 2. 3. 4. 5. 6.–13. 14.
1919	**Treaty of Versailles is signed.** →	15. What terms of the treaty specifically affected Germany?
		16. What were the weaknesses of the treaty?
1920	**Senate rejects Treaty of Versailles.** →	17. Why did Henry Cabot Lodge object to the treaty?
1921	**Senate again rejects Treaty of Versailles.** →	18. How did Wilson help bring about the Senate's rejection of the treaty?
	U.S. signs separate treaty with Germany. →	19. What circumstances at this time would eventually lead many Germans to support Adolf Hitler?

Politics of the Roaring Twenties

Americans Struggle with Postwar Issues

Terms and Names

nativism Suspicion of foreign-born people

isolationism Pulling away from world affairs

communism An economic system that supports government control over property to create equality

anarchists People who opposed any form of government

Sacco and Vanzetti Immigrant anarchists accused of murder

quota system A system that established the maximum number of people who could enter the United States from each country

John L. Lewis President of the United Mine Workers

Before You Read

In the last section, you read about the end of the First World War. In this section, you will see how Americans adjusted to the end of the war.

As You Read

Use a chart to take notes on the aftereffects of World War I.

POSTWAR TRENDS (Page 412)
How did World War I affect America?

World War I left much of the American public divided about the League of Nations. The end of the war hurt the economy. Returning soldiers took jobs away from many women and minorities, or faced unemployment themselves. A wave of **nativism** and **isolationism** swept over America as people became suspicious of foreigners and wanted to pull away from world affairs.

1. What attitudes became prevalent in America after WWI?

_____

_____

FEAR OF COMMUNISM
(Pages 413–414)
Why did Americans fear communism?

Americans saw **communism** as a threat to their way of life. Communism is an economic and political system that supports government control over property to create equality. Some communists said there should be only one political party: the Communist Party. Communists came to power in Russia through violent revolution.

World War I created economic and political problems in Russia. In 1917, the Russian czar, or emperor, stepped down. Later, a group of revolutionaries called

Guided Reading Workbook

Bolsheviks took power. Their leader was Vladimir I. Lenin. They established the world's first communist state. This new government called for worldwide revolution. Communist leaders wanted workers to seize political and economic power. They wanted to overthrow capitalism.

In the United States, about 70,000 people joined the Communist Party. Still, the ideas of the communists, or "Reds," frightened many people. A fear of communism, known as the "Red Scare," swept the nation.

Attorney General A. Mitchell Palmer set up an agency in the Justice Department to arrest communists, socialists, and **anarchists,** who opposed all forms of government. (The agency later became the Federal Bureau of Investigation, or FBI.)

Palmer's agents trampled on people's civil rights. Many radicals were sent out of the country without trial. But Palmer found no evidence of a plot to overthrow the government. Many suffered because of abuses of power during the Red Scare. One case involved two Italian immigrants, Nicola Sacco and Bartolomeo Vanzetti. **Sacco and Vanzetti** were arrested for robbery and murder in Massachusetts. They admitted they were anarchists. But they denied committing any crime. The case against them was weak. But they were convicted anyway. Many people protested the conviction. They believed it was based on a fear of foreigners. Sacco and Vanzetti were executed in 1927.

2. How did Americans show their fear of communism?

_____

_____

LIMITING IMMIGRATION
(**Pages** 414–415)
How did Americans show their Nativist feelings?

Some Americans used the Red Scare as an excuse to act against any people who were different. For example, the Ku Klux Klan, which had threatened African Americans during Reconstruction, revived.

Now the Klan turned against blacks, Jews, Roman Catholics, immigrants, and union leaders. They used violence to keep these groups "in their place." The Klan briefly gained political power in several states.

As a result of nativism, or anti-immigrant feelings, Congress passed the Emergency Quota Act of 1921. It established a **quota system.** This set a limit on how many immigrants from each country could enter the United States every year. In 1924, a new quota limited immigration from Eastern and Southern Europe, mostly Jews and Roman Catholics.

The 1924 law also banned immigration from Japan. People from the Western Hemisphere still entered the United States in large numbers.

3. What was the quota system?

_____

_____

A TIME OF LABOR UNREST
(**Pages** 417–418)
What were the three major strikes of 1919?

Strikes were not allowed during World War I because they might have hurt the war effort. But in 1919, three important strikes occurred.

Guided Reading Workbook

Boston police officers went on strike for a living wage. The cost of living had doubled since their last raise. Massachusetts governor Calvin Coolidge used force to put down the strike.

A strike by steelworkers began at U.S. Steel Corporation. Workers demanded the right to join unions, which employers prohibited. In 1923, a report revealed the harsh conditions in steel mills. Public opinion turned against the steel companies, and workers were given an eight-hour day. But they still had no union.

A more successful strike was led by **John L. Lewis,** the president of the United Mine Workers. When Lewis's workers closed the coal mines, President Wilson tried to help to settle the dispute between the miners and mine owners. The miners got higher wages, but they did not get shorter hours.

In 1925, A. Philip Randolph founded the Brotherhood of Sleeping Car Porters, an African-American union of railroad workers. But few blacks belonged to other unions. Overall, the 1920s was a bad time for unions. Union membership declined from 5 million to 3.5 million for the following reasons: (1) immigrants were willing to work in poor conditions, (2) language barriers made organizing people difficult; (3) farmers who had migrated to cities were used to relying on themselves, and (4) most unions excluded African Americans.

4. Why did union membership decline?

_____

_____

As you read this section, take notes to answer questions about postwar conditions in America and the fear of communism.

After World War I, many Americans feared that Communists would take over the country.

1. How did the Justice Department under A. Mitchell Palmer respond to this fear? →	2. Why did Palmer eventually lose his standing with the American public?
3. How did the Ku Klux Klan respond to this fear? →	4. Why did the Klan eventually lose popularity and membership?

Public opinion turned against labor unions as many Americans came to believe that unions encouraged communism.

5. Why was the strike by Boston police unpopular with the public? →	6. Why did Massachusetts governor Calvin Coolidge become so popular?
7. Why was the strike at U.S. Steel unpopular? →	8. How did President Wilson respond to the steel strike?

The Harding Presidency

Terms and Names

Warren G. Harding 29th president of the United States

Charles Evans Hughes Secretary of state under Harding

Fordney-McCumber Tariff High tax on imports adopted in 1922

Ohio gang Harding's friends and advisors

Teapot Dome scandal Scandal surrounding Albert Fall

Albert B. Fall Secretary of the interior under Harding

Before You Read

In the last section, you learned about some of the issues Americans faced following World War I. In this section, you will read about President Harding and the issues his administration faced at home and abroad.

As You Read

Use a chart to take notes on the effects of the major events of Harding's presidency.

HARDING STRUGGLES FOR PEACE (Pages 419–420)
How did Harding handle foreign affairs?

In 1921, **Warren G. Harding** invited several major world powers to the Washington Naval Conference. Once there, Secretary of State **Charles Evans Hughes** urged that no more warships should be built for ten years and that the five major naval powers—the U.S., Great Britain, Japan, France and Italy—would scrap many of their existing warships. For the first time, nations agreed to disarm or reduce their weapons. In 1928, long after Harding left office, 64 nations signed the Kellogg-Briand Pact. By signing the Pact, these nations said they would give up war as national policy.

Americans wanted to stay out of world affairs. But the United States still wanted

France and Britain to repay the money they had borrowed during World War I.

Those two nations had suffered during the war. Their economies were too weak for them to repay the loans. To make matters worse, Congress passed the **Fordney-McCumber Tariff** in 1922. This tariff protected American business from foreign competition. But the tariff made it impossible for Britain and France to sell their goods in the United States.

As a result, France and Britain put pressure on Germany to pay its promised reparations. But Germany's economy had been destroyed. When Germany failed to make payments to France, French troops marched into Germany. To avoid another war, American banker Charles Dawes negotiated a settlement to end the loan crisis. Under the Dawes Plan, as the solution was called, the U.S. loaned

---

money to Germany to pay back Britain and France which then repaid their American loan. Thus, the U.S. ended up getting paid with its own money. The solution left bitter feelings. Britain and France saw the U.S. as a miser for not paying its fair share of the costs of war; the U.S. felt Britain and France were financially irresponsible.

1. How did the Fordney-McCumber Tariff affect other countries?

_____

_____

SCANDAL HITS HARDING'S ADMINISTRATION
(Pages 420–421)
How **did scandal hurt Harding's administration?**

Some of Harding's cabinet appointments were excellent. But others caused problems. Three honest members of his cabinet were Charles Evans Hughes, Herbert Hoover, and Andrew Mellon. Hughes was secretary of state. He later became chief justice of the Supreme Court. The talented Herbert Hoover became secretary of commerce. Secretary of the Treasury Andrew Mellon reduced the national debt by about a third.

Other cabinet appointments caused problems. Some were part of the so-called **Ohio gang**. These were the president's poker-playing buddies from back home. They caused the president a great deal of

embarrassment. It became apparent to some that the president's main problem was that he didn't understand many of the country's financial issues. This left him in the dark about practices going on in his own cabinet. He had to comply with whatever his advisers told him. Many of these people took advantage of the situation.

Charles R. Forbes, the head of the Veterans Bureau, was caught selling government and hospital supplies to private companies, and pocketing the money. Colonel Thomas W. Miller, the head of the Office of Alien Property, was caught taking a bribe.

One of the worst cases of corruption was known as the **Teapot Dome scandal**. It involved pieces of land called Teapot Dome and Elk Hills. This land was owned by the government and held large reserves of oil. **Albert B. Fall**, Harding's secretary of the interior, secretly leased the land to two oil companies. He received money and property in return.

Harding was not charged with corruption himself. He suddenly died in 1923, and Calvin Coolidge became president. Coolidge was then elected president in 1924.

2. What does the Teapot Dome scandal tell about President Harding?

_____

_____

In the blank boxes below, write one or two words that describe how each nation, person, or group felt about the issues listed.

1. Americans→Kellogg- Briand Pact		2. Britain and →Dawes Plan France	
3. Americans → Immigrants		4. Ohio gang →Public service	
5. Harding→Administration scandals		6. Americans → Harding	

Section 3

The Business of America

Terms and Names

Calvin Coolidge President of the U.S. (1923–1929) succeeded to presidency on death of Harding, elected in 1924

urban sprawl The outward expansion of cities

installment plan An easy way to borrow money to buy goods

Before You Read

In the last section, you read about Harding's presidency. In this section, you will read about the economy of the 1920s.

As You Read

Use a web diagram to take notes on the changes in business and technology in the 1920s.

AMERICA'S INDUSTRIES FLOURISH (Pages 422–424)
How did the success of certain industries affect American life?

The new president, **Calvin Coolidge** said, "The chief business of the American people is business." Both Coolidge and his Republican successor, Herbert Hoover, favored government policies that promoted business and limited government interference.

The automobile changed the American landscape. New roads were built, and new businesses sprang up such as gas stations, repair shops, public garages, motels, tourist camps and shopping centers. Automobiles ended the isolation of rural families and gave young people and women more independence. Cars also made it possible for people to live farther from their jobs. This led to **urban sprawl**, as cities spread out in all directions.

Cities in Ohio and Michigan grew as major centers of automobile manufacturing. States that produced oil

such as California and Texas also prospered.

The automobile also became a status symbol. Everyone wanted to have one. By the late 1920s, about 80 percent of all the cars in the world were in the United States.

The airline industry also grew. Planes carried the nation's mail. Passenger service began.

1. Name three ways the automobile changed American life.

   _____

   _____

AMERICA'S STANDARD OF LIVING SOARS (Pages 425–426)
How did the American household change?

Another major change was the spread of electricity. In the 1920s, electric power stretched beyond big cities to the suburbs. Still, farms lacked electricity.

Americans began to use all kinds of electrical appliances. Radios, washing machines, and vacuum cleaners became popular. These appliances made housework easier. One result was more leisure time for families. Another effect was to increase the number of women working outside the home.

More consumer goods appeared on the market. Businesses used advertising to sell these goods. Ads didn't just give information about the product. Now, they used psychology. They tried to use people's desire for youth, beauty, and popularity to sell products. Things that once were luxuries became necessities. Some brand names became known nationwide.

Businesspeople formed organizations to do charity work. They also formed organizations to promote business.

2. How did advertising change American life?

_____

_____

A SUPERFICIAL PROSPERITY
(**Pages** 426–427)
***What* hidden problems did the economy have?**

Most Americans had confidence in the prosperity of the 1920s. The national income rose from $64 billion in 1921 to $87 billion in 1929. Most businesses seemed to make fortunes. The stock market reached new heights. But this prosperity hid two big problems.

First, business was not as healthy as it seemed. As workers produced more goods, businesses grew. Large businesses bought up, or merged with, smaller ones. But as businesses grew, business managers made much more money than workers did. Also, mining companies, railroads, and farms were not doing well.

Second, consumer debt rose to high levels. Businesses needed to sell all the goods they were now producing. So they encouraged customers to buy on the **installment plan**. This was a form of borrowing. Customers could make low payments over a period of time. That way people could afford to buy more. Banks provided money at low interest rates. Advertising also pushed the idea of buying on credit. Average Americans were spending more money than they actually had.

3. Describe two economic problems hidden by the business boom of the 1920s.

_____

_____

In the first column, write notes to describe how the inventions and trends
of the 1920s changed American life. In the second column, write the name
of a related company or product that contributed to the boom of the 1920s.

Invention or Trend	Effects of the Invention or Trend	Company or Product
1. Automobiles		
2. Airplane industry		
3. Alternating electrical current		
4. Modern advertising		
5. Installment plan		

Why should Americans in the 1920s have shown greater concern for their
future? Note three things that were, or might have been, seen as "clouds in
the blue skies of prosperity."

1.	2.	3.

Changing Ways of Life

Terms and Names

Prohibition The era that prohibited the manufacture and sale of alcoholic beverages

speakeasy Hidden saloons and nightclubs that illegally sold liquor

bootlegger Smugglers who brought alcohol in from Canada and the Caribbean

fundamentalism Religious movement based on the belief that everything written in the Bible was literally true

Clarence Darrow Famous trial lawyer

Scopes trial Trial of John Scopes for teaching evolution

Before You Read

In the last section, you learned about American business in the 1920s. In this section, you will read about new lifestyles and values that emerged in the 1920s.

As You Read

Use a diagram to show how the government attempted to deal with problems thought to stem from alcohol use and with the teaching of evolution.

RURAL AND URBAN DIFFERENCES
(**Pages** 434–437)
What was Prohibition?

The 1920 census showed a change in America. For the first time, more Americans lived in large towns and cities than in small towns and on farms.

The values that most Americans had grown up with were small-town values. They included conservative social standards, hard work, thriftiness, and close families. People knew their neighbors and followed the teachings of their churches.

By the 1920s, urbanization, or the movement of Americans from rural areas to the cities, had increased. New York, Chicago, and Philadelphia had become huge cities. There were over 65 cities with more than 100,000 people. Two million

people a year left their farms and small towns for the cities.

Urban values began to dominate the nation. Life in big cities was different from in small towns. People with different backgrounds came into contact with one another.

City people were more open to new ideas in art, science, and politics. They went out at night. They were more tolerant of drinking and gambling. Life was fast-paced. Sometimes it was impersonal and lonely. Many people who were new to city life found it hard to adjust.

One clash between small-town and city values led to an era known as **Prohibition.** Prohibition was the ban on alcoholic beverages set forth in the Eighteenth Amendment. It took effect in 1920. Most

Guided Reading Workbook

support for prohibition came from religious rural white Protestants.

Even though it was the law, the effort to stop drinking was doomed. The government did not have enough officers to enforce it. People made their own alcohol illegally.

In cities, even respectable middle-class people flocked to **speakeasies.** These were hidden saloons and nightclubs that served liquor illegally.

People also bought liquor from **bootleggers,** or smugglers who brought it in from Canada and the Caribbean. Bootleggers created a chain of corruption by bribing police officers and judges.

Prohibition caused a general disrespect for the law. It also caused a great deal of money to flow out of lawful businesses and into organized crime. Underworld gangs took control of the illegal liquor business. The most famous gang was headed by Chicago's Al Capone. Chicago became known for bloody gang killings.

This rise in crime and violence led many people to demand the repeal of prohibition. By the middle of the decade, only 19 percent of Americans supported it. Prohibition was repealed by the Twenty-first Amendment in 1933.

1. How did prohibition affect the nation?

_____

_____

SCIENCE AND RELIGION CLASH
(**Pages** 438–439)
What was the Scopes Trial?

During the 1920s, the nation saw the rise of Christian **fundamentalism.** This religious movement was based on the belief that everything written in the Bible was literally true. Fundamentalists rejected the growing trust in science that most

Americans had. They were also against the religious faiths of other people, especially immigrants.

These beliefs led fundamentalists to reject Charles Darwin's theory of evolution. According to that theory, plant and animal species had developed over millions of years.

Fundamentalists believed that the Bible was correct in stating that the world and all its plants and animals were created by God in six days. They did not want evolution taught in schools.

Fundamentalist preachers drew large crowds to religious revivals, especially in the South and West. Fundamentalists also gained political power. In 1925, Tennessee passed a law making it a crime to teach evolution.

Many people opposed this law. The American Civil Liberties Union (ACLU) promised to defend in court any teacher who would challenge the law.

John Scopes, a young biology teacher from Dayton, Tennessee, challenged the law. He openly taught about evolution. He was arrested, and his case went to trial. The ACLU hired **Clarence Darrow,** the most famous trial lawyer in the nation, to defend Scopes. William Jennings Bryan was the prosecutor.

Scopes was guilty because he broke the law. But the trial was really about evolution. It was also about religion in schools. Reporters came from all over the world to cover the **Scopes trial.** Huge crowds gathered.

The highlight of the trial was when William Jennings Bryan took the stand. Darrow questioned Bryan until Bryan said that while the earth was made in six days, they were "not six days of 24 hours." Bryan was admitting that the Bible could be interpreted in different ways.

Even so, Scopes was found guilty. His conviction was later overturned by the state Supreme Court. But the ban on teaching evolution remained a law in Tennessee.

2. How did fundamentalist beliefs lead to the Scopes trial?

_____

_____

As you read about how the 1920s reflected conflicts and tensions in
American culture, take notes to answer the questions below.

In January 1920, Prohibition went into effect.

1. a. Who tended to be supporters of Prohibition at this time? b. Why did they support it?	2. a. Who tended to be opponents of Prohibition at this time? b. Why did they oppose it?
3. Why was Prohibition repealed?	

In July 1925, Clarence Darrow and William Jennings Bryan faced each other in the Scopes trial.

4. a. Who were Darrow's main supporters? b. Why did they support him?	5. a. Who were Bryan's main supporters? b. Why did they support him?
6. What was the outcome of the case?	

Section 2

The Twenties Woman

Terms and Names

flapper Young woman who embraced the new fashions and values of the 1920s

double standard Set of principles granting one group more freedom than another group

Before You Read

In the last section, you read about some lifestyle changes in the 1920s. In this section, you will learn how women's lives changed during the 1920s.

As You Read

Use a web diagram to take notes on the changes women experienced in the 1920s.

YOUNG WOMEN CHANGE THE RULES (Pages 440–441)
What was a flapper?

In some ways, the spirit of the twenties was a reaction to World War I. Many young soldiers had witnessed horrible events in Europe. This led them to rebel against traditional values. They wanted to enjoy life while they could.

Young women also wanted to take part in the rebellious, pleasure-loving life of the twenties. Many of them demanded the same freedom as men.

The new urban culture also influenced many women. Their symbol was the **flapper.** She was an emancipated young woman. She held new independent attitudes and liked the sophisticated new fashions of the day.

She wore make-up, short skirts, short hair, and more jewelry than would have been proper only a few years before. She often smoked cigarettes and drank alcohol in public. She went dancing to new, exciting music.

Other attitudes changed, too. Many young men and women began to see marriage as more of an equal partnership.

At the same time, churches and schools protested the new values. The majority of women were not flappers. Many people felt torn between the old values and the new ones.

One result of this clash between old values and the image of the flapper was the **double standard.** This was a set of principles or values generally accepted by society. One American double standard allowed men to have greater sexual freedom than women. Women still had to observe stricter standards of behavior than men did.

1. How did the flapper represent the spirit of the twenties?

_____

_____

Guided Reading Workbook

WOMEN SHED OLD ROLES AT HOME AND AT WORK

(**Pages** 441–443)

How did women's roles change?

Many women had gone to work outside the home during World War I. This trend continued in the twenties. But their opportunities had changed after the war. Men returned from the war and took back traditional "men's jobs." Women moved back into the "women's professions" of teaching, nursing, and social work.

Big business provided another role for women: clerical work. Millions of women became secretaries. Many others became salesclerks in stores. Many women also worked on assembly lines in factories. By 1930, 10 million women had paid jobs outside the home. This was almost one-fourth of the American work force.

Women did not find equality in the workplace. Few women rose to jobs in management. Women earned less than men. Men regarded women as temporary workers whose real job was at home keeping house and raising children. In the twenties, patterns of discrimination against women in the business world continued.

Family life changed, too. Families had fewer children. Electrical appliances made housework easier. Many items that had been made at home—from clothing to bread—could now be bought ready-made in stores.

Public agencies took over some family responsibilities, too. They provided services for the elderly and the sick. Nevertheless, most women remained homemakers. Some women had to work and also run their homes. It was hard for them to combine these roles.

In the 1920s, marriages were more often based on romantic love than arranged by families. Children were no longer part of the work force. They spent their days in school and other activities with people of their own age. Peer pressure began to be an important influence on teens' behavior. This reflected the conflict between traditional attitudes and modern ways of thinking.

2. Describe two changes in women's roles in the workplace.

_____

_____

As you read about women's changing roles in the 1920s, fill out the chart
by writing notes in the appropriate spaces.

Social Life in the 1920s	
1. Note two ways women's fashions changed.	
2. Note two ways women's social behavior changed.	
3. Note two words that describe the attitude reflected by these changes.	

Work and Home Life in the 1920s	
4. Note one way women's work opportunities improved.	
5. Note two ways women's home and family life improved.	

6. Note three negative effects that accompanied women's changing roles in the 1920s.	

Section 3

Education and Popular Culture

Terms and Names

Charles A. Lindbergh First person to fly solo across the Atlantic

George Gershwin Composer

Georgia O'Keeffe Artist

Sinclair Lewis Novelist

F. Scott Fitzgerald Novelist

Edna St. Vincent Millay Poet

Ernest Hemingway Novelist

Before You Read

In the last section, you learned about women in the 1920s. In this section, you will read about education and popular culture during the 1920s.

As You Read

Use a time line to take notes on the key events in popular culture in the 1920s.

SCHOOLS AND THE MASS MEDIA SHAPE CULTURE (Pages 446–448)
How **did popular culture change in America?**

America was becoming more prosperous. Business and industry required a more educated work force. These two factors caused a huge increase in the number of students going to high school. In 1914, only 1 million American students went to high school after elementary school. In 1926, the number was nearly 4 million.

Schools changed as they grew. Before the 1920s, high schools were mostly for students who were going on to college. In the twenties, high schools had a wide range of students. Schools offered vocational, or work-related, training for industrial jobs. They offered home economics courses for future homemakers.

High schools also saw an increase in the number of children of immigrants. Many of these students did not speak English. Even so, the nation's schools were successful in teaching large numbers of Americans to read.

As a result of increased literacy, more people read newspapers than before. Newspaper circulation rose. Big city papers and newspaper chains swallowed up small town newspapers.

National magazines were also popular. Some of them delivered the news. Other magazines published fiction and articles.

The most powerful of the mass media was radio. Radio networks with stations in many cities were formed in the twenties. The networks did research to find out what people wanted to hear—and gave it to them. Radio networks created something new in America: the shared national experience of hearing things as they happened. By 1930, 40 percent of American households had radios.

1. What was an effect of increased literacy in the United States?

_____

_____

AMERICA CHASES NEW HEROES AND OLD DREAMS (Pages 448–451)
Who was Charles Lindbergh?

In the 1920s, Americans had more money and more free time than ever before. Fads, including puzzles and games, swept the nation. People also spent a great deal of money at sports events.

The twenties were called the Golden Age of Sports. Many talented athletes set new records. These athletes were portrayed as superheroes by the media. They became heroes to many Americans.

Charles A. Lindbergh thrilled the nation by becoming the first person to fly solo across the Atlantic Ocean. Lindbergh took off from New York City in his plane, *The Spirit of St. Louis*. After 33 hours, Lindbergh landed outside of Paris, France. On his return to the United States, Lindbergh became the idol of America. In an age of sensationalism and excess, Lindbergh stood for the honesty and bravery the nation seemed to have lost.

Even before the introduction of sound, movies became a national pastime. *The Jazz Singer*, the first movie with sound, was released in 1927. Walt Disney's *Steamboat Willie*, the first animated film with sound was made the next year. By 1930, the "talkies" had caused movie attendance to double.

In the 1920s, American artists broke away from European traditions. Eugene O'Neill wrote plays about the confusion of modern American life. Composer **George Gershwin** merged jazz with traditional elements creating music with a new American sound.

American painters recorded the America they saw and felt. Edward Hopper painted the loneliness of American life. **Georgia O'Keeffe** showed the grandeur of New York City. She later became famous for her paintings of the Southwest.

Many gifted American writers criticized American society. **Sinclair Lewis** was the first American to win a Nobel Prize for Literature. His novels *Main Street* and *Babbitt* made fun of middle-class America's conformity and materialism.

Novelist **F. Scott Fitzgerald** coined the term "Jazz Age" to describe the twenties. His books, such as *This Side of Paradise* and *The Great Gatsby*, showed the negative side of the age. But the poems of **Edna Vincent Millay** celebrated youth and freedom from traditional restrictions.

Some Americans disliked American culture so much they went to live abroad. Many gathered in Paris. The writer Gertrude Stein called them the Lost Generation. They included Fitzgerald and **Ernest Hemingway**. Hemingway introduced a tough, simple style of writing that changed American literature.

2. Why did Lindbergh become an American idol?

_____

_____

Section 3, *continued*

As you read this section, take notes summarizing how public education changed.

	Education Before the 1920s	Education During the 1920s
1. Enrollments		
2. Types of courses		
3. Immigrants		
4. Financing		

As you read about how America's popular culture developed in the 1920s, give at least two specific examples of each area of popular culture.

1. Magazines	2. Radio
3. Sports	4. Movies
5. Theater, music, and art	6. Literature

Guided Reading Workbook

The Harlem Renaissance

Terms and Names

James Weldon Johnson Poet and civil rights leader

Marcus Garvey Black nationalist leader

Harlem Renaissance African-American artistic movement

Claude McKay Poet

Langston Hughes Poet

Zora Neale Hurston Anthropologist and author

Paul Robeson Actor, singer, and civil-rights leader

Louis Armstrong Jazz musician

Duke Ellington Jazz musician

Bessie Smith Blues singer

Before You Read

In the last section, you read about education and popular culture in the 1920s. In this section, you will learn about the Harlem Renaissance.

As You Read

Use a chart to take notes on the achievements of the Harlem Renaissance.

AFRICAN-AMERICAN VOICES IN THE 1920S (Pages 452–454)
How did African Americans approach civil rights in the 1920s?

Between 1910 and 1920, hundreds of thousands of African Americans had moved from the South to the big cities of the North. This was called the Great Migration. It was a response to racial violence and economic discrimination against blacks in the South. By 1929, 40 percent of African Americans lived in cities. As a result, racial tensions increased in Northern cities. There were race riots.

The National Association for the Advancement of Colored People (NAACP) worked to end violence against

African Americans. W. E. B. Du Bois led a peaceful protest against racial violence.

The NAACP also fought to get laws against lynching passed by Congress. **James Weldon Johnson**, a poet and lawyer, led that fight. While no law against lynching was passed in the twenties, the number of lynchings gradually dropped.

Marcus Garvey voiced a message of black pride that appealed to many African Americans. Garvey thought that African Americans should build a separate society. He formed a black nationalist group called the Universal Negro Improvement Association (UNIA).

Garvey promoted black-owned businesses. He also urged African

Guided Reading Workbook

Americans to return to Africa to set up an independent nation.

1. How did the NAACP and Marcus Garvey's followers respond to racial discrimination?

_____

_____

THE HARLEM RENAISSANCE FLOWERS IN NEW YORK
(Pages 454–457)
What **was the Harlem Renaissance?**

In the 1920s, many African Americans moved to Harlem, a section of New York City. So did blacks from the West Indies, Cuba, Puerto Rico, and Haiti. Harlem became the world's largest black urban community.

This neighborhood was also the birthplace of the **Harlem Renaissance.** This literary and artistic movement celebrated African-American culture.

Above all, the Harlem Renaissance was a literary movement. It was led by well-educated middle-class blacks. They took pride in their African heritage and their people's folklore. They also wrote about the problems of being black in a white culture. An important collection of works by Harlem Renaissance writers, *The New Negro*, was published by Alain Locke in 1925.

The Harlem Renaissance produced many outstanding poets. **Claude McKay** wrote about the pain of prejudice. He urged African Americans to resist discrimination.

One of the most famous Harlem Renaissance poets was **Langston Hughes.** In the 1920s, he wrote about the daily lives of working-class blacks. He wove the tempos of jazz and the blues into his poems.

Zora Neale Hurston was the most famous female writer of the Harlem Renaissance. She collected the folklore of poor Southern blacks. Hurston also wrote novels, short stories, and poems.

Music and drama were important parts of the Harlem Renaissance, too. Some African-American performers became popular with white audiences. **Paul Robeson** became an important actor and singer. He starred in Eugene O'Neill's play *The Emperor Jones* and in Shakespeare's *Othello*.

Jazz became more popular in the twenties. Early in the 20th century, musicians in New Orleans blended ragtime and blues into the new sound of jazz. Musicians from New Orleans traveled North, and they brought jazz with them. The most important and influential jazz musician was **Louis Armstrong.**

Many whites came to Harlem to hear jazz in night clubs. Edward Kennedy **"Duke" Ellington** led an orchestra there. He was a jazz pianist and one of the nation's greatest composers.

The outstanding singer of the time was **Bessie Smith.** Some black musicians chose to live and perform in Europe. Josephine Baker became a famous dancer, singer, and comedy star in Paris.

2. Describe the contributions of one artist of the Harlem Renaissance.

_____

_____

Name the organization with which each leader was associated. Then note
their beliefs and goals as well as the tactics they believed necessary to
achieve them.

1. W. E. B. Du Bois and James Weldon Johnson	2. Marcus Garvey
Organization:	Organization:
Beliefs, goals, and tactics:	Beliefs, goals, and tactics:

Describe briefly what each of the following artists was known for.

African-American Writers
1. Claude McKay
2. Langston Hughes
3. Zora Neale Hurston

African-American Performers
4. Paul Robeson
5. Louis Armstrong
6. Duke Ellington
7. Bessie Smith

The Great Depression Begins

The Nation's Sick Economy

Terms and Names

price support Law that keeps prices above a set level

credit Short-term loans to buy goods with promises to pay later

Alfred E. Smith Democratic presidential candidate in 1928

Dow Jones Industrial Average Index of stock prices of select companies

speculation Investments in high-risk ventures

buying on margin Buying stock by paying only a portion of the full cost up-front with promises to pay the rest later

Black Tuesday October 29,1929, the day the stock market crashed

Great Depression Period of bad economic times in the United States that lasted from 1929 to 1940

Hawley-Smoot Tariff Act Law that raised taxes on imports and worsened the Depression

Before You Read

In the last section, you learned about the Harlem Renaissance in the 1920s. In this section, you will read about the economic problems that led to the Great Depression.

As You Read

Use a web diagram to take notes on the causes of the 1929 stock market crash.

ECONOMIC TROUBLES ON THE HORIZON (Pages 464–466)
Why was the nation's economy sick in the late 1920s?

During the 1920s, the economy boomed. But there were economic problems under the surface. Industries, such as clothing, steel-making, and mining, were hardly making a profit.

Many industries had been successful in the early 1920s. But by the late 1920s, they were losing money. These industries included auto manufacturing, construction, and consumer goods.

The biggest problems were in farming. After the war, the demand for food dropped and farmers suffered. Farmers' incomes went down. Many could not make the mortgage payments on their farms. As a result, many farmers lost their land.

Congress tried to help farmers by passing **price supports.** With price supports, the government would not allow food prices to fall below a certain level. But Calvin Coolidge vetoed the bill. Farmers' incomes continued to drop.

Farmers were not the only problem with the economy. Americans were buying less. Many found that prices were rising faster than their salaries. Many people bought goods on **credit**—an arrangement in which consumers agreed to make monthly payments with interest. But too many Americans were accumulating debt they could not afford to pay off.

In the late 1920s, much of America seemed prosperous, but there was an uneven distribution of income. A small number of rich people were getting richer. But a large number of people were not doing well and falling further behind.

1. What problems did farmers face in the 1920s?

_____

_____

HOOVER TAKES THE NATION
(**Pages** 466–467)
How **healthy was the stock market?**

Few people recognized the problems with the economy in 1928. The Republican Herbert Hoover easily defeated the Democratic challenger, **Alfred E. Smith.** People believed Hoover when he said the American economy was healthy. The **Dow Jones Industrial Average,** a measure of 30 popular stocks, was way up. People rushed to buy stocks. Many people were engaging in **speculation,** buying risky stocks in hopes of a quick profit. To do so, they were **buying on margin**—paying just a small down payment and borrowing the rest. The problem of buying on margin was that there was no way to pay off the loan if the stock price declined sharply.

2. What was dangerous about how Americans bought stock?

_____

_____

THE STOCK MARKET CRASHES
(**Pages** 467–469)
What **was Black Tuesday?**

Stock prices did begin to fall in September 1929. On Tuesday, October 29, 1929, called **Black Tuesday,** prices fell so sharply that people said the market had "crashed." People frantically tried to sell their shares which drove prices down further. There were no buyers. Many people lost all their savings. By mid-November, $30 billion—more than America had spent in World War I—had been lost.

3. What happened on Black Tuesday?

_____

_____

FINANCIAL COLLAPSE
(**Pages** 469–471)
How **did the stock market crash affect businesses?**

The stock market crash signaled the **Great Depression.** This period of bad economic times when many people were out of work lasted from 1929 to 1940. Although the crash did not cause the Depression, it did make it worse. After the crash, many people panicked and took their money out of banks. Many banks were forced to close. When the banks failed, other depositors lost the savings they had in the banks.

Businesses also began to close. Millions of Americans lost their jobs. Workers who kept their jobs experienced pay cuts or reduced hours.

The Depression spread around the world. Germany was still paying war reparations. Other European countries were struggling with debts from the war. With Americans unable to buy their goods

Guided Reading Workbook

now, European economies suffered even more.

The situation became worse when Congress passed the **Hawley-Smoot Tariff Act**. Congress hoped that higher tariffs would push Americans to buy goods made in the United States. The result would be to help American industry. Instead, when the United States charged more to bring goods in, imports from Europe declined. Then Europeans had even less money to spend on U.S. goods, and American industry suffered.

The Great Depression had several causes:

- Tariffs and war debt policies that cut down the foreign market for American goods

- A crisis in the farm sector
- The availability of easy credit
- An unequal distribution of income

These factors led to a falling demand for consumer goods. The federal government hurt the economy with its policy of low interest rates causing businesses and consumers to borrow easily and build up too much debt.

4. Why did many banks fail after the stock market crashed?

_____

_____

As you read this section, take notes to describe the serious problems in each area of the economy that helped cause the Great Depression.

1. Industry	2. Agriculture

3. Consumer spending	4. Distribution of wealth	5. Stock market

Hardship and Suffering During the Depression

Terms and Names

shantytown A neighborhood where people live in shacks

soup kitchen Place where free food is served to the needy

bread line A line of people waiting for free food

Dust Bowl Area of the Great Plains made worthless for farming by drought and dust storms in the 1930s

direct relief Money or food given directly from the government to the needy

Before You Read

In the last section, you learned about the start of the Great Depression. In this section, you will read about the hardships caused by the Depression.

As You Read

Use a Venn diagram to take notes on the effects of the Great Depression on farmers and city dwellers. Find the similarities and the differences.

THE DEPRESSION DEVASTATES PEOPLE'S LIVES (Pages 472–474)
How did the Depression affect people in cities and on farms?

The Depression brought suffering and hardship to many Americans. The hard economic times ruined many lives. Millions of people lost their jobs. Some went hungry or became homeless. Those who could not meet their housing payments were thrown out of their homes.

Cities across the country were full of these homeless people. Some slept in parks and wrapped themselves up in newspapers to keep warm. Others built **shantytowns,** where they lived in little shacks they made out of scrap material. Some ate in **soup kitchens,** where charities served meals to the needy. Those who could not afford to buy food stood in **bread lines** to receive free food.

African Americans and Latino Americans who lived in the cities had a very hard time. They had a higher unemployment rate than whites. If they did have work, they were paid less than white workers.

There was even violence directed against African Americans and Latinos. Angry whites who had lost their jobs did not want to compete against these minority groups for the few jobs that were left. They sometimes attacked African Americans. They demanded that Latino Americans be sent back to the countries they came from.

The Depression hurt people in rural areas, too. Food prices continued to go down as the Depression deepened.

Farmers earned less and less. Many farm families could not meet their mortgage payments. More and more of them lost their farms. From 1929 to 1932, about 400,000 farmers lost their land.

To make matters worse, a long drought hit the Great Plains. There was little rain from Texas to North Dakota. Much of this area had been grassland that farmers broke up with their plows in order to grow crops.

The soil was now exhausted from over-farming. The grass that had once held the soil in place was gone. When powerful winds swept across the Great Plains, the soil simply blew away. This dry area of blowing soil was called the **Dust Bowl.** Huge dust storms covered the plains and blew dust as far away as the East Coast.

The hardest hit region included parts of Kansas, Oklahoma, Texas, New Mexico, and Colorado. Many Oklahoma farmers packed up their belongings and started for California to look for work. They became migrant workers, moving from place to place to pick crops. Because so many of them came from Oklahoma, migrant workers were often called Okies.

1. How did people in the cities and in rural areas suffer during the Great Depression?

_____

_____

EFFECTS ON THE AMERICAN FAMILY (Pages 474–477)
How did the Depression affect families?

The Depression put a heavy strain on family life. Many families pulled together during the hard times. They shared what they earned. Instead of going out for entertainment, parents and children often stayed home. They played board games or listened to the radio.

But some families broke apart under the strain of poverty and unemployment. Many men felt ashamed because they had lost their jobs. Some of them simply left their families and wandered the country looking for work.

Women tried to find work, too. But they were usually paid less than men. Many people complained that employers should not hire women. They thought that men should have the jobs instead. These people argued that men were the ones who supported families, so it was more important for them to have jobs.

Children suffered terribly from poverty and the break-up of families. Many children had poor diets and no health care. Their parents could not afford to buy healthy food or to pay doctor bills. Many children suffered from malnutrition and diet-related illnesses like rickets. Many children ran away from home, hopping rides aboard freight trains. It was exciting, but also dangerous. Many were robbed or killed by criminals or beaten by railroad guards.

During the early years of the Great Depression, the federal government did not give **direct relief**—cash or food directly to poor people. Charities and some city governments struggled to help. But they could not provide enough relief to keep people out of poverty.

Because so many people were out of work, cities and states collected less tax money. They had to cut their budgets for programs like child welfare. Some cities could not afford to keep their schools open for a full term. Many school boards shortened the school year. Other schools simply closed. Children often went to work to try to help their families survive.

Guided Reading Workbook

The Great Depression caused great suffering. Rates of suicide and mental illness increased dramatically. Hardship forced young people to give up dreams of college.

While the Great Depression caused much suffering, it sometimes brought out the best in individuals, families, and communities. Many people shared resources with their neighbors or gave food and clothing to the needy.

2. Describe two ways the Great Depression affected families.

_____

_____

Name _____ Class _____ Date _____

As you read about how people coped with hard times, use the chart below
to summarize the Great Depression's effects on various aspects of
American life.

1. Employment
2. Housing
3. Farming
4. Race relations
5. Family life
6. Physical health
7. Emotional health

Guided Reading Workbook

Section 3

Hoover Struggles with the Depression

Terms and Names

Herbert Hoover 31st president

Boulder Dam Dam on the Colorado River built during the Depression to create jobs

Federal Home Loan Bank Act Law passed in 1931 to reduce mortgage rates to save farmers from foreclosure

Reconstruction Finance Corporation Agency established in 1932 to provide emergency relief to large businesses, insurance companies, and banks

Bonus Army Unemployed World War I veterans who marched to Washington to demand their war bonuses

---

Before You Read

In the last section, you read about how the Depression affected common people. In this section, you will learn how President Hoover tried to stop the Depression.

As You Read

Use a web diagram to take notes on President Hoover's response to the Great Depression.

HOOVER TRIES TO REASSURE THE NATION (Pages 478–481)
How could the nation recover?

Economic slowdowns occur regularly. Over time, economies go through cycles. There are times of economic growth and prosperity. They are followed by slumps when the economy slows down. In the 1930s, many experts believed that it was best not to interfere with these economic cycles. They argued that slumps would end on their own and good times would return.

At first, President **Herbert Hoover** believed that the Great Depression was just another slowdown that would end on its own. His advisors thought that it was best to do nothing. The economy would

heal itself. Hoover believed the government should take some action. But he also believed that government should not take too much power or give direct aid to poor people.

Hoover believed government should help different groups work together to improve the economy. For example, Hoover thought government should help managers and workers find solutions to their problems. But he did not think government should decide on the solution.

Hoover also believed in "rugged individualism"—the idea that people should succeed through their own efforts. He believed people should take care of themselves and each other, and that the government should encourage private

---

groups to help the needy. He thought that charities—not government—should give food and shelter to people who were poor or out of work. Hoover felt that government could guide these private relief efforts. None of these steps made a difference. The economy shrank and unemployment continued to go up.

One project that did help was the **Boulder Dam,** a huge dam on the Colorado River. Still, economic difficulties increased, the country turned against Hoover. In the 1930 elections, the Democrats gained more seats in Congress. Farmers burned crops and dumped milk rather than sell it for less than it cost them to produce it. People called the shantytowns that sprang up "Hoovervilles." Despite public criticism, Hoover stuck to his principles.

Hoover met with bankers, businessmen, and labor leaders. He urged them to work together to help improve the economy. He asked employers not to fire workers or to lower their pay. He asked labor leaders not to ask for higher pay or to strike.

1. What did Hoover think government should do in bad economic times?

_____

_____

HOOVER TAKES ACTION; GASSING THE BONUS ARMY
(**Pages** 481–483)
What did Hoover do?

Hoover did not offer direct aid to the poor. But he did worry about the suffering of the people. He took steps to use the government to improve the economy.

Hoover used the Boulder Dam project as a model of how the federal government could encourage cooperation between private groups. He tried to help farmers with the Federal Farm Board, and banks by creating the National Credit Corporation. Another program tried to raise the prices farmers received for their crops. Hoover also urged bankers to join a credit organization. It gave loans to banks that were in danger of failing.

By 1931, the economy had not improved. Congress passed the **Federal Home Loan Bank Act.** This law lowered mortgage rates. Congress hoped that low mortgage rates would help farmers change the terms of their mortgages. This would help protect their farms from foreclosure.

Hoover also created the **Reconstruction Finance Corporation.** The RFC provided money for projects to create jobs.

Hoover became less popular with the public. His popularity fell even more in 1932 when World War I veterans came to the capital. These veterans had been promised bonuses to make up for their poor wartime pay. Congress was about to vote on a bill to give the veterans their bonuses immediately.

Thousands of veterans and their families came to Washington. This so-called **Bonus Army** set up tents to live in near the Capitol building. Hoover first sent the veterans food. But after the bonus was voted down in Congress, Hoover told the veterans to leave. About 2,000 stayed. Hoover ordered the army to remove them. The sight of U.S. Army troops using tear gas on citizens outraged many people.

2. What actions did Hoover take to improve the economy?

_____

_____

As you read about President Hoover's response to the Great Depression,
write notes in the appropriate boxes to answer the questions.

Philosophy
1. What was Hoover's philosophy of government?

Response and Economic Results
2. What was Hoover's initial reaction to the stock market crash of 1929?
3. a. What was the nation's economic situation in 1930?   b. How did voters in 1930 respond to this situation?
4. a. What did Hoover do about the economic situation?   b. How did the economy respond to his efforts?
5. a. How did Hoover deal with the economic problem posed by the Bonus Army?   b. How did his efforts affect his own political situation?

Guided Reading Workbook

The New Deal

A New Deal Fights the Depression

Terms and Names

Franklin Delano Roosevelt 32nd president

New Deal Franklin Roosevelt's programs to end the Depression

Glass-Steagall Act Law that created insurance for bank deposits

Federal Securities Act Law to regulate stock information

Agricultural Adjustment Act (AAA) Programs to help farmers

Civilian Conservation Corps (CCC) Program to employ young men in work projects

National Industrial Recovery Act (NIRA) Programs to help industry

deficit spending Spending more than the government receives in revenue

Huey Long Political leader from Louisiana who criticized the New Deal

Before You Read

In the last section, you read about Herbert Hoover's reaction to the Great Depression. In this section, you will learn about Franklin Delano Roosevelt's programs to fight the Depression.

As You Read

Use a chart to take notes on the problems Roosevelt faced at the beginning of his presidency and how he tried to solve them.

AMERICANS GET A NEW DEAL
(Pages 488–490)
***What* were the goals of the New Deal?**

By the end of 1932, Americans were ready for a change. Democratic candidate **Franklin Delano Roosevelt**—often called FDR—beat Hoover in the presidential election of 1932 by a landslide. Democrats also won large majorities in the House and Senate.

Roosevelt and his advisors planned programs to end the Depression. These programs became known as the **New Deal.**

It had three goals: relief for the needy, economic recovery, and financial reform.

In the first Hundred Days, Congress quickly passed many important laws. These laws expanded the federal government's role in the nation's economy.

Roosevelt declared a "bank holiday." He closed the banks to prevent more bank failures. Then Congress passed the Emergency Banking Relief Act, which allowed healthy banks to reopen. This restored public confidence in banks. So did the **Glass-Steagall Act.** It established the Federal Deposit Insurance Corporation (FDIC), which protects the savings people put in banks. Congress also passed the **Federal Securities Act.** This law made companies give accurate information in its stock offerings. Later, Congress created the Securities and Exchange Commission (SEC) to regulate stock markets.

FDR spoke directly to the American people in radio talks called "fireside chats." He explained the New Deal measures and asked for public support. These chats did a lot to restore the nation's confidence.

1. Describe the three goals of the New Deal.

_____

_____

HELPING THE AMERICAN PEOPLE
(Pages 491–492)
Who did the New Deal help?

Roosevelt worked to help farmers and other workers. The **Agricultural Adjustment Act (AAA)** helped to raise crop prices by lowering production.

The New Deal included programs that gave relief through work projects and cash payments. The **Civilian Conservation Corps (CCC)** put young men to work building roads and planting trees. The Federal Emergency Relief Administration (FERA) provided direct relief of food, clothing, and cash to the needy.

The **National Industrial Recovery Act (NIRA)** set codes of fair practice for industries. It also guaranteed the workers' right to organize unions. The NIRA set up the National Recovery Administration (NRA) to stop the trend of wage cuts, falling prices, and layoffs.

The Home Owners Loan Corporation (HOLC) was set up to provide government

loans to homeowners who faced foreclosure because they could not make their loan payments. The Federal Emergency Relief Administration (FERA) provided direct relief to the needy.

2. How did the New Deal provide help to different groups of Americans?

_____

_____

THE NEW DEAL COMES UNDER ATTACK (Pages 492–494)
Who criticized the New Deal?

Roosevelt reluctantly financed the New Deal through **deficit spending**—spending more money than the government receives in revenue. Although the New Deal programs benefited many people and helped restore public confidence, some people criticized it. Some liberals said it did not do enough to help the poor. Conservative critics said it gave the federal government too much control over agriculture and business.

The Supreme Court found two important parts of the New Deal unconstitutional. The Court struck down the NIRA and the AAA. This upset Roosevelt. He proposed a bill to allow him to appoint more new Supreme Court justices.

Critics claimed that Roosevelt was trying to "pack the Court" with justices who supported him. Protest over this proposal cost Roosevelt support. But as justices resigned from the Court, Roosevelt was able to appoint seven new justices. Court decisions began to favor the New Deal.

Three critics of Roosevelt were particularly important. Father Charles Coughlin was a Roman Catholic priest. He used his popular radio sermons to criticize

Roosevelt. His anti-Jewish views eventually cost him support.

Dr. Francis Townsend proposed a pension plan to give monthly payments to the elderly. Many elderly voters liked Townsend's plan.

The most serious challenge to the New Deal came from Senator **Huey Long** of Louisiana. He was an early supporter of the New Deal. But he wanted to become president himself. Long proposed a program called Share Our Wealth. In 1935, at the height of his popularity, Long was assassinated.

3. List two critics of the New Deal and describe their arguments.

_____

_____

As you read about President Roosevelt's New Deal, take notes to answer
questions about each new federal program. The first one is done for you.

Federal Program	What was its immediate purpose?	What was its long-term goal?
Business Assistance and Reform 1. Emergency Banking Relief Act (EBRA)	*Authorized the Treasury Department to inspect and close banks*	*To restore public confidence in banks*
2. Glass-Steagall Banking Act of 1933		
3. Federal Securities Act		
4. National Industrial Recovery Act (NIRA)		
Farm Relief/Rural Development 5. Agricultural Adjustment Act (AAA)		
6. Tennessee Valley Authority (TVA)		
Employment Projects 7. Civilian Conservation Corps (CCC)		
8. Federal Emergency Relief Administration (FERA)		
9. Public Works Administration (PWA)		
10. Civil Works Administration (CWA)		
Housing 11. Home Owners Loan Corporation (HOLC)		

Section 2

The Second New Deal Takes Hold

Terms and Names

Eleanor Roosevelt First lady, social reformer, political adviser

Works Progress Administration (WPA) New Deal jobs program

National Youth Administration Program to provide aid and jobs to young people

Wagner Act Law to protect workers' rights

Social Security Act Program that provided aid to people with disabilities and pensions for retired workers

Before You Read

In the last section, you read about the early days of the New Deal. In this section, you will learn about the Second New Deal.

As You Read

Use a chart to take notes on how the programs of the Second New Deal helped groups such as farmers, the unemployed, youth, and retirees.

THE SECOND HUNDRED DAYS
(Pages 495–496)
***What* did voters think about the New Deal?**

The economy improved in the first two years of Roosevelt's presidency. But it did not improve much. Still, the New Deal was very popular. Democrats increased their majority in Congress in the midterm elections of 1934.

FDR launched a second wave of reforms— sometimes called the Second New Deal. These were programs designed to help poor people. The president's wife, **Eleanor Roosevelt,** traveled around the country. She reported to the president on the suffering of the poor. She spoke up for women and minorities.

The 1936 election was an overwhelming victory for Roosevelt, the Democrats, and the New Deal. It also marked the first time most African Americans voted Democratic.

And it was the first time that labor unions supported a single candidate. They supported Roosevelt.

1. What did the elections of 1934 and 1936 tell about the New Deal?

_____

_____

HELPING FARMERS (Pages 496–498)
***How* did the Second New Deal help farmers?**

Things were still tough for farmers in the mid 1930s. The first AAA had helped some farmers before it was struck down by the Supreme Court.

Now Congress passed new laws to replace the first AAA. One program paid farmers to use soil conservation measures in managing their land. The second AAA was passed without the tax that had made the first one unconstitutional.

Other laws helped sharecroppers and tenant farmers. They provided loans to help farmers buy land. New laws also helped migrant workers by providing better housing for them.

2. What action did the Second New Deal take to help farmers?

_____

_____

ROOSEVELT EXTENDS RELIEF
(Pages 498–499)
What were the WPA and NYA?

A new agency called the **Works Progress Administration (WPA)** set out to create jobs as quickly as possible. The WPA used millions of workers to build airports, roads, libraries, schools, and hospitals. Sewing groups made clothes for the needy.

Some people criticized the WPA as a make-work program that created useless jobs just to give people a paycheck. But the WPA created works of lasting value. And it gave working people a sense of hope and dignity along with their paychecks.

The WPA also employed teachers, writers, artists, actors, and musicians. And it made special efforts to help women, minorities, and the young.

The **National Youth Administration (NYA)** provided aid and part-time jobs to many high school and college students. This allowed them to get an education even in tough economic times.

3. How did the WPA and NYA help people?

_____

_____

IMPROVING LABOR AND OTHER REFORMS (Pages 499–501)
How did the Second New Deal help workers?

The Second New Deal created important reforms for labor. Congress passed the National Labor Relations Act to replace the NIRA, which the Supreme Court struck down. This law is often called the **Wagner Act.**

The Wagner Act supported workers' right to collective bargaining. It also banned unfair labor practices. The Wagner Act set up the National Labor Relations Board (NLRB) to enforce these reforms.

The Fair Labor Standards Act of 1938 set maximum hours and a minimum wage for the first time. It set a workweek of 44 hours. It also banned child labor in factories.

The **Social Security Act** was one of the most important achievements of the New Deal. It had three parts:
- Old-age insurance—supplemental retirement plan that provided funds from what workers and employers paid into the system
- Unemployment compensation— payments to workers who lost their jobs
- Aid to the disabled and families with children—this helped people who could not be expected to work

The Second New Deal also extended electricity to rural areas through the Rural Electrification Administration (REA).

4. How did the Second New Deal try to protect workers?

_____

_____

As you read this section, take notes to answer questions about the second
phase of Roosevelt's New Deal policies.

Group	What problems did each group face during the Depression?	What laws were passed and agencies established to deal with these problems?
1. Farmers, migrant workers, and others living in rural areas		
2. Students and other young people		
3. Teachers, writers, artists, and other professionals		
4. All workers, including the unemployed		
5. Retired workers		
6. The disabled, the needy elderly, and dependent mothers and children		

The New Deal Affects Many Groups

Terms and Names

Frances Perkins Secretary of labor

Mary McLeod Bethune Head of the Office of Minority Affairs in the NYA

John Collier Commissioner on Indian Affairs

New Deal coalition Voters from different groups that supported the Democratic party because of the New Deal

Congress of Industrial Organizations (CIO) Labor union

Before You Read

In the last section, you read about the Second New Deal. In this section, you will learn about some of the effects of the New Deal.

As You Read

Use a chart to take notes on how the New Deal affected minorities and other groups.

THE NEW DEAL BRINGS NEW OPPORTUNITIES (Pages 504–505)
How did the New Deal affect women?

Women made some important gains during the New Deal. More women were appointed to important federal jobs.

Frances Perkins became the first female cabinet member as secretary of labor. Perkins helped create the Social Security system. Roosevelt also appointed women as federal judges. Roosevelt hoped that these appointments would make him more popular among women voters.

Many New Deal agencies did not discriminate in hiring. This gave women more opportunities. But some government agencies and many businesses did not hire as many women as men. For example, the Civilian Conservation Corps hired men only. And women were almost always paid less than men. For instance, the

National Recovery Administration set lower wage levels for women than for men.

1. Describe two ways that the New Deal expanded and limited opportunities for women.

_____

_____

AFRICAN-AMERICAN ACTIVISM (Pages 505–506)
How did the New Deal affect African Americans?

President Roosevelt gave a number of African Americans a voice in government. **Mary McLeod Bethune** was an educator who became head of the Minority Affairs Office of the National Youth Administration.

She worked to ensure that the NYA hired some African Americans. Bethune also helped organize the "Black Cabinet." This was a group of influential African Americans that advised Roosevelt on racial issues.

However, President Roosevelt did not push for full civil rights for African Americans. He was afraid of losing the support of white Southerners.

2. What gains did African Americans make during the New Deal?

_____

_____

MEXICAN-AMERICAN FORTUNES; NATIVE AMERICAN GAINS
(Pages 506–507)
What gains did Mexican Americans and Native Americans make?

Mexican Americans tended to support the New Deal. But they received few benefits from New Deal programs. Many were farm workers who were not covered by federal laws. Some New Deal agencies discriminated against them.

Native Americans got support from the New Deal. In 1933, Roosevelt made **John Collier** commissioner on Indian affairs. He was a strong supporter of Native American rights. Collier helped pass the Indian Reorganization Act. This law strengthened Native American land claims.

3. How did Mexican Americans and Native Americans fare under the New Deal?

_____

_____

FDR CREATES THE NEW DEAL COALITION (Pages 507–509)
Who supported the New Deal?

Roosevelt got votes from Southern whites, city people, African Americans, and workers who belonged to unions. Together these groups of voters formed a coalition that supported FDR. It became known as the **New Deal coalition.**

Labor unions made gains in the 1930s. New Deal laws made it easier for workers to form unions and to bargain with employers. Union membership soared from 3 million to more than 10 million.

Divisions emerged between labor unions. The American Federation of Labor (AFL) was made up of mostly crafts unions, such as plumbers or carpenters. Other unions wanted to represent workers in a whole industry, such as the automobile industry. These unions broke away to form the **Congress of Industrial Organizations (CIO).**

Labor employed a new kind of strike in the 1930s—a sit-down strike. In a sit-down strike, workers did not leave their workplace. They remained inside but refused to work. That prevented factory owners from using strikebreakers or scabs to get the work done.

Some strikes led to violence. On Memorial Day, 1937, police killed ten people during a steel strike in Chicago. The National Labor Relations Board stepped in. It forced the steel company to negotiate with the union. This helped labor gain strength.

The Democratic Party got a great deal of support from people living in cities. Powerful city political organizations helped build this support. So did New Deal programs that helped the urban poor. Roosevelt also appealed to people of many

· Guided Reading Workbook

ethnic groups. He appointed people of urban-immigrant backgrounds to important government jobs.

4. What was the New Deal coalition?

_____

_____

As you read, write notes about each group in Roosevelt's New Deal coalition.

1. Women Example(s) of appointees to important government positions:	Gains women made under the New Deal:	Problems of women not solved by the New Deal:

2. African Americans Example(s) of appointees to important government positions:	Gains African Americans made under the New Deal:	Problems of African Americans not solved by the New Deal:

3. Labor unions Example(s) of union(s) organized during the New Deal:	Gains unions made under the New Deal:	Problems of unions not solved by the New Deal:

4. Other coalition groups Other groups:	Reasons they supported the Democratic party:

The New Deal

Section 4

Culture of the 1930s

Terms and Names

Gone With the Wind Popular movie

Orson Welles Actor, director, and filmmaker

Grant Wood Artist

Richard Wright Author

The Grapes of Wrath Novel by John Steinbeck

Before You Read

In the last section, you learned about the New Deal coalition. In this section, you will learn about American culture during the Depression.

As You Read

Use a web diagram to take notes on the cultural figures of the 1930s in the fields of radio, literature, movies, and the arts.

THE LURE OF MOTION PICTURES AND RADIO (Pages 510–512)
What did Americans do for fun during the Depression?

The 1930s were a golden age for the radio and film industries in spite of the hard economic times. Movie tickets were not expensive, and films provided an escape from the problems of Depression life. About two-thirds of Americans went to a movie once a week.

Hollywood studios made a wide variety of movies and created many new movie stars. One of the most popular films of all time was *Gone With the Wind* (1939). Fred Astaire and Ginger Rogers were dancing partners who made many movies together. Other popular movies in the 1930s included *The Wizard of Oz* and the Disney animated film, *Snow White and the Seven Dwarfs*. Audiences flocked to see comedies starring the Marx Brothers and also to see dark, gritty gangster movies. Frank Capra made a different type of

movie. In his movies, honest, kind-hearted people won out over greedy people.

Radio showed the democratic spirit of the times. There were radios in nearly 90 percent of American homes. Most American families listened to their favorite radio shows together. The radio offered inexpensive entertainment. There were comedy and variety shows, news programs, soap operas, and children's shows. There were also excellent dramas and mysteries.

Radio made people like Bob Hope, Jack Benny, and George Burns and Gracie Allen stars long before they had success on television. In order to reach the greatest number of people, President Roosevelt went on the radio during his famous fireside chats.

The most famous radio broadcast was by **Orson Welles.** He was an actor, director, and filmmaker. His fictional radio show "The War of the Worlds" was so realistic that it convinced many

Americans that Martians had landed in New Jersey. It showed the power of radio at a time when many Americans got their news that way.

1. What was the appeal of movies and radio during the Depression?

_____

_____

THE ARTS IN DEPRESSION AMERICA (Pages 512–514)
How did the New Deal help artists?

The art and literature of the Depression was more serious and sober than radio and movies. Many artists used realism to show the hardships of Depression life. Some criticized American society. Others praised the strength of character and the democratic values of the American people.

Some people believed that the government should not play any role in funding arts projects. But New Deal officials believed the arts were important for the nation. They created several programs to put artists to work.

The Federal Arts Project was part of the WPA. It paid artists to create posters, murals, and other works of art for public places. Artists such as Thomas Hart Benton and **Grant Wood** painted rural midwestern subjects. Wood's *American Gothic*, a portrait of a serious-looking man and woman standing in front of their farmhouse, remains symbolic of life during the Depression.

The Federal Theater Project was another part of the WPA. It helped support American playwrights. It also brought live drama to many communities around the country.

Woody Guthrie was a folksinger who used music to capture the hardships of the Depression. Guthrie traveled the country and met thousands of people struggling to get by and wrote songs about what he saw. The Federal Writers' Project funded writers. Saul Bellow was one of these writers. He later won a Pulitzer Prize. **Richard Wright** was an African-American writer. He received financial help while writing *Native Son*. This novel shows the problems racism caused for a young African-American man.

John Steinbeck also got help from the FWP. His novel *The Grapes of Wrath* is one of the most famous books about the Depression. It shows the problems faced by Oklahoma farmers who were forced from their homes during the Dust Bowl. They became migrant workers. They made it to California, but their hardships continued.

Another notable book of the Depression was by the writer James Agee and the photographer Walker Evans. *Let Us Now Praise Famous Men* showed the dignity of Alabama sharecroppers in the face of hardship. The play *Our Town* by Thornton Wilder captured the warmth and beauty of small-town life.

2. Describe two New Deal programs that supported the arts.

_____

_____

As you read about how the Depression and New Deal influenced American culture, write notes in the appropriate boxes to answer the questions about each work.

Films and Radio Drama		
1. Gone with the Wind	What was it? Who created or appeared in it?	What was its theme?
2. Mr. Smith Goes to Washington	What was it? Who created or appeared in it?	What was its theme?
3. The War of the Worlds	What was it? Who created or appeared in it?	What was its theme?
4. Waiting for Lefty	What was it? Who created or appeared in it?	What was its theme?
Art and Literature		
5. Native Son	What was it? Who created or appeared in it?	What was its theme?
6. The Grapes of Wrath	What was it? Who created or appeared in it?	What was its theme?
7. Our Town	What was it? Who created or appeared in it?	What was its theme?
8. American Gothic	What was it? Who created or appeared in it?	What was its theme?

Section 5

The Impact of the New Deal

Terms and Names

Federal Deposit Insurance Corporation (FDIC) Insurance for savings

Securities and Exchange Commission (SEC) Agency to regulate stock markets

National Labor Relations Board (NLRB) Agency to regulate business

parity An equal or fair amount

Tennessee Valley Authority (TVA) Regional work project of lasting value

---

Before You Read

In the last section, you learned about American culture during the Depression. In this section, you will read about the legacy of the New Deal.

As You Read

Use a web diagram to take notes on the lasting effects of the New Deal.

NEW DEAL REFORMS ENDURE
(Pages 515–518)
What do critics say about the New Deal?

By the end of the 1930s, the economy had improved somewhat. Industrial production had reached 1929 levels. Unemployment was still high. But it was much lower than during the worst days of the Depression. Congress urged Roosevelt to cut back on New Deal programs. Roosevelt did, and the economy slid back a bit. Still, Roosevelt did not start another phase of the New Deal.

One reason FDR did not launch another New Deal was that he did not want any more deficit spending. Roosevelt was also more and more worried about events in Europe, particularly the rise of Hitler.

People still disagree over whether the New Deal was good or bad for the country. Conservative critics say that the New Deal made the government too big and too powerful. They say that it got in

the way of free enterprise: They feel that government should not be so involved in the economy.

Liberal critics say that the New Deal did not go far enough. They think it should have done more to change the economy. They think that Roosevelt should have done more to end the differences in wealth between the rich and the poor.

Supporters of the New Deal say that it was well balanced between saving capitalism and reforming it. They point to many lasting benefits of the New Deal.

The New Deal expanded the power of the federal government. It gave the federal government and particularly the president, a greater role in shaping the economy. It did this by putting millions of dollars into the economy, creating federal jobs, regulating supply and demand, and participating in settling labor disputes. The government also created agencies such as the **Federal Deposit Insurance Corporation (FDIC)** and the **Securities**

---

and Exchange Commission (SEC) to regulate banking and investment activities. To do all this, the government went deeply into debt. In the end, what really ended the depression was the massive spending for World War II.

The New Deal left a lasting impact on workers' rights, banking, and investment. Today the **National Labor Relations Board (NLRB)** still mediates labor disputes. And the FDIC and SEC help regulate the banking and securities industries.

1. How did some liberals and conservatives criticize the New Deal?

_____

_____

SOCIAL AND ENVIRONMENTAL EFFECTS (Pages 518–519)
How did the New Deal make the economy more stable?

New Deal reforms had lasting effects. They helped make the economy more stable. The nation has had economic downturns. But none have been as bad as the Great Depression. And people's savings are insured.

One of the most important and lasting benefits of the New Deal is the Social Security system. It provides old-age insurance and unemployment benefits. It also helps families with dependent children and those who are disabled. For the first time, the federal government took responsibility for the welfare of its citizens.

The Second Agricultural Adjustment Act made loans to farmers. The loans were based on the **parity** value—a price based on 1910–1914 levels—of farmers' surplus crops. Projects that spread electric power to rural areas also helped farmers.

The New Deal also helped the environment. Roosevelt was very interested in protecting the nation's natural resources. New Deal policies promoted soil conservation to prevent a repeat of the Dust Bowl. The **Tennessee Valley Authority (TVA)** helped prevent floods and provided electricity. And New Deal programs also added to the national park system. They set up areas to protect wildlife. However, the TVA did contribute to pollution through strip mining.

2. What are two continuing benefits of the New Deal?

_____

_____

As you read about the impact of New Deal reforms, take notes about the lasting effects of those reforms on American society.

	New Deal Laws and Agencies	Lasting Effects of These Laws and Agencies on American Government and Life
1. Labor		
2. Agriculture and rural life		
3. Banking and finance		
4. Social welfare		
5. Environment		

Guided Reading Workbook

World War Looms

Dictators Threaten World Peace

Terms and Names

Joseph Stalin Communist dictator of the Soviet Union

totalitarian Government that has complete control over its citizens and puts down all opposition

Benito Mussolini Fascist dictator of Italy

fascism Political system based on a strong, centralized government headed by a dictator

Adolf Hitler Nazi dictator of Germany

Nazism Fascist political philosophy of Germany under Nazi dictator Hitler

Francisco Franco Fascist dictator of Spain

Neutrality Acts Laws passed by Congress to ban the sale of arms or loans to nations at war

Before You Read

In the last section, you saw the effects of the New Deal reforms in the United States during the Great Depression. In this section, you will see how economic and political conditions in Europe and Asia in the 1930s gave rise to expansionist totalitarian states.

As You Read

Use a web diagram to take notes on the ambitions of the dictators of the 1930s.

NATIONALISM GRIPS EUROPE AND ASIA (Pages 528–533)
How did dictators take power in Europe and Asia?

Woodrow Wilson had hoped that the Treaty of Versailles would provide a "just and lasting peace," among the world's most powerful nations. However, the Treaty mostly caused anger and resentment. The German government was angry about losing territory it considered Germany's, as well as being blamed for

starting the war. The Soviet Union resented losing its own territories.

The peace settlement failed to make the world "safe for democracy" as Woodrow Wilson had hoped. New democratic governments, hurt by economic and social problems, floundered and turned to dictatorships.

In the Soviet Union, **Joseph Stalin** came to power in 1924. He was a ruthless leader who let nothing stand in his way. Stalin focused on creating a model communist state. He wanted to stamp out private enterprise. He did away with private farms and created collectives, or huge state-owned farms. The state also took over industry. Stalin made the Soviet Union into a leading industrial power.

But he also made it into a police state. Anyone who criticized him or his policies was arrested by the secret police. Many were executed. Millions of others died in famines caused by Stalin's restructuring of Soviet society. It is believed that Stalin was responsible for between 8 and 13 million deaths in the Soviet Union. Stalin created a **totalitarian** government—a government with complete control over its citizens. Individuals had no rights, and the government put down all opposition.

At the same time, **Benito Mussolini** was creating a totalitarian state in Italy. His political movement was called **fascism.** It was based on a strong, centralized government headed by a dictator. Fascism grew out of extreme nationalism. Mussolini, called *Il Duce*, or the leader, was known for his efficiency in running all aspects of Italian life. But he did not want the government to own farms and factories. Fascism was actually anti-communist.

In Germany, another fascist party came to power under the leadership of **Adolf Hitler.** Hitler's political philosophy was called **Nazism.** He hoped to unite all German-speaking people into a new German empire, or Reich. He believed that Germans—especially blond, blue-eyed "Aryans"—were the master race. According to Hitler, Aryans were meant to have power over all "inferior races," such as Jews and nonwhites. Hitler believed Germany needed to expand—to gain territory—so that the German people could thrive.

Nazism combined extreme nationalism, racism, and expansionism. It appealed to unemployed, desperate, and resentful Germans during the Great Depression. In the 1932 elections, the Nazi Party gained power. Hitler became chancellor in January 1933. He did away with the Weimar Republic and set up the Third Reich, or third German empire.

Meanwhile, in Asia, military leaders had taken over Japan. They believed that Japan needed more land and resources. Japan attacked Manchuria, a province of China, in 1931. The League of Nations protested, but Japan left the League and kept Manchuria.

The League's failure to stop Japan made Hitler and Mussolini bolder. Hitler sent troops into the Rhineland and rebuilt the German army. These acts broke the Versailles Treaty. Mussolini captured the African nation of Ethiopia. Haile Selassie, the leader of Ethiopia, asked the League for help. When the League did nothing, he said, "It is us today. It will be you tomorrow."

In Spain, the fascist general **Francisco Franco** led a rebellion to overthrow the elected government. Many American volunteers went to Spain to fight the fascists. These volunteers felt that Spain was the place to stop fascism and defend democracy. The governments of the Western democracies sent only food and clothing to democratic forces in Spain. Hitler and Mussolini supported Franco with troops and weapons. When Franco won in 1939, Europe had another totalitarian government.

1. What five major countries were ruled by dictatorships in the 1930s?

_____

_____

THE UNITED STATES RESPONDS CAUTIOUSLY (Pages 534–535)

How did the United States respond to the rise of dictators?

Most Americans wanted the United States to stay out of foreign conflicts. Many people thought that the United States had made a mistake in getting involved in World War I. Anti-war rallies were held. Isolationism became more popular.

Congress passed the **Neutrality Acts.** These laws banned loans or arms sale to nations at war. Because of the Spanish Civil War, the Neutrality Acts included those involved in civil wars.

In 1937, Roosevelt found a way around the Neutrality Acts. Since Japan had not declared war on China, Roosevelt felt free to send military aid to China. He gave a speech in which he talked of "quarantining the aggressors," but growing criticism from isolationists forced FDR to back down.

2. How did the United States react to the rise of expansionist dictatorships in Europe and Asia?

_____

_____

As you read this section, take notes about the rise of dictators in Europe and Asia.

	1. Joseph Stalin	2. Benito Mussolini	3. Adolf Hitler
Nation			
Political movement and beliefs			
Aggressive actions taken in the 1920s and 1930s			

	4. Japanese Militarists	5. Francisco Franco
Nation		
Political movement and beliefs		
Aggressive actions taken in the 1920s and 1930s		

Section 2

War in Europe

Terms and Names

Neville Chamberlain Prime minister of Great Britain before World War II

Winston Churchill Prime minister of Great Britain during World War II

appeasement Trying to pacify an aggressor in order to keep the peace

nonaggression pact Agreement between Germany and Russia not to fight each other

blitzkrieg Lightning war strategy used by Germany against Poland

Charles de Gaulle Head of the French government in exile in England

---

Before You Read

In the last section, you saw how dictatorships rose in Europe and Asia in the 1930s. In this section, you will see how the expansionist policies of Hitler led to World War II in Europe.

As You Read

Use a time line to take notes on major events in German expansion from 1937 to 1940.

AUSTRIA AND CZECHOSLOVAKIA FALL (Pages 536–538)
How did Britain and France react to Hitler's aggression?

Hitler decided that the new living space the German people needed would come from nearby nations. He would annex, or add, Austria and Czechoslovakia. And he was willing to use force to do it.

A majority of Austria's six million people were German-speaking and favored unification with Germany. In March 1938, German troops marched into Austria. They met no opposition. Germany announced an Anschluss, or "union" with Austria.

Then Hitler claimed that the Czechs were mistreating German-speaking people in an area called the Sudetenland. He

massed troops on the border. France and Britain promised to defend Czechoslovakia. Their leaders met with Hitler in Munich, Germany. Hitler promised that the Sudetenland would be his "last territorial demand." France, Britain, and Germany signed the Munich Pact in September 1938. It gave the Sudetenland to Germany.

Neville Chamberlain was the British prime minister who signed the Munich Pact. He called it "peace with honor." Another British leader, **Winston Churchill,** disagreed. He called the Pact dishonorable **appeasement.** That means giving up your principles in order to pacify an aggressor. Churchill predicted that appeasement would eventually lead to war.

Guided Reading Workbook

1. How did Hitler begin to expand Germany's territory?

_____

_____

THE GERMAN OFFENSIVE BEGINS
(**Pages** 538–540)
What **did Britain and France do about Nazi and Soviet aggression?**

Hitler did not keep the promise he made at Munich. In March of 1939, he conquered the rest of Czechoslovakia.

Then Hitler began to claim that Germans living in Poland were being persecuted. Many people thought Hitler would never attack Poland. They thought he would be afraid that the Soviet Union, on Poland's eastern border, would then fight Germany. But Germany and the Soviet Union signed a **nonaggression pact,** an agreement not to fight each other. In a secret part of this treaty, Hitler and Stalin also agreed to divide Poland between them.

On September 1, 1939, Hitler launched World War II by attacking Poland. The Germans used a new strategy called a *blitzkrieg,* or lightning war. They used tanks and planes to take the enemy by surprise and crush them quickly. Poland fell to the Germans in a month. Britain and France declared war on Germany. Meanwhile, the Soviets attacked Poland from the east, and grabbed some of its territory.

For the next few months, not much happened. This was called the "phony war." French and British troops gathered on the French border. German troops also waited.

Meanwhile, Stalin seized regions that the Soviet Union had lost in World War I. He took the Baltic states in September and October of 1939. Finland resisted, and was conquered only after fierce fighting in March 1940.

In April, Hitler launched surprise invasions of Denmark and Norway. Then in May, he quickly took the Netherlands, Belgium, and Luxembourg. This war was very real indeed.

2. How did Hitler conquer much of Europe so quickly?

_____

_____

FRANCE AND BRITAIN FIGHT ON
(**Pages** 540–541)
How **did Hitler's attacks on France and on Britain turn out?**

Germany attacked France in May 1940—but not where the Allies expected. It cut off Allied forces in the north. The British sent all kinds of boats—from fishing vessels to yachts—to bring nearly 340,000 British, French, and other Allied troops safely across the English Channel.

Meanwhile, Italy joined the war on the side of Germany. The Italians attacked France from the south. France surrendered quickly, in June 1940. The Germans occupied the northern part of France while a Nazi-controlled puppet government, called the Vichy government, ruled the southern part of France. The French general **Charles de Gaulle** set up a French government in exile in England. He promised to free France from the Nazis.

Hitler now made plans to invade Britain. He began with air raids over England. The Germans bombed London night after night in August 1940. The British air force (RAF) defended Britain against these attacks. They used a new technology called radar, and shot down hundreds of German planes. This air war was called the Battle of Britain. The new prime minister, Winston Churchill, rallied the spirits of the British people and declared that Britain would never surrender. Hitler gave up the idea of invading Britain.

3. What happened to Hitler's plans for conquering France and Britain?

_____

_____

Name _____ Class _____ Date _____

Section 2, *continued*

As you read this section, take notes to answer questions about how Germany started World War II. Note the development of events in the time line.

1938 **March** — Germany invades Austria. **September** — Munich Pact is signed by Germany, France, and Britain.	1. Why did Neville Chamberlain sign the Munich Pact? / 2. Why did Winston Churchill oppose the pact?
1939 **March** — Germany invades Czechoslovakia. **August** — Germany and USSR sign nonaggression pact and secret agreement. **September** — Germany invades Poland. **November** — USSR invades Finland.	3. What did Germany and the USSR agree to in their accords? 4. What happened to Poland as a result of the invasion, and how did Britain and France respond to it?
1940 **Spring** — Germany invades Norway, Denmark, the Netherlands, Belgium, and Luxembourg. **June** — France surrenders to Germany. **Summer** — USSR overruns Baltic states. Battle of Britain begins.	5. What were the surrender terms offered to France? 6. What type of battle was the Battle of Britain, and why was England's victory so important?

Guided Reading Workbook

The Holocaust

Terms and Names

Holocaust Systematic murder of 11 million Jews and other people in Europe by the Nazis

Kristallnacht Name given the night of November 9, 1938, when Nazis in Germany attacked Jews, their businesses, and their synagogues

genocide Deliberate and systematic killing of an entire people

ghetto A segregated neighborhood

concentration camp Prison camps operated by the Nazis where Jews and others were starved while doing slave labor, or murdered

Before You Read

In the last section, you saw how Hitler began World War II. In this section, you will see how Hitler put his plan of Aryan domination into place by killing Jews and other groups he considered inferior.

As You Read

Use a chart to take notes on the events that led to the Holocaust.

THE PERSECUTION BEGINS
(Pages 542–544)
How **did the persecution of the Jews begin in Germany?**

Part of Hitler's plan for Germany was to make the country racially pure. In 1933, just three months after taking power, Hitler ordered all non-Aryans out of government jobs. Then Hitler began an organized persecution of non-Aryans, particularly of Jews. This resulted in the **Holocaust**—the systematic murder of over 11 million people across Europe. Over half of the murdered people were Jews.

Anti-Semitism, or hatred of Jews, had a long history in Germany and in other parts of Europe. For a long time, Germans had used Jews as a scapegoat, someone to blame for their own failures and frustrations. Therefore, when Hitler

blamed Jews for Germany's defeat in World War I, many Germans agreed. When Hitler blamed the Jews for Germany's economic problems, many Germans supported him.

Persecution of Jews increased under Hitler. In 1935, new laws took away Jews' civil rights and their property. Jews were forced to wear yellow stars of David on their clothing.

On November 9, 1938, organized, violent persecution began with *Kristallnacht.* (*Kristallnacht* is a German word meaning "crystal night," or night of broken glass.) Gangs of Nazi storm troopers attacked Jewish homes, businesses, and synagogues across Germany. The streets were littered with broken glass. Then the Nazis blamed Jews for the destruction. Many Jews were arrested; others were fined.

Guided Reading Workbook

Many Jews started to flee Germany. Nazis were in favor of this, but other nations did not want to accept the Jewish refugees. Some refugees, including Albert Einstein and Thomas Mann, were allowed into the United States. But the United States would not change its immigration quotas. This was partly American anti-Semitism. It was also because many Americans feared competition for the few jobs during the Depression.

Once war broke out in Europe, Americans said they feared that refugees would be "enemy agents." The Coast Guard even turned away a ship carrying refugees who had emigration papers for the United States. Three-quarters of those passengers were killed by the Nazis after the ship was forced to return to Europe.

1. How did the world react to Germany's persecution of the Jews?

_____

_____

HITLER'S "FINAL SOLUTION"
(Pages 544–546)
How did the Nazis try to kill off the Jews and others?

In 1939, there were only about a quarter of a million Jews left in Germany. But other countries that Hitler occupied had millions more Jews. Hitler's ultimate goal was to get rid of all of Europe's Jews. He began implementing the "final solution." This plan amounted to genocide, the deliberate and systematic killing of an entire population.

The "final solution" was based on the Nazi belief that "Aryans" were a superior people and that their strength and racial purity must be preserved. To accomplish this, the Nazis arrested people they identified as "enemies of the state,"

condemning these people to slavery and death. In addition to Jews, the Nazis rounded up political opponents— Communists, Socialists, liberals— and other groups including Gypsies, Freemasons, Jehovah's Witnesses, homosexuals, the disabled, and the terminally ill.

Some Jews were forced into ghettos— segregated Jewish areas where they were made to work in factories or left to starve. Despite brutal conditions, Jews hung on, resisting the Germans and setting up schools and underground newspapers.

2. Who were the targets of the "final solution"?

_____

_____

THE FINAL STAGE (Pages 547–549)
How did the Nazis kill so many people?

Most Jews were sent to concentration camps, where they suffered hunger, illness, overwork, torture, and death. The early concentration camps did not kill Jews fast enough for the Nazis. In 1941, six death camps were built in Poland. These camps had gas chambers that could kill 12,000 people a day. Prisoners were separated upon arrival at death camps by SS doctors. Those who were too old or too weak to work were led to the gas chambers and killed. At first bodies were buried or burned in huge pits. Then the Nazis built huge ovens called crematoriums that destroyed the bodies and all evidence of the mass murder that had taken place. Other prisoners were shot or hanged or subjected to horrible medical experiments by camp doctors.

Six million Jews died in death camps and Nazi massacres. Some Jews, however, were saved. Ordinary people sometimes risked their own lives to hide Jews or to help them escape.

Some Jews even survived the concentration camps. Elie Wiesel, who won the Nobel Peace Prize in 1986, is a survivor of Auschwitz. He has written memorably about his concentration camp experiences and the need to prevent such genocide from ever happening again.

3. Why were certain people separated from the others and led to the gas chambers?

_____

_____

As you read, take notes to answer questions related to the time line.

1925	In *Mein Kampf*, Hitler presents his racist views on "Aryans" and Jews.	
1933	Hitler comes to power. Soon after, he orders non-Aryans to be removed from government jobs and begins to build concentration camps.	
	Thousands of Jews begin leaving Germany. →	1. Why didn't France and Britain accept as many German Jews as they might have?
1935	Nuremberg laws are passed. →	2. What did the Nuremberg laws do?
1938	*Kristallnacht* occurs. →	3. What happened during *Kristallnacht?*
1939	As war breaks out in Europe, U.S. Coast Guard prevents refugees on the *St. Louis* from landing in Miami. →	4. Why didn't the United States accept as many German Jews as it might have?
1941	Nazis build six death camps in Poland. →	5. What groups did the Nazis single out for extermination?
1945 to 1949	After war in Europe ends in 1945, many Nazi leaders are brought to justice for their crimes against humanity. →	6. How did the Nazis go about exterminating the approximately 11 million people who died in the Holocaust?

World War Looms

Section 4

America Moves Toward War

Terms and Names

Axis powers Germany, Italy, and Japan

Lend-Lease Act Law that allowed lending or leasing arms to any nation "whose defense was vital to the United States"

Atlantic Charter British and American statement of goals for fighting World War II

Allies Group of nations, including the United States, Britain, and the Soviet Union, who opposed the Axis powers

Hideki Tojo Prime minister of Japan during World War II

Before You Read

In the last section, you saw how Hitler's plan to make Germany racially pure killed millions of people. In this section, you will see how the United States moved closer to entering the war against the Nazis.

As You Read

Use a time line to take notes on the events that led to the entry of the United States into World War II.

THE UNITED STATES MUSTERS ITS FORCES (Pages 550–551)
How did the United States try to stay out of war but be prepared?

According to the Neutrality Acts, the United States could not enter the war in Europe. However, President Roosevelt asked for a change in the Acts. He suggested a cash-and-carry provision. Such a provision would allow Britain and France to buy and transport American arms. Congress passed this new Neutrality Act in November 1939.

In 1940, Germany, Italy, and Japan signed a mutual defense treaty. They became the **Axis powers.** The treaty meant that if the United States went to war against any one of them, all three would

fight. That would put America at war on two fronts: in Europe and in Asia. Nevertheless, Roosevelt gave the British "all aid short of war" to help them fight Hitler.

Roosevelt assured the nation that the United States would stay out of war. But he prepared for war. Congress increased spending for national defense. It passed the nation's first peacetime draft in September 1940.

FDR broke the tradition of a two-term presidency and ran for re-election in 1940. His opponent, Wendell Willkie, shared Roosevelt's beliefs that the United States should help Britain, but that it should not get involved in war. Voters chose the candidate they knew. FDR won a third term.

Guided Reading Workbook

1. How did the United States slowly move toward war?

_____

_____

"THE GREAT ARSENAL OF DEMOCRACY" (Pages 552–553)
Why did the United States change its policy of neutrality?

After the election, Roosevelt spoke to the American people. He said that the United States could not stand by and let Hitler conquer the world. America would become "the great arsenal of democracy." At that time, Britain could no longer pay for arms and supplies. Roosevelt suggested lending or leasing arms to any nation "whose defense was vital to the United States." Isolationists bitterly opposed his policy. But Congress passed the **Lend-Lease Act** in March 1941.

Meanwhile, Germany invaded its former ally, the Soviet Union. The United States gave lend-lease support to the Soviets as well as to Britain.

Nazi submarines called U-boats attacked and sank ships carrying arms across the Atlantic to Germany's enemies. In June 1941, Roosevelt ordered the U.S. Navy to protect lend-lease ships. He also gave American warships permission to attack German U-boats in self-defense.

2. Name two ways in which the United States became the "arsenal of democracy."

_____

_____

FDR PLANS FOR WAR (Page 554)
How did the United States move toward war?

In August 1941, Roosevelt met secretly with British Prime Minister Winston Churchill. Roosevelt did not actually commit the United States to war. But he and Churchill did sign the **Atlantic Charter.** That was a statement of the goals for fighting World War II. These goals included protecting peoples' rights to choose their own form of government and building a secure peace.

Later, 26 nations signed a similar agreement. These nations, called the **Allies,** were united in fighting Germany, Italy, and Japan.

On September 4, 1941, a German U-boat fired on an American merchant ship. President Roosevelt ordered the U.S. Navy to fire on German ships on sight. U-boats responded by sinking several American ships, and American seamen were killed. The Senate finally allowed the arming of merchant ships. Full scale war seemed inevitable.

3. What events moved the United States closer to war?

_____

_____

JAPAN ATTACKS THE UNITED STATES (Pages 554–557)
What brought the United States into conflict with Japan?

In Japan, expansionists had long dreamed of creating a huge empire. Japan was now acting on this dream. It began seizing Asian territory held as colonies by European nations. The United States also owned islands in the Pacific.

When Japan invaded Indochina, the United States cut off trade with Japan. Japan needed American oil to run its war machine. The new prime minister of Japan was a militant general named **Hideki Tojo.** He started peace talks with the United States, but he also prepared for war.

The United States broke Japan's secret communications code. The Americans knew Japan was preparing for a military strike. But they did not know when or where the strike would be.

On December 7, 1941—during the peace talks—Japan attacked the main U.S. naval base at Pearl Harbor in Hawaii. The Japanese crippled the U.S. Pacific fleet in one blow. Planes and ships were destroyed. Over 2,400 people were killed.

Roosevelt was grim. He did not want to fight a war on two fronts. He had expected to enter the war in Europe, not to fight in Asia, too. On December 8, 1941, Roosevelt addressed Congress asking for a declaration of war against Japan. He said: "Yesterday, December 7, 1941, a date which will live in infamy . . . [the Japanese launched] an unprovoked and dastardly attack." Congress quickly agreed to declare war. Germany and Italy then declared war on the United States.

4. What event caused the American declaration of war against Japan?

_____

_____

_____

As you read, take notes about how the United States entered World War II.

1939	**Congress passes Neutrality Act.** →	1. What did the Neutrality Act allow?
1940	**Axis powers form alliance.** →	2. Who were the Axis powers? What did their alliance mean for the United States?
1941	**Congress passes Lend-Lease Act.** →	3. What did the Lend-Lease Act do?
	Germany invades USSR.	
	Japan takes over French military bases in Indochina. →	4. What did the United States do to protest Japan's action?
	Congress extends the draft.	
	Churchill and Roosevelt draft the Atlantic Charter. →	5. What pledges were contained in the Atlantic Charter?
	"A Declaration by the United Nations" is signed by the Allies. →	6. Who were the Allies?
	Hideki Tojo becomes Japan's prime minister.	
	U.S. Senate allows arming of merchant ships.	7. What did the attack do to the U.S. Pacific fleet?
	Japan launches a surprise attack on Pearl Harbor. →	
	As U.S. declares war on Japan, Germany and Italy declare war on U.S. →	8. Why did Germany and Italy declare war on the United States?

Section 1

Mobilizing for Defense

Terms and Names

George Marshall Army chief of staff during World War II

Women's Auxiliary Army Corps (WAAC) Women volunteers who served in non-combat positions

A. Philip Randolph Important African-American labor leader

Manhattan Project Secret research project that resulted in the Atomic Bomb

Office of Price Administration (OPA) Agency of the federal government that fought inflation

War Production Board (WPB) Government agency that decided which companies would make war materials and how to distribute raw materials

rationing Restricting the amount of food and other goods people may buy during wartime to assure adequate supplies for the military

Before You Read

In the last section, you learned the reasons why the United States entered World War II. In this section, you will learn how Americans joined in the war effort.

As You Read

Use a web diagram to take notes on how the United States prepared for war.

AMERICANS JOIN THE WAR EFFORT (Pages 562–564)
How did Americans react to Pearl Harbor?

The Japanese had expected Americans to react with fear and despair to the attack on Pearl Harbor. Instead, Americans reacted with rage. "Remember Pearl Harbor" became a rallying cry. Five million men volunteered for military service.

But fighting a war on two fronts—in Europe and in the Pacific—required huge numbers of soldiers. Another ten million men were drafted. New soldiers received eight weeks of basic training. Then they were officially "GIs," a nickname coming from the term "Government Issue."

To free more men for combat, Army Chief of Staff General **George Marshall** suggested using women for noncombat military tasks. Congress created the **Women's Auxiliary Army Corps (WAAC)** in 1942. About 25,000 women served in the military. They did not receive the same pay or benefits as men.

Men and women from minority groups also served in World War II. They included Mexican Americans, Asian Americans, and Native Americans. Some African Americans had mixed feelings about defending a country where they were often segregated and denied the basic rights of citizenship. But they also knew they would be worse off under any of the

Axis powers. More than a million African Americans served, but in racially segregated units. These units were not even allowed into combat until the last year of the war.

1. How did women and minorities join in the war effort?

_____

_____

A PRODUCTION MIRACLE
(**Pages** 564-567)
What changes took place in American life?

The nation's factories quickly switched to war production. Automobile factories made planes and tanks. Pencil-makers turned out bomb parts. Shipyards and defense plants expanded. They produced warships with amazing speed.

About 18 million workers kept these war industries going. Some 6 million new factory workers were women. At first, industry did not want to hire women. Men feared women would not be able to handle the heavy work. Once women proved they could do the work, factories hired them. But they paid women only 60 percent as much as men.

Before the war, most defense contractors had refused to hire African Americans. **A. Philip Randolph**, the president of the Brotherhood of Sleeping Car Porters, was an important African-American labor leader. He threatened to have African Americans march on Washington to demand an end to this discrimination. Roosevelt feared such a march. He issued an executive order banning discrimination in defense industries.

Even Hollywood contributed to the war effort with patriotic films. They also made escapist romances and comedies. Public

hunger for news of the war made magazines and radio more popular.

The government hired scientists to develop new weapons and medicines. They made improvements in radar and sonar, and in "miracle drugs" like penicillin. The government also set up the **Manhattan Project,** which developed the atomic bomb.

2. How did the war change life at home?

_____

_____

THE FEDERAL GOVERNMENT TAKES CONTROL (**Pages** 567-568)
How did the federal government get involved in the economy?

The federal government was worried about economic issues. Congress wanted to prevent the high inflation that had occurred during World War I. Congress set up the **Office of Price Administration (OPA)**. It successfully fought inflation by "freezing," or not increasing, prices on most goods. Congress also raised taxes. The **War Production Board (WPB)** decided which companies would make war materials and how to distribute raw materials.

The OPA also set up a system of **rationing**. Families were issued coupons to be used for buying scarce items, such as meat and gasoline. Most Americans cooperated with the rationing system. They also bought war bonds and collected goods, such as tin cans and paper, that could be recycled, or reused, for the war effort.

3. How did the federal government regulate American life during the war?

_____

_____

As you read about how the United States mobilized for war, note how each
of the following contributed to that effort.

1. Selective Service System	6. Office of Scientific Research and Development (OSRD)
2. Women	7. Entertainment industry
3. Minorities	8. Office of Price Administration (OPA)
4. Manufacturers	9. War Production Board (WPB)
5. A. Philip Randolph	10. Rationing

The War for Europe and North Africa

Terms and Names

Dwight D. Eisenhower American general

D-Day Allied invasion to liberate Europe

Omar Bradley American general

George Patton American general

Battle of the Bulge German counteroffensive in December 1944

V-E Day Victory in Europe Day, May 8, 1945

Harry S. Truman 33rd president of the United States

Before You Read

In the last section, you saw how the American involvement in World War II affected life on the home front. In this section, you will see how the United States, Britain, and the Soviet Union combined to defeat Germany and its partners in Europe.

As You Read

Use a timeline to take notes on major events influencing the fighting in North Africa and Europe.

THE UNITED STATES AND BRITAIN JOIN FORCES
(Pages 569–570)
What **were the goals of the American and British alliance?**

In late December 1941, a few weeks after Pearl Harbor, President Roosevelt met with British Prime Minister Winston Churchill. They planned their war strategy. They agreed that the first thing to do was to defeat Hitler's Germany. Roosevelt and Churchill began a lasting friendship and a strong alliance between America and Britain.

After war was declared, German U-boats increased attacks on American ships in the Atlantic. Many American ships were sunk. The Allies organized convoys, or groups, for shared protection. Warships and airplanes escorted the convoys. They used sonar and radar to find and destroy many German submarines.

The United States also started building ships at a rapid pace. Soon there were more Allied cargo ships, or Liberty ships, being made than being sunk. By mid-1943, the tide of the Battle of the Atlantic had turned in favor of the Allies.

1. What was the Battle of the Atlantic, and how did the Allies win it?

_____

_____

THE EASTERN FRONT AND THE MEDITERRANEAN (Pages 571–573)
What happened in the Soviet Union, North Africa, and Italy?

By the summer of 1943, the Allies were winning on land as well as on the sea.

The German invasion of the Soviet Union had begun in 1941. When it stalled early in 1942, Hitler changed his tactics. He moved to capture Soviet oil fields and to take the industrial city of Stalingrad. The Germans bombed Stalingrad until almost the whole city was on fire.

But Stalin refused to give up. In three months of horrible hand-to-hand combat, the Germans took most of Stalingrad. Then the Soviets counterattacked. They trapped a large German force just as winter came. The Germans froze and starved. In February 1943, the few German soldiers who were still alive surrendered. The Battle of Stalingrad was a turning point. From then on, Soviet forces moved steadily west towards Germany.

Meanwhile, in November 1942, the Allies invaded North Africa. North Africa at the time was controlled by the Axis. American forces led by General **Dwight D. ("Ike") Eisenhower** defeated German troops under General Erwin Rommel. The Germans surrendered in May 1943.

Next, in July 1943, the Allies invaded Italy. They captured Sicily. The war-weary Italian king stripped Prime Minister Mussolini of power and had him arrested. But then Hitler seized Italy. It took 18 long and bloody months of fighting for the Allies to drive the Germans out of Italy. In the Italian campaign, segregated units of African Americans, Mexican Americans, and Japanese Americans all won honors for bravery.

2. How were the Allies victorious in the Soviet Union, North Africa, and Italy?

_____

_____

THE ALLIES LIBERATE EUROPE (Pages 574–577)
Why did the Allies invade Normandy?

The Americans and British had been building a huge invasion force for two years. It was designed to liberate Europe. June 6, 1944, was **D-Day**—the day the Allies crossed the English Channel and landed in Normandy, France. This invasion was the largest land-sea-air operation in history.

British, American, and Canadian forces landed on the beaches of Normandy. They met fierce German resistance, and many were killed. But they took the beaches. Over 1 million Allied troops landed in France, and began to advance. General **Omar Bradley** opened a huge hole in the German lines. It allowed American General **George Patton** and his Third Army to liberate Paris in August. By September, the Allies had liberated other European nations and had entered Germany itself.

In the United States, Roosevelt won reelection to a fourth term as president.

To the Allies' surprise, Hitler began a counterattack in December. At first, the Germans cut deeply into Allied lines. After a month of fierce fighting, the Allies pushed the Germans back. The Germans had lost so many men and weapons in this **Battle of the Bulge** that they could only retreat.

Guided Reading Workbook

Meanwhile, the Soviets pushed through Poland toward Germany. The Soviets were the first to liberate death camps and to describe the unbelievable horrors they saw there. By April 25, the Soviets were in Berlin. Hitler responded to certain defeat by shooting himself.

On May 8, 1945, General Eisenhower accepted the unconditional surrender of Nazi Germany. That became known as

V-E Day—Victory in Europe Day. Roosevelt died on April 12, 1945 before V-E Day. Vice President **Harry S. Truman** became president.

3. How did the Allies liberate Europe and defeat Germany?

_____

_____

As you read about the Allied war effort, take notes to explain what made
each event a critical moment or turning point in the war.

February 1943	End of Battle of Stalingrad	→	1.
May 1943	End of Operation Torch	→	2.
Mid-1943	Victory in Battle of the Atlantic	→	3.
June 1944	D-Day	→	4.
July 1944	Liberation of Majdanek	→	5.
August 1944	Liberation of France	→	6.
October 1944	Capture of Aachen	→	7.
January 1945	End of Battle of the Bulge	→	8.
Spring 1945	End of Italian campaign	→	9.
May 1945	V-E Day	→	10.

The United States in World War II

Section 3

The War in the Pacific

Terms and Names

Douglas MacArthur American commander in the Philippines

Chester Nimitz Commander of American naval forces in the Pacific

Battle of Midway American victory that was the turning point in the Pacific War

kamikaze Japanese suicide flight

J. Robert Oppenheimer Scientist who led the Manhattan Project

Hiroshima City that was the site of the first atomic-bomb drop in Japan

Nagasaki Japanese city that was the site of the second atomic-bomb drop

Nuremberg Trials Tribunal that tried Nazi leaders for war crimes

Before You Read

In the last section, you saw how the Allies won victory in Europe. In this section, you will see how the Allies defeated Japan in the Pacific.

As You Read

Use a chart to take notes on military actions in the Pacific and their significance.

THE ALLIES STEM THE JAPANESE TIDE (Pages 578–580)

What was so important about the Battle of Midway?

In the first six months after Pearl Harbor, the Japanese military had great success. They conquered huge areas of the Asian mainland and many islands in the Pacific. In 1942, Japanese forces threatened the American army in the Philippines. General **Douglas MacArthur** was the commander of the American army. In March 1942, MacArthur left the Philippines but told people left behind, "I shall return."

The United States started to fight back against the Japanese. In the spring of 1942, Lt. Colonel James Doolittle led a bombing raid on Tokyo. The U.S. Navy defeated the Japanese at the Battle of Coral Sea. This ended the Japanese threat to invade Australia.

Then, in June 1942, the Japanese steamed toward Midway, an island northwest of Hawaii. American forces broke the Japanese code and knew of their plans. Admiral **Chester Nimitz** commanded American forces that crushed the Japanese. The **Battle of Midway** was a turning point in the Pacific War. After Midway, the Allies began "island hopping," moving closer to Japan.

1. Why was the Battle of Midway important?

_____

_____

THE ALLIES GO ON THE OFFENSIVE (Pages 581–583)
What were the important battles in the Pacific?

American forces, led by General MacArthur, now went island-hopping towards Japan. They avoided islands that were well defended by the Japanese. Airfields were built on captured islands. Planes could then bomb Japanese supply lines.

American marines stormed the island of Guadalcanal in August 1942. This marked Japan's first defeat on land. In October 1944, Americans landed on the island of Leyte in the Philippines. The Japanese launched **kamikaze** raids. In these suicide attacks, Japanese pilots crashed their planes into Allied ships supporting the invasion. Still, Japan lost so many ships in the Battle of Leyte Gulf that the Japanese Navy was essentially knocked out of the war.

The Americans took the island of Iwo Jima in March 1945. This extremely bloody battle gave the United States a base to launch heavy bombers that could reach Japan itself.

A fierce battle raged over the island of Okinawa. The island was Japan's last defensive outpost. The Americans finally won on June 22, 1945, but it cost 7,600 American lives. Japan lost 110,000 men. The Allies feared the human cost of invading Japan.

2. Why was the Battle of Leyte Gulf so important?

_____

_____

THE ATOMIC BOMB ENDS THE WAR (Pages 583–585)
Why did the United States use the atomic bomb?

As American forces neared Japan in March 1945, President Roosevelt died.

Vice-President Harry S. Truman became president.

President Truman was told about the Manhattan Project. This was the secret development of the atomic bomb led by **J. Robert Oppenheimer**. On July 16, 1945, the first atomic bomb was tested. It was even more powerful than predicted. Many scientists felt it would be immoral to drop the bomb on Japan. Others said it would shorten the war and save lives. It would also give the United States an advantage over the Soviets after the war. Truman decided to use the bomb.

On August 6, 1945, an atomic bomb was dropped on **Hiroshima**, Japan. Almost every building collapsed into dust. But Japan did not surrender. A second bomb was dropped on **Nagasaki,** killing 200,000. Emperor Hirohito was horrified. Japan surrendered September 2, 1945. The war was over.

3. Why did Truman decide to use the atomic bomb?

_____

_____

REBUILDING BEGINS (Pages 585–587)
How did the Allies try to shape the postwar world?

In February 1945, Roosevelt, Churchill, and Stalin met at the Yalta Conference. Stalin and Churchill disagreed on how to treat Germany. Roosevelt made concessions to Stalin. He wanted Stalin to help in the fight to defeat Japan. And he wanted Stalin to support the United Nations. At Yalta, the allies agreed to divide Germany into four zones. Stalin agreed to allow free elections in Poland and other Eastern European countries now occupied by the Soviet Army.

The **Nuremberg Trials**, trials held by an international tribunal, were held to try Nazi leaders. For the first time, a nation's leaders were held legally responsible for their wartime acts. They were tried for starting the war; for acts against the customs of war, such as killing prisoners; and for the murder and enslavement of civilians.

American forces, headed by General MacArthur, occupied Japan for six years. First, Japanese officials were put on trial for war crimes. Then, the Americans helped Japan set up a free-market economic system and create a new democratic constitution.

4. How did the Yalta Conference shape the postwar world?

_____

_____

Name _____ Class _____ Date _____

Section 3, *continued*

As you read about the Allied war effort, take notes to explain what made each event a critical moment or turning point in the war.

The War in the Pacific		
Date and Place	Leader Involved	What happened?
1. April 1942, Bataan		
2. June 1942, Midway		
3. August 1942, Guadalcanal		
4. October 1944, Leyte Gulf		
5. March 1945, Iwo Jima		
6. June 1945, Okinawa		
7. September 1945, Tokyo Bay		

The Science of War		
Date and Place	Leaders Involved	What happened?
8. July 1945, Los Alamos		
9. August 1945, Hiroshima, Nagasaki		

Planning and Rebuilding or Peace		
Date and Place	Leaders Involved	What happened?
10. February 1945, Yalta		
11. April 1945, San Francisco		
12. 1945–1949, Nuremberg		

Guided Reading Workbook

The United States in World War II

The Home Front

Terms and Names

GI Bill of Rights Law passed by Congress to help servicemen readjust to civilian life

James Farmer Civil rights leader who founded the Congress of Racial Equality

Congress of Racial Equality (CORE) Interracial organization formed to fight discrimination

internment Confinement under guard, especially during wartime

Japanese American Citizens League (JACL) Civil rights group formed by Japanese Americans

Before You Read

In the last section, you saw how the Allies prepared for the postwar world. In this section, you will see how the war changed the United States.

As You Read

Use a chart to take notes on the effects of the war on the home front.

OPPORTUNITY AND ADJUSTMENT
(Pages 590–592)
How did the war create opportunities at home?

World War II was a time of opportunity for many Americans. The economy boomed. There were plenty of jobs. Wages rose. Farmers also did well.

Women had many job opportunities during the war. The share of women in the work force rose to 35 percent. (They lost some of these jobs when the men returned from military service.) Women also did a wide range of jobs and entered professions that had not been open to them before the war.

Many Americans relocated—picked up and moved. They moved to where there were defense jobs. States with military bases or defense plants saw huge gains in population. Some city populations grew by one third. The result was a housing shortage. Even though workers had the

money to pay, there was no housing to rent. There were also food shortages in some areas.

People had to adjust to new family situations. Many fathers were in the armed forces, so women had to work and raise children on their own.

The war also caused a boom in marriages. Many couples married before the men went overseas. But when the men returned after years of military service, many of these marriages failed. The divorce rate increased.

In 1944, Congress passed the **GI Bill of Rights,** which was designed to help servicemen readjust to civilian life. This bill paid for veterans to attend college or technical school. Over half the returning soldiers took advantage of this opportunity. It also gave federal loan guarantees to veterans buying homes or farms or starting businesses. The GI Bill gave many people opportunities they otherwise would never have had.

1. What opportunities did the war create at home?

_____

_____

DISCRIMINATION AND REACTION
(**Pages** 592–593)
How **did the war affect African Americans and Mexican Americans?**

On the home front, many African Americans left the South and moved to the West Coast. There they found skilled jobs that paid well. But they also found prejudice. In 1942, civil rights leader **James Farmer** formed a new interracial organization to fight discrimination. It was called the **Congress of Racial Equality (CORE)**.

African Americans also moved into the crowded cities of the North. Tension among the races grew. In 1943 it led to race riots. The worst one was in Detroit, where over 30 people were killed. President Roosevelt had to send federal troops to restore order. In response, many communities formed committees to improve race relations.

Mexican Americans experienced prejudice during the war years as well. In 1942, there were anti-Mexican riots in Los Angeles. In the "zoot-suit" riots, Mexican Americans were beaten by white service men and civilians.

2. How did World War II affect African Americans and Mexican Americans?

_____

_____

INTERNMENT OF JAPANESE AMERICANS (**Pages** 594–595)
What **happened to Japanese Americans during the war?**

Japanese Americans endured terrible treatment during the war. After Pearl Harbor, panic-striken Americans believed Japanese Americans living in the U.S. were disloyal to the United States. In Hawaii, the commanding general ordered the **internment**, or confinement of about 1 percent of Japanese-American residents.

On February 19, 1942, President Roosevelt ordered the internment of all Japanese Americans living in California, and parts of other western states. More than 100,000 people were rounded up and shipped to internment camps.

No charges were ever filed against Japanese Americans. No evidence of subversion was ever found. In 1944, in the case of *Korematsu* v. *United States*, the Supreme Court said the government policy was justified by "military necessity." After the war, the **Japanese American Citizens League (JACL)** pushed the government to compensate, or pay back those sent to the camps.

Over the years, Congress passed bills to repay those who had been interned for the loss of their property. Finally, in 1990, cash payments were sent to all former internees. In a letter that year, President Bush said the nation "recognized the injustice done to Japanese Americans during World War II."

3. What reason was given for the internment of Japanese Americans?

_____

_____

As you read this section, write notes to answer questions about the impact
of the war on various segments of American society.

How did the war and its immediate aftermath affect the following?	
1. Labor	2. Agriculture
3. Population centers	4. Family life
5. Returning GIs	

How did these groups react to discrimination and racism during and after the war?
6. African Americans
7. Mexican Americans
8. Japanese Americans

Cold War Conflicts

Origins of the Cold War

Terms and Names

United Nations (UN) Peacekeeping body of nations

satellite nation Country dominated by the Soviet Union

containment Effort to block Soviet influence by making alliances and supporting weaker nations

iron curtain The division of Europe between free and communist countries

Cold War State of hostility between the Soviet Union and the United States but without military action

Truman Doctrine U.S. policy of sending aid to any nation trying to prevent a Communist takeover

Marshall Plan Program under which the United States gave economic aid to rebuild postwar Western Europe

Berlin Airlift Resupply of West Berlin by U.S. and British planes during Soviet blockade of 1948

North Atlantic Treaty Organization (NATO) Defensive military alliance of the United States, Canada, and ten European nations

Before You Read

In the last section, you saw the social and economic changes that would reshape postwar America. In this section, you will see how the Allied coalition that won the war fell apart and the United States and the Soviet Union came into conflict.

As You Read

Use a chart to take notes on U.S. actions and Soviet actions that contributed to the beginning of the Cold War.

FORMER ALLIES CLASH
(**Pages** 602–604)
What caused Soviet-American problems?

The United States and the Soviet Union were wartime allies. But there had been trouble between them for some time. A major reason was that they had opposing political and economic systems. In addition, the Soviets were angry that the United States had taken so long to launch an attack against Hitler in Europe. Stalin also did not like that the United States had kept the development of the atomic bomb a secret. Americans were upset that Stalin had signed a treaty with Hitler before World War II. Still, at the end of the war, people hoped that the **United Nations (UN)** would help bring a time of peace. Instead, the UN became a place where the two superpowers competed and tried to influence other nations.

Meanwhile, Roosevelt had died. Harry S. Truman had become president. Truman was a plain, self-educated man. But he had honesty, self-confidence, and a willingness to make tough decisions.

Truman met with the British and Soviet leaders at the Potsdam Conference in July 1945. He reminded Stalin of his promise at Yalta to allow free elections in Eastern Europe. But Stalin would not listen to Truman. Soviet troops occupied Eastern Europe and Stalin was not going to allow free elections.

1. What were three issues that led to hard feelings between the Soviet Union and the United States?

_____

_____

TENSION MOUNTS (Pages 604–605)
What did Stalin and Truman want for postwar Europe?

Truman and Stalin disagreed over the future of Europe. Truman wanted strong democratic nations. He wanted the United States to be able to buy raw materials in Eastern Europe. He also wanted Eastern European markets for American products.

Stalin wished to spread communism. He also wanted to control Eastern Europe to prevent another invasion of Soviet territory. He wanted to use the resources of Germany and Eastern Europe to rebuild his war-torn nation. Stalin also felt that war between the Soviet Union and the West could not be avoided.

Stalin set up Communist governments in the European nations occupied by Soviet troops. They became **satellite nations,** countries that depended on and were dominated by the Soviet Union. The United States answered with a policy of **containment.** This was an effort to block

Soviet influence by making alliances and supporting weaker nations.

In 1946, Winston Churchill described "an **iron curtain**" coming down across Europe. It separated the nations in the "Soviet sphere" from the capitalist democracies of the West.

2. How did Truman's and Stalin's plans differ?

_____

_____

COLD WAR IN EUROPE (Page 606)
What were the Truman Doctrine and the Marshall Plan?

The conflicting aims of the United States and the Soviet Union led to the **Cold War.** This was a state of hostility between these superpowers, but one without military action. Each tried to spread its political and economic influence worldwide.

Truman's first test of containment was when Greece and Turkey needed economic and military aid in 1947. In the **Truman Doctrine,** the president argued that aid should be sent to any nation trying to stop Communists from taking over. Congress agreed. Aid was sent to Turkey and Greece.

Western Europe was also in terrible economic shape. Factories and fields had been destroyed. A terrible winter in 1946–1947 increased hardship. Secretary of State George Marshall wanted to send aid to nations that cooperated with American economic goals. Then Soviet troops took over Czechoslovakia in 1949. Congress saw the need for strong, stable governments to resist communism. It approved the **Marshall Plan.** The plan was a great success in rebuilding Western

Europe and halting the spread of communism.

3. How did the United States begin to send aid to nations fighting communism?

_____

_____

SUPERPOWERS STRUGGLE OVER GERMANY (Pages 607–608)
How did the Soviets and the West disagree over Germany?

East and West also disagreed over Germany. Stalin wanted to keep it weak and divided. The Western allies thought Europe would be more stable if Germany were united and productive. Britain, France, and the United States combined their occupied zones into the nation of West Germany.

Berlin was also divided into four occupied zones. But it was located in Soviet-controlled East Germany. The

Soviets cut off all transportation to West Berlin. West Berlin was the name given the zones occupied by Britain, France, and the United States. The Soviets said they would hold the city hostage until the West gave up the idea of German reunification. Instead, the United States and Britain started the **Berlin Airlift.** For 327 days, planes brought food and supplies to West Berlin. Finally, the Soviets gave up the blockade.

The blockade made the West worry about Soviet aggression. The United States and Canada joined with ten European nations in a defensive military alliance called the **North Atlantic Treaty Organization (NATO).** Members agreed that an attack on one was an attack on all.

4. What led to the Berlin blockade?

_____

_____

Name _____ Class _____ Date _____

Section 1, *continued*

As you read this section, complete the cause-and-effect diagram with the specific U.S. actions made in response to the Soviet actions listed. Use the following terms and names in filling out the diagram:

containment   Truman Doctrine   Berlin airlift   NATO

Effect: U.S. Action
1.

Cause: Soviet Action

Soviet leader Joseph Stalin refused free elections in Eastern Europe and set up satellite nations.

Effect: U.S. Action
2.

Effect: U.S. Action
3.

Cause: Soviet Action

Soviets blockaded Berlin for almost a year.

Effect: U.S. Action
4.

Section 2

The Cold War Heats Up

Terms and Names

Chiang Kai-shek Leader of the Nationalist forces in China

Mao Zedong Leader of the Communist forces in China

Taiwan Island off the coast of China

38th parallel Imaginary line that divides Korea at 38 degrees north latitude

Korean War War begun when North Korea invaded South Korea in 1950

Before You Read

In the last section, you read about postwar Europe. In this section, you will read about the postwar situation in Asia and about the Korean War.

As You Read

Use a time line to take notes on the major events of the Korean War.

CHINA BECOMES A COMMUNIST COUNTRY (Pages 609–611)
How did the Communists gain control of China?

For two decades the Chinese Communists struggled against the Nationalist government led by **Chiang Kai-shek.** The United States supported Chiang because he opposed communism and sent him aid. But U.S. officials knew that Chiang's government was inefficient and corrupt. He overtaxed the Chinese people even during times of famine. He did not have the support of the people.

Mao Zedong led the Communist forces in the North. He won the support of many Chinese peasants. Mao distributed land to them and reduced rents. He had an experienced army with high morale.

President Truman refused to send American troops to help the Nationalists

fight communism. But he did send aid. Even so, in 1949, Chiang and his forces had to flee to **Taiwan,** an island off the coast of China. China was now Communist. Containment in China had failed!

American conservatives said that the United States had "lost" China because not enough had been done to help the Nationalists. Truman's followers said that the Communist success was because Chiang could not win the support of the Chinese people. Conservatives claimed that the U.S. government was filled with Communist agents. American fear of communism began to burn out of control.

1. How did Communists gain control of China?

_____

_____

_____

THE KOREAN WAR; THE UNITED STATES FIGHTS IN KOREA
(**Pages** 611–615)
What caused the Korean War?

Japan had ruled Korea since 1910. At the end of World War II, Japanese forces in the north surrendered to the Soviets. In the south, the Japanese surrendered to the Americans. Two nations then developed. They were separated by the **38th parallel,** an imaginary line that divides Korea at 38 degrees north latitude.

In 1948, South Korea became an independent nation. North Korea became a Communist nation. Each claimed the right to rule all of Korea.

In June 1950, North Korea started the **Korean War** by invading South Korea. Truman was afraid another Asian nation was about to fall to communism. He ordered air and naval support for South Korea. Then the United Nations agreed to help South Korea. Troops from 16 nations—most of them American—were sent to South Korea. They were led by General Douglas MacArthur.

North Korean troops moved steadily south. They conquered the South Korean capital of Seoul. Then MacArthur launched a counterattack. His forces trapped about half the North Korean Army, which surrendered. MacArthur's success in Korea made him a national hero.

UN and South Korean forces advanced toward the 38th parallel. If they crossed it, the war would become an offensive rather than a defensive one. In October 1950, the UN told MacArthur to cross the 38th parallel and reunite Korea.

The Chinese opposed UN forces moving into North Korea. China said it would not let the Americans near its border. The UN ignored the threat and advanced. Then Chinese troops entered North Korea. They drove UN forces back. In January 1951, the Communists recaptured Seoul.

For two years, fighting continued. But neither side advanced. MacArthur wanted to extend the war into China. He even suggested dropping atomic bombs on China. Truman was against this strategy. The Soviets were allies of the Chinese. Truman felt bombing China would start World War III.

MacArthur continued to argue for his plan. He spoke to the press and to Republican leaders. Truman felt that he could no longer allow MacArthur's insubordination. He fired MacArthur as commander. At first, the American public sided with MacArthur. Later, they came to agree with Truman's idea of a limited war.

Meanwhile, a cease-fire went into effect in June 1951. Both sides agreed on a demilitarized zone at the 38th parallel. An armistice was signed in July 1953. The agreement was a stalemate. Korea was still divided between Communist North Korea and non-Communist South Korea.

Many people felt that American lives had been lost for little gain. As a result, the American people rejected the party in power, the Democrats, in the 1952 election. Republican Dwight D. Eisenhower was elected president. Americans also became even more worried about Communist expansion abroad and Communist spies at home.

2. What was gained by the Korean War?

_____

_____

Guided Reading Workbook

As you read this section, fill out the chart below by writing answers to the questions in the appropriate boxes.

	Civil War in China	Civil War in Korea
1. Which side did the United States support, and why?		
2. What did the United States do to affect the outcome of the war?		
3. What was the outcome of the war?		
4. How did the American public react to that outcome, and why?		

Cold War Conflicts

The Cold War at Home

Terms and Names

HUAC House Committee on Un-American Activities

Hollywood Ten People called before HUAC who did not cooperate

blacklist List of people in the Hollywood film industry who were refused jobs because they did not cooperate with HUAC

Alger Hiss Former State Department official

Ethel and Julius Rosenberg Activists in the American Communist Party who were executed as spies

Joseph McCarthy Republican Senator who claimed Communists were taking over the federal government

McCarthyism Term used to refer to tactic of accusing people of disloyalty without producing evidence

Before You Read

In the last section, you read about the Cold War abroad. In this section, you will read about the effects of the Cold War at home.

As You Read

Use a web diagram to take notes on the ways that anticommunist fear gripped the United States.

FEAR OF COMMUNIST INFLUENCE
(Pages 616–618)
How did Americans react to the threat of Communist influence?

Many Americans felt threatened by the rise of Communist governments in Europe and Asia. Some even felt that Communists could threaten the U.S. government from within. These fears increased when people found out about some spies selling U.S. government secrets to the Soviets.

Republicans accused the Truman administration of being "soft on communism." In response to this pressure, Truman set up a Loyalty Review Board. The Board investigated over 3 million people. About 200 were fired. Many

people felt that these investigations were unconstitutional. The accused were not allowed to see the evidence against them or to face their accusers.

In 1947, Congress set up the House Committee on Un-American Activities **(HUAC)**. Its purpose was to look for Communists both inside and outside government. HUAC concentrated on the movie industry because of suspected Communist influences in Hollywood. Many people were brought before HUAC. Some agreed that there had been Communist infiltration of the movie industry. They informed on others to save themselves.

Ten people called before HUAC refused to testify. They said the hearings were unconstitutional. The **Hollywood Ten,** as they were called, were sent to prison for their refusal.

In response to the HUAC hearings, Hollywood executives created a list of some 500 people they thought were Communist-influenced. They refused to hire the people on this **blacklist.** Many people's careers were ruined.

In 1950, Congress passed the McCarren Act. It outlawed the planning of any action that might lead to a totalitarian dictatorship in the United States.

1. What are three ways that the United States reacted to fear of communism at home?

_____

_____

SPY CASES STUN THE NATION
(Pages 618–620)
How did spies increase fear of communism?

Two spy cases added to the fear of communism sweeping the nation. One involved an official of the State Department named **Alger Hiss.** A former Soviet spy accused Hiss of spying for the Soviet Union. He had documents that implicated Hiss. Hiss claimed the documents were forgeries. Hiss was convicted of perjury—for lying about the documents—and went to jail.

In 1949, the Soviet Union tested an atomic bomb. Most people thought that it would take the Soviets much longer to develop their own atomic bomb. A British scientist admitted giving the Soviets secret information about the American bomb. He also implicated two Americans: **Ethel and Julius Rosenberg.**

The Rosenbergs were members of the American Communist Party. They denied the charges of spying. But they were convicted and sentenced to death. People from all over the world appealed for clemency for the Rosenbergs. They said the evidence against them was weak. The Supreme Court refused to overturn the decision, and the Rosenbergs were executed in 1953.

2. What two spy cases increased fear of communism in the United States?

_____

_____

MCCARTHY LAUNCHES HIS "WITCH HUNT" (Pages 620–621)
Who was Senator McCarthy?

In the early 1950s, Republican Senator **Joseph McCarthy** made headlines. He claimed that Communists were taking over the government. He also said the Democrats were guilty of treason for allowing this Communist infiltration.

McCarthy never produced any evidence to support his charges. These unsupported attacks on suspected Communists became known as **McCarthyism.** Later, McCarthyism also came to mean the unfair tactic of accusing people of disloyalty without producing evidence.

Many Republicans encouraged McCarthy. They thought that a strong anti-Communist position would help them win the 1952 elections. But some complained that McCarthy was violating people's constitutional rights.

In 1954, McCarthy made accusations against the U.S. Army. The Senate hearings were broadcast on national television. The American people watched McCarthy bully witnesses but produce no evidence. McCarthy lost public favor. The Senate voted to condemn him.

There had been much support for Communist witch hunts in the early 1950s. Many people were forced to take loyalty oaths in order to get jobs. States passed laws making it a crime to speak of overthrowing the government. These laws violated the constitutional right of free speech. But people became afraid to speak

their views. Fear of communism made many Americans willing to give up their constitutional rights.

3. What was McCarthyism?

_____

_____

Name _____ Class _____ Date _____

Section 3, *continued*

As you read this section, fill out the charts below by writing answers to the questions in the appropriate boxes.

	a. What were they accused of?	b. How were they affected by the accusations?	c. Do the accusations seem to have been fair? Explain.
1. The Hollywood Ten			
2. Alger Hiss			
3. Ethel and Julius Rosenberg			

McCarthyism		
4. What seems to have motivated it?	5. Why did it succeed at first?	6. Why did it fall out of favor?

Guided Reading Workbook

Cold War Conflicts

Two Nations Live on the Edge

Terms and Names

H-bomb Hydrogen bomb

Dwight D. Eisenhower President of the United States

John Foster Dulles Secretary of state

brinkmanship Willingness to go to the edge, or brink, of war

CIA Intelligence-gathering, or spy, agency of the United States government

Warsaw Pact Military alliance of the Soviet Union and its satellite nations

Eisenhower Doctrine Policy of the United States that it would defend the Middle East against attack by any Communist country

Nikita Khruschev Soviet leader

Francis Gary Powers Pilot of an American U-2 spy plane

U-2 incident Downing of a U.S. spy plane and the capture of its pilot by the Soviet Union in 1960

Before You Read

In the last section, you saw how the fear of communism affected life in the United States. In this section, you will see how Cold War tensions increased as both the United States and the Soviet Union tried to spread their influence around the world.

As You Read

Use a chart to take notes on the involvement of the United States in Cold War trouble spots around the world.

BRINKMANSHIP RULES
U.S. POLICY (Pages 622–623)
What was the arms race?

The Soviet Union exploded its first atomic bomb in 1949. American leaders wanted to develop a more powerful weapon. In 1952, the United States exploded the first hydrogen bomb, or **H-bomb.**

But the Soviets tested their own H-bomb in 1953. **Dwight D. Eisenhower** was president. His secretary of state, **John Foster Dulles,** was very anti-Communist. He said America must not compromise. The United States must be prepared to use all of its nuclear weapons against any aggressor. This willingness to go to the edge, or brink, of war was called **brinkmanship.**

The United States began making more nuclear weapons. So did the Soviet Union. This was called the arms race. Many

Americans feared a nuclear attack at any time. They had air-raid drills and fallout shelters to prepare for these attacks.

1. Why did the arms race begin?

_____

_____

THE COLD WAR SPREADS AROUND THE WORLD
(**Pages** 623–626)
What events increased Cold War tensions?

The United States was in competition with the Soviet Union all over the world. President Eisenhower began to rely on the **Central Intelligence Agency (CIA).** The CIA used spies to get information abroad. It also carried out covert actions, or secret operations, to weaken or overthrow governments unfriendly to the United States.

One CIA action involved Iran. In 1953, the CIA convinced the Shah, or monarch, of Iran to get rid of a prime minister who was not friendly to the West. In 1954, the CIA took action in Guatemala. Eisenhower believed Guatemala was friendly to the Communists. The CIA trained an army that overthrew Guatemala's government.

Soviet dictator Josef Stalin died in 1953. At first, tensions eased between the superpowers. People called it a thaw in the Cold War. But when West Germany joined NATO, the Soviet Union formed a military alliance with its satellite nations in 1955. This alliance was called the **Warsaw Pact.**

In 1956, a crisis developed in the Middle East. Egypt seized control of the Suez Canal. The Canal was located in Egypt but owned by Britain and France, who had built it. Egypt was an ally of the Soviet Union. Britain, France, and Israel invaded Egypt to take the Canal back. The Soviets threatened to bomb Britain and France. The United States threatened to retaliate. War was prevented when the UN imposed a cease-fire. During the crisis, Eisenhower issued a warning, known as the **Eisenhower Doctrine.** It said the United States would defend the Middle East against Communist attack.

In 1956, the people of Hungary rose in revolt and called for a democratic government. The new government promised free elections. But when the Hungarians asked to leave the Warsaw pact in 1956, Soviet tanks rolled into Hungary. They crushed the reform movement. Many Hungarian reformers were killed, and others fled the country.

2. How did hostilities increase between the United States and the Soviet Union during the 1950s?

_____

_____

THE COLD WAR TAKES TO THE SKIES (**Pages** 626–627)
What was the missile race?

The Soviet leader, **Nikita Khrushchev,** came to power in the years after Stalin's death. Unlike Stalin, he believed communism could triumph through peaceful means.

On October 4, 1957, the Soviets shocked the world by launching Sputnik I. It was the first artificial satellite to orbit the earth. American scientists also worked hard to catch up. The first attempt to launch a U.S. satellite was a humiliating failure. On January 31, 1958, the United States successfully launched its first satellite.

Guided Reading Workbook

Meanwhile, the United States had been flying spy missions over the Soviet Union. The CIA used U-2 aircraft that flew so high they could not be shot down. Or so the Americans thought. On May 1, 1960, a U-2 spy plane was shot down over the Soviet Union. The pilot, **Francis Gary Powers,** was captured and convicted of spying. However, he was soon released in exchange for a Soviet spy.

This **U-2 incident** happened right before a meeting between Eisenhower and Khrushchev. At the meeting, Khrushchev criticized the United States and walked out. The U-2 incident hurt Eisenhower's ability to deal with the Soviets.

3. In what two ways was the Cold War fought in the skies?

_____

_____

As you read this section, write your answers to the question in the appropriate boxes.

	How did the United States react, and why?
1. The Soviet Union exploded its first atomic bomb in 1949.	
2. In 1951, the Iranian prime minister placed the oil industry in Iran under the Iranian government's control.	
3. The Guatemalan head of government gave American-owned land in Guatemala to peasants.	
4. In 1956, Britain, France, and Israel invaded Egypt and occupied the Suez Canal.	
5. Soviet tanks invaded Hungary and fired on protesters in 1956.	
6. In 1957, the Soviet Union launched Sputnik.	
7. In 1960, the Soviet Union brought down an American U-2 piloted by Francis Gary Powers.	

Section 1

Postwar America

Terms and Names

GI Bill of Rights Law that provided financial and educational benefits for World War II veterans

suburb Residential town or community near a city

Harry S. Truman President after World War II

Dixiecrat Southern Democrat who left the party

Fair Deal President Truman's economic and social program

Before You Read

In the last section, you read about the developments in the Cold War at home and abroad. In this section, you will read about the economic boom in the United States after World War II.

As You Read

Use a time line to take notes on the key events in postwar America.

READJUSTMENT AND RECOVERY
(Pages 634–636)
How did the end of World War II affect America?

After World War II, millions of returning veterans used the **GI Bill of Rights** to get an education and to buy homes. At first, there was a terrible housing shortage. Then developers such as William Levitt built thousands of inexpensive homes in the **suburbs,** small residential communities near the cities. Many veterans and their families moved in.

The United States changed from a wartime to a peacetime economy. After the war, many defense workers were laid off. Returning veterans added to unemployment. When wartime price controls ended, prices shot up. Congress eventually put back economic controls on wages, prices, and rents.

The economy began to improve on its own. There was a huge pent-up demand for consumer goods. People had been too poor to buy these goods during the Depression. Many items had not been available during the war. Now Americans bought cars and appliances and houses. The Cold War increased defense spending and employment.

1. What were three effects of the end of World War II on American society?

_____

_____

MEETING ECONOMIC CHALLENGES; SOCIAL UNREST PERSISTS (Pages 636–639)
What were postwar problems?

President **Harry S. Truman** faced a number of problems immediately after the war. One was labor unrest. In 1946, a

---

Guided Reading Workbook

steel-workers' strike was followed by a coal miners' strike. In addition, the railroad unions threatened to stop all rail traffic in the nation.

Truman was pro-labor. But he would not let strikes cripple the nation. He threatened to draft striking workers into the army and then order them back to work. The unions gave in.

During this time, before the economy turned around, many Americans were disgusted with shortages, rising inflation, and strikes. Voters became more conservative. In the 1946 election, conservative Republicans gained control of Congress.

After the war, there was racial violence in the South. African-American veterans demanded their rights as citizens. Truman met with African-American leaders. They asked for a federal anti-lynching law, an end to the poll tax, and a commission to prevent discrimination in hiring.

Truman put his career on the line for civil rights. But Congress would not pass any of his civil rights measures. Finally, Truman acted on his own. In 1948, he issued an executive order to desegregate the armed forces. He also ordered an end to discrimination in hiring government employees.

Meanwhile, the Supreme Court said that African Americans could not be kept from living in certain neighborhoods. These acts marked the beginning of a federal commitment to deal with racial issues.

Truman was nominated for president in 1948. He insisted on a strong civil rights plank in the Democratic Party platform. This split the party. Many Southern Democrats left the Democratic Party. These **Dixiecrats** were against civil rights. They wanted to preserve the "Southern way of life." They formed the States' Rights Party. Some liberals left the

Democratic Party to form the Progressive Party.

It didn't look like Truman could win. But he took his ideas to the people. He criticized the "do-nothing Congress." Truman won a narrow victory. Democrats took control of Congress.

Truman tried to pass economic and social reforms. He called his program the **Fair Deal.** Health insurance and a crop-subsidy program for farmers were both defeated by Congress. But an increase in the minimum wage, extension of Social Security, and financial aid for cities passed.

2. What were some issues Truman fought for?

_____

_____

REPUBLICANS TAKE THE MIDDLE ROAD (Pages 639–640)
Why did Eisenhower win?

Truman did not run for reelection in 1952. The big issues of that campaign were (1) the stalemate in the Korean War, (2) anti-Communist hysteria and McCarthyism, (3) the growing power of the federal government, (4) strikes, and (5) inflation. Voters wanted a change. The Republicans nominated war hero General Dwight D. Eisenhower. He easily beat Democrat Adlai Stevenson.

Eisenhower was a low-key president with middle-of-the-road policies. He did have to deal with one controversial issue—civil rights. In 1954, the Supreme Court ruled in *Brown* v. *Board of Education* that public schools could not be segregated. Eisenhower believed that the federal government should not be involved in desegregation. But he upheld the law. When the governor of Arkansas tried to keep African-American students out of a white high school, Eisenhower sent federal troops to integrate the school.

The America of the mid-1950s was a place of "peace, progress, and prosperity." Eisenhower won a landslide reelection in 1956.

3. What two important civil rights actions occurred during Eisenhower's presidency?

_____

_____

Guided Reading Workbook

As you read this section, describe the solutions offered to deal with postwar problems.

1. Problem: Millions of veterans thrown out of work as they return to civilian life	
Solution offered by the Truman administration and Congress	

2. Problem: Severe housing shortage	
Solution offered by developers such as William Levitt	
Solutions offered by Congress under the Truman and Eisenhower administrations	

3. Problem: Runaway inflation	
Solution offered by the Truman administration and Congress	

4. Problem: Labor strikes that threaten to cripple the nation	
Solution offered by the Truman administration	

5. Problem: Discrimination and racial violence	
Solutions offered during the Truman administration	

Section 2

The American Dream in the Fifties

Terms and Names

conglomerate Major corporation that owns smaller companies in unrelated industries

franchise Company that offers similar products or services in many locations

baby boom Soaring birthrate from 1946 to 1964

Dr. Jonas Salk Developer of a vaccine to prevent polio

consumerism Excessive concern with buying material goods

planned obsolescence Purposely making products to become outdated or wear out quickly

---

Before You Read

In the last section, you read about the postwar boom in the United States. In this section, you will read how many Americans achieved their dreams of material comfort and prosperity, but some found the cost of conformity too high.

As You Read

Use a chart to take notes on specific goals that characterized the American Dream for suburbanites of the 1950s.

THE ORGANIZATION AND THE ORGANIZATION MAN
(Pages 641–643)
What changes took place in the American workplace in the 1950s?

The economy grew rapidly in the 1950s. By 1956, more Americans were white-collar workers in offices than were in blue-collar factory jobs. White-collar workers were paid better. They usually worked in service industries, such as sales and communications.

Businesses also expanded. They formed **conglomerates,** or major corporations that own smaller companies in unrelated industries. Other businesses expanded by franchising. A **franchise** is a company that offers similar products or services in many locations, such as fast-food restaurants.

These large companies offered well-paying, secure jobs to certain kinds of workers. These workers were conformists, or team players. They were "company people" who would fit in and not rock the boat. Businesses rewarded loyalty rather than creativity. They promoted a sameness, or standardization, of people as well as products. Books such as *The Organization Man* and *The Man in the Gray Flannel Suit* criticized this conformity.

---

1. What changes occurred in the American work force and workplace in the 1950s?

_____

_____

THE SUBURBAN LIFESTYLE
(**Pages** 643–645)
What was life like in the 1950s?

Many Americans enjoyed the benefits of the booming economy. Many worked in cities but lived in suburbs. They had the American dream of a single-family home, good schools, and a safe neighborhood with people just like themselves.

There was an increase in births called the **baby boom.** It was caused by the reuniting of families after the war and growing prosperity. Medical advances also wiped out childhood diseases. **Dr. Jonas Salk** developed a vaccine to prevent polio. Polio had killed or crippled 58,000 children a year.

The baby boom created a need for more schools and products for children. Suburban family life revolved around children. Many parents depended on advice from a popular baby-care book by Dr. Benjamin Spock. He said it was important that mothers stay at home with their children. The role of homemaker and mother was also glorified in the media. But many women felt alone and bored at home.

By 1960, 40 percent of mothers worked outside the home. But their career opportunities usually were limited to "women's fields." These included secretarial work, nursing, and teaching. Even if women did the same work as men, they were paid less.

Americans had more leisure time. They spent time and money on leisure activities, such as sports. They also watched sports on

television and read books and magazines. Youth activities, such as Scouts and Little League, became popular too.

2. What was life like in the suburbs in the 1950s?

_____

_____

THE AUTOMOBILE CULTURE
(**Pages** 646–647)
Why were cars so important?

Easy credit for buying cars and cheap gasoline led to a boom in automobile ownership. In the 1950s, the number of American cars on the road grew from 40 to 60 million.

A car was a necessity in the suburbs. There was no public transportation. People needed to drive to their jobs in the cities. They also had to drive to shop and do errands. Therefore, more and better roads were also needed. In 1956, the United States began building a nationwide highway network. In turn, these roads allowed long-distance trucking. This led to a decline in the railroads.

Americans loved to drive. They went to drive-in restaurants and movies. They drove long distances on vacation. Motels and shopping malls were built to serve them. These new industries were good for the economy. But the increase in driving also caused problems. These included stressful traffic jams and air pollution. Many white people left the cities. Jobs and industries followed. This left mostly poor people in crowded inner cities.

3. How did cars change American life?

_____

_____

CONSUMERISM UNBOUND

(Pages 648–649)

Why did Americans turn to consumerism in the 1950s?

By the mid-1950s, nearly 60 percent of Americans were in the middle class. They had the money to buy more and more products. They measured success by their **consumerism,** or the amount of material goods they bought.

American business flooded stores with new products. Consumers had money to spend and leisure time. They bought household appliances like washing machines, dryers, and dishwashers, and recreational items such as television sets, barbecue grills, and swimming pools.

Manufacturers also tried a new marketing strategy called **planned obsolescence.** They purposely made products to become outdated or to wear out quickly. Americans began to throw away items in order to buy "new models." Easy credit, including the introduction of credit cards, encouraged people to buy. Private debt grew.

The 1950s were "the advertising age." Ads were everywhere—even on the new medium of television. They tried to persuade Americans to buy things they didn't need. They appealed to people's desire for status and for a sense of belonging.

4. How was consumerism encouraged in the 1950s?

_____

_____

As you read this section, write notes about how Americans were affected by various trends of the 1950s.

Trends	Effects
1. Business expansion: conglomerates and franchises	
2. Suburban expansion: flight from the cities	
3. Population growth: the baby boom	
4. Dramatic increase in leisure time	
5. Dramatic increase in the use of the automobile	
6. The rise of consumerism	

Popular Culture

Terms and Names

mass media Means of communication that reach large audiences

Federal Communications Commission (FCC) Government agency that regulates the communications industry

beat movement Writers who made fun of the conformity and materialism of mainstream American society

rock 'n' roll Form of popular music, characterized by heavy rhythms and simple melodies, that developed from rhythm and blues in the 1950s

jazz A style of music characterized by improvisation

Before You Read

In the last section, you read about the American dream in the 1950s. In this section, you will read that popular culture in the 1950s reflected white, middle-class America, and a subculture challenged that conformity.

As You Read

Use a chart to take notes on the popular culture idols of the 1950s and their contributions.

NEW ERA OF MASS MEDIA
(**Pages** 652–655)
What **influence did TV have?**

Mass media—the means of communication that reach large audiences—include radio, television, newspapers, and magazines. Television became the most important means of communication in the 1950s. It both showed and influenced popular culture of the time.

The number of homes with television jumped. It went from 9 percent of all homes in 1950 to 90 percent in 1960. At first, the number of television stations was limited by the **Federal Communications Commission (FCC).** The FCC is the government agency that regulates the communications industry. Soon, however,

TV stations spread across the country. Many shows became widely popular all over the nation.

The 1950s were the "golden age of television." Comedy shows starring Milton Berle and Lucille Ball were popular. Edward R. Murrow introduced on-the-scene reporting and interviews. There were also westerns, sports events, and original dramas. At first, all shows were broadcast live.

Advertisers took advantage of this new medium, especially of its children's shows. Young fans wanted to buy everything that was advertised on their favorite shows. TV magazines and TV dinners— frozen meals to heat and eat— became popular.

Television reflected the mainstream values of white suburban America. These values were secure jobs, material success, well-behaved children, and conformity. Critics objected to the stereotypes of women and minorities. Women were shown as happy, ideal mothers. African Americans and Latinos hardly appeared at all. In short, TV showed an idealized white America. It ignored poverty, diversity, and problems such as racism.

As dramas and comedies moved to TV, radio changed. It began to focus on news, weather, music, and local issues. The radio industry did well. Advertising increased and so did the number of stations.

The movie industry suffered from competition by television. The number of moviegoers dropped 50 percent. But Hollywood fought back. It responded by using color, stereophonic sound, and the wide screen to create spectacular movies.

1. Was the picture of America portrayed on television accurate?

_____

_____

A SUBCULTURE EMERGES
(**Page** 655)
What was the beat movement and rock 'n' roll?

Television showed the suburban way of life. But two subcultures presented other points of view. One was the **beat movement** in literature. These writers made fun of the conformity and materialism of mainstream American society.

Their followers were called beatniks. They rebelled against consumerism and the suburban lifestyle. They did not hold steady jobs and lived inexpensively. They read their poetry in coffee houses. Their

art and poetry had a free, open form. Major works of the beat generation include Allen Ginsberg's long poem *Howl,* Jack Kerouac's novel *On the Road,* and Lawrence Ferlinghetti's *A Coney Island of the Mind.*

2. How did the beat movement criticize mainstream culture?

_____

_____

AFRICAN AMERICANS AND ROCK 'N' ROLL (**Pages** 655–657)
What role did African-American artists play in the 1950s?

Some musicians also took a new direction. They added electronic instruments to the African-American music called rhythm and blues. The result was **rock 'n' roll.** The new music had a strong beat. Its lyrics focused on the interests of teenagers, including alienation and unhappiness in love. And teenagers responded. They bought millions of records. The biggest star of all—the King of Rock 'n' Roll—was Elvis Presley. He had 45 songs that sold more than one million copies.

Some adults criticized rock 'n' roll. They said it would lead to teenage crime and immorality. But television and radio helped bring rock 'n' roll into the mainstream.

Many of the great performers of the 1950s were African American. Nat "King" Cole, Lena Horne, Harry Belafonte, and Sidney Poitier were popular with white audiences. They led the way for later African-American stars. **Jazz** musicians like Miles Davis and Dizzy Gillespie also entertained audiences of both races. The most popular black performers were the

Guided Reading Workbook

early rock 'n' roll stars, like Little Richard and Chuck Berry.

Television was slow to integrate. One of the first programs to do so was Dick Clark's popular rock 'n' roll show *American Bandstand*. In 1957, *Bandstand* showed both black couples and white couples on the dance floor.

Before integration reached radio audiences, there were stations that aimed specifically at African-American listeners.

They played the popular black artists of the day. They also served advertisers who wanted to reach black audiences.

3. How did African Americans influence the entertainment industry of the 1950s?

_____

_____

As you read this section, take notes to answer questions about innovations
and trends in 1950s popular culture.

1. Television	a. What are some of the most popular shows produced?	b. What kinds of subjects did television tend to present?	c. What kinds of subjects did it tend to avoid?
2. Radio	a. How did radio change to compete with television?	b. What role did it play in popularizing African-American culture?	
3. Film	How did movies change to compete with television?		
4. The beat movement	a. Who were the most famous beat writers?	b. What were the movement's chief characteristics?	
5. Rock 'n' roll	a. Who helped to popularize rock 'n' roll?	b. What were rock's chief characteristics?	

Section 4

The Other America

Terms and Names
urban renewal Plan to tear down decaying neighborhoods and build low-cost housing
bracero Farm workers entering the United States from Mexico
termination policy Federal government decision to end federal responsibility for Native American tribes

Before You Read

In the last section, you read about mainstream American society in the 1950s. In this section, you will read about Americans who were not part of the American mainstream.

As You Read

Use a diagram to take notes on the problems faced by African Americans, Mexican Americans, and Native Americans in the 1950s.

THE URBAN POOR (Pages 660–661)
What **was the plight of the inner cities?**

Prosperity reached many Americans in the 1950s. But it did not reach all Americans. In 1962, one out of every four Americans was poor. Many of these poor people were members of minority groups.

In the 1950s, millions of middle-class white people left the cities for the suburbs. This was called "white flight." Meanwhile, many poor African Americans moved from the rural South to Northern cities. Businesses—and jobs—followed whites out of the cities. Cities also lost the taxes these people and businesses had paid. City governments could no longer afford to keep up the quality of schools, public transportation, or other services. The urban poor suffered as their neighborhoods decayed.

Many suburban, middle-class Americans could not believe that a

country as rich as the United States had such poverty in its cities. However, Michael Harrington's 1962 book, *The Other America: Poverty in the United States,* made many Americans aware of the problem.

One way the government tried to solve the problem of the inner cities was called **urban renewal.** Minorities could not afford the new homes that had been built in the suburbs during the 1950s. Also, minorities were not welcome in the white suburbs. As a result, inner-city neighborhoods became very overcrowded.

Urban renewal was designed to tear down decaying neighborhoods and build low-cost housing. However, sometimes highways and shopping centers were built instead. The people who had lived in the old slums ended up moving to other slums—rather than into better housing.

Guided Reading Workbook

1. What were some reasons for the decay of America's inner cities?

_____

_____

POVERTY LEADS TO ACTIVISM
(**Pages** 662–663)
How **were Mexican Americans and Native Americans treated?**

During World War II, there was a shortage of laborers to harvest crops. The federal government allowed **braceros,** or hired hands, to enter the United States from Mexico. They were supposed to work on American farms during the war, and then go back to Mexico. However, when the war ended, many braceros stayed illegally. Many other Mexicans entered the United States illegally to find jobs.

Mexican Americans suffered prejudice and discrimination, too, even though they were citizens. When Mexican-American veterans came home from the war, they wanted to be treated fairly. They formed an organization to protest injustices. Other groups worked to help Mexican Americans register to vote. Pressure from these groups forced California to stop placing Mexican-American children in segregated classes. Mexican Americans began to have a nationwide political voice.

Native Americans also struggled for equal rights. This struggle was complicated by federal involvement in Native American affairs. At first, the government had supported assimilation, or absorbing Native Americans into mainstream American culture. That forced Native Americans to give up their own culture. In 1934, the Indian Reorganization Act changed that policy. The government now wanted Native Americans to have more control over their own affairs.

In 1944, Native Americans formed an organization to work for their civil rights and for the right to keep their own customs. After World War II, Native Americans got less financial help from the government. Outsiders grabbed tribal lands for mining and development.

In 1953, the federal government decided to end its responsibility for Native American tribes. This **termination policy** stopped federal economic support. It also ended the reservation system and distributed tribal land among individual Native Americans. One result of this policy was that many acres of tribal lands were sold to developers.

As part of the termination policy, the Bureau of Indian Affairs also moved thousands of Native Americans to the cities. It helped them find jobs and housing. This program was a failure. Native Americans did not have the skills to succeed in the cities. They were cut off from medical care. And they suffered job discrimination. The termination policy was ended in 1963.

2. How did Mexican Americans and Native Americans work for equal rights after World War II?

_____

_____

As you read about problems faced by the "other" America of the 1950s,
note some causes of each problem, solutions that were offered, and some
effects of those solutions. (Notice that two answers have been provided for
you.)

Problem: Decaying Cities		
1. Causes:	Solution Offered: *Urban renewal*	2. Effects of solution:

Problem: Discrimination Against Mexican Americans	
Causes: *Prejudice against Hispanics; hard feelings toward braceros who stayed to work in the U.S. after World War II; illegal aliens escaping poor conditions in Mexico*	3. Solutions offered:

Problem: Economic Hardship for Native Americans		
4. Causes:	5. Solutions offered:	6. Effects of solutions:

The New Frontier and the Great Society

Section 1

Kennedy and the Cold War

Terms and Names

John F. Kennedy 35th president of the United States

flexible response Policy of using nonnuclear weapons to fight a war

Fidel Castro Ruler of Cuba

Berlin Wall Barrier built to keep East Germans from fleeing to West Berlin

hot line Direct phone line between the White House and the Kremlin

Limited Test Ban Treaty Treaty that barred nuclear testing in the atmosphere

---

Before You Read

In the last section, you read about the poverty that existed in the United States in the 1950s. In this section, you will read how John F. Kennedy became president and how he handled a period of intense foreign affairs.

As You Read

Use a diagram to take notes on the outcomes of the major foreign crises that the Kennedy administration faced.

THE ELECTION OF 1960; THE CAMELOT YEARS (Pages 670–672.)
How did Kennedy win the election?

In 1960, President Eisenhower's term came to a close. By then, many Americans were worried about the future. The economy was in a recession. In addition, the Soviet Union was gaining strength. As a result, some wondered whether the United States was losing the Cold War.

John F. Kennedy and Richard M. Nixon faced off in the 1960 presidential election. Kennedy was a Democratic senator from Massachusetts. Nixon was Eisenhower's vice-president. Kennedy won the election by a slim margin. Two main factors led him to victory.

During a televised debate, Kennedy impressed viewers with his strong, forceful personality. Nixon appeared nervous and ill at ease.

The second factor was Kennedy's response to the arrest of Dr. Martin Luther King Jr., in October 1960. Kennedy called King's wife to express sympathy and persuaded the judge to release King from jail. His actions won him the support of African-American voters.

President Kennedy and his wife Jacqueline charmed many Americans. Jacqueline Kennedy influenced fashion and culture. People talked of the Kennedy Administration as a kind of *Camelot*, the story of King Arthur that was made into a popular Broadway musical. Kennedy surrounded himself with advisers that one journalist called "the best and brightest."

1. What two factors helped Kennedy win the 1960 presidential election?

_____

_____

A NEW MILITARY POLICY; CRISES OVER CUBA (Pages 673–677)
What two crises involving Cuba did Kennedy face?

Upon entering the White House, Kennedy focused on foreign affairs. He urged a tough stand against the Soviet Union. He also supported a policy called **flexible response.** This policy called for the use of conventional weapons rather than nuclear weapons in the event of a war. Conventional weapons included jets, tanks, missiles, and guns. In order to build more conventional weapons, Kennedy increased defense spending.

Kennedy's first foreign policy test came from Cuba. Cuba's leader was **Fidel Castro.** Castro had seized power in 1959. Soon after that, he declared himself a Communist. He then formed ties with the Soviet Union.

Kennedy approved a plan to remove Castro from power. The plan called for Cuban exiles to invade Cuba and overthrow Castro. The U.S. government would supply air support for the exiles.

The attack failed. Many exiles were captured. The failed invasion became known as the Bay of Pigs. It left the Kennedy administration greatly embarrassed.

A year later, the United States and Cuba clashed again. Pictures from U.S. spy planes revealed that the Soviets were building nuclear missile bases in Cuba. Some bases already contained missiles ready to launch. These weapons could be aimed at the United States.

President Kennedy demanded that the Soviets remove the missiles. In October 1962, he surrounded Cuba with U.S. Navy ships. These ships forced Soviet vessels trying to reach Cuba to turn around. A tense standoff followed. It appeared that war might break out. However, Soviet leader Nikita Khrushchev finally agreed to remove the missiles.

The crisis damaged Khrushchev's prestige in the Soviet Union and the world. Kennedy also endured criticism. Some Americans thought Kennedy had acted too boldly and nearly started a nuclear war. Others claimed he had acted too softly. These critics believed that Kennedy should have invaded Cuba and ousted Castro.

2. Name the two Cuban crises that the Kennedy administration faced.

_____

_____

CRISIS OVER BERLIN
(Pages 677–678)
How did the U.S. and Soviets try to ease tensions?

Cuba was not Kennedy's only foreign policy problem. In 1961, the president faced a growing problem in Berlin. The city was still divided. East Berlin was under Communist control. West Berlin was under the control of Great Britain, France, and the United States. By 1961, almost 3 million East Germans had fled into West Berlin.

Khrushchev threatened to block all air and land routes into West Berlin. Kennedy warned the Soviet leader against such action. As a result, Khrushchev changed his plan. He built a large concrete barrier along the border between East and West Berlin. It was known as the **Berlin Wall.** It prevented any more East Germans from fleeing to West Berlin.

Despite their battles, Kennedy and Khrushchev did attempt to reach agreements. They established a **hot line** between their two nations. This special telephone hookup connected Kennedy and Khruschchev. It allowed them to talk directly when a crisis arose. The two leaders also agreed to a **Limited Test Ban Treaty.** This treaty barred nuclear testing in the atmosphere.

3. Name two ways the U.S. and Soviet Union worked to ease tensions between them.

_____

_____

As you read this section, complete the time line by taking notes about the
election of John F. Kennedy and about his handling of several Soviet-
American confrontations.

1957	**Launch of *Sputnik 1***	1. What were some of the factors that helped John F. Kennedy win the presidency?
1960	**U-2 incident**	
	Alignment of Cuba with the Soviet Union	
	U.S. presidential election →	
1961	**Bay of Pigs** →	2. What were the results of the Bay of Pigs invasion?
	Berlin crisis →	3. How was the Berlin crisis resolved?
1962	**Cuban missile crisis** →	4. What were the effects of the Cuban missile crisis?
1963	**Installation of hot line** →	5. Why was the hot line installed?
	Negotiation of Limited Test Ban Treaty →	6. What would the Limited Test Ban Treaty eventually do?

The New Frontier

Terms and Names

New Frontier The name given to Kennedy's domestic program

mandate An overwhelming show of support by voters

Peace Corps A program that enlisted volunteers to help in poor countries

Alliance for Progress A program that supplied aid to Latin America

Warren Commission The body that investigated the assassination of President Kennedy

Before You Read

In the last section, you read about how President Kennedy dealt with explosive foreign matters. In this section, you will read about Kennedy's domestic agenda and how his presidency—and life—was cut short.

As You Read

Use a diagram to take notes about Kennedy's New Frontier programs.

THE PROMISE OF PROGRESS
(Pages 679–682)
What **were Kennedy's domestic plans?**

President Kennedy called his domestic program the **New Frontier.** However, Kennedy had a difficult time getting Congress to support his program. Conservative Republicans and southern Democrats blocked many of his bills. These included bills to provide medical care for the aged, rebuild cities, and aid education.

One reason for Kennedy's difficulties was that he was elected by a small margin. As a result, he lacked a popular **mandate,** or a clear indication that the voters approved of his plans. Because he lacked overwhelming support, Kennedy rarely pushed hard for his bills.

Kennedy did succeed with some proposals. To help the economy grow, the Kennedy administration used deficit spending. This occurred when the

government spent more money than it received in taxes. Kennedy hoped that increased spending on defense would help boost the economy.

Kennedy also introduced the **Peace Corps.** This was a program of volunteers working in poor nations around the world. The purpose of this program was to decrease poverty abroad. It was also meant to increase goodwill toward the United States. The Peace Corps was a huge success. People of all ages and backgrounds signed up to work for the organization. By 1968, more than 35,000 volunteers had served in 60 nations around the world.

Another program was the **Alliance for Progress.** This program gave aid to Latin American countries. One reason for this program was to keep communism from spreading to these countries.

In 1961 the Soviets launched a person into orbit around the earth. The news stunned America. A space race began between the United States and Soviet Union. President Kennedy pledged that the nation would put a man on the moon by the end of the decade. That goal was reached on July 20, 1969, when Neil Armstrong stepped onto the moon.

The space race affected American society in many ways. Schools taught more science. Researchers developed many new technologies. The space race also contributed to economic growth.

The Kennedy administration also tried to solve the problems of poverty and racism. In 1963, Kennedy called for a national effort to fight American poverty. He also ordered the Justice Department to investigate racial injustices in the South.

1. Name two successful programs of the Kennedy administration.

_____

_____

TRAGEDY IN DALLAS
(**Pages** 682–683)
Who killed President Kennedy?

On November 22, 1963, President and Mrs. Kennedy arrived in Dallas, Texas. Kennedy had come there to improve relations with the state's Democratic Party. Large crowds greeted the Kennedy's as they rode along the streets

of downtown Dallas. Then, rifle shots rang out. Kennedy had been shot. The president died about an hour later at a nearby hospital.

The tragic news spread across the nation and then around the world. Millions of Americans sat glued to their televisions over the next few days. They watched on live television as a gunman shot and killed the president's accused killer, Lee Harvey Oswald.

The events seemed too strange to believe. Many people wondered if Oswald had acted alone or with others. Chief Justice Earl Warren headed a commission to investigate the assassination. The **Warren Commission** determined that Oswald acted alone. However, many people continue to believe that Oswald was part of a conspiracy.

The assassination taught Americans that their system of government could survive an upset. Lyndon Johnson took office on Kennedy's death and promised to carry on his programs.

2. What did the Warren Commission determine?

_____

_____

As you read this section, take notes to answer questions about President
Kennedy's attempts to solve domestic and international problems.

The New Frontier: Fulfilled Promises

Problems	What did Kennedy believe the government could do to solve the problem?	What programs, laws, and accomplishments resulted from Kennedy's beliefs?
1. Economic recession		
2. Poverty abroad		
3. Soviet successes in space		

The New Frontier: Unfulfilled Promises

Rejected Proposals	Later Proposals
4. What reform proposals did Kennedy make that were rejected by a conservative Congress?	5. In 1963, what proposals did Kennedy make but never had the chance to guide through Congress?

The New Frontier and the Great Society

Section 3

The Great Society

Terms and Names

Lyndon Baines Johnson 36th president of the United States

Economic Opportunity Act Act that created numerous antipoverty measures

Great Society Name given to Johnson's domestic agenda

Medicare and Medicaid Health benefits for the elderly and poor

Immigration Act of 1965 Established new immigration system that allowed more immigrants into the U.S.

Warren Court The Supreme Court under Chief Justice Earl Warren

reapportionment The way in which states redraw their election districts

Before You Read

In the last section, you read about President Kennedy's domestic programs. In this section, you will read about Lyndon Johnson's bold plan to reshape America.

As You Read

Use a chart to take notes on the programs of the Great Society and the decisions of the Warren Court.

LBJ'S PATH TO POWER; JOHNSON'S DOMESTIC AGENDA (Pages 686–688)
How did Johnson wage a "war" on poverty?

Lyndon Baines Johnson, a Texan, was Senate majority leader in 1960. Johnson was a skilled lawmaker. He demonstrated a great ability to negotiate and reach agreements. During the 1960 presidential campaign, Kennedy's advisers thought that Johnson would make the perfect running mate. They believed that Johnson's connections in Congress and his Southern background would help Kennedy's presidential chances. Kennedy asked Johnson to be his vice-presidential candidate. Johnson agreed. He helped Kennedy win important states in the South.

Upon Kennedy's death, Johnson became president. Under President Johnson's leadership, Congress passed two bills that President Kennedy had proposed. One was a tax cut to help stimulate the economy. The other was the Civil Rights Act of 1964.

Johnson then launched his own program—a "war on poverty." He worked with Congress to pass the **Economic Opportunity Act.** This law created youth programs, antipoverty measures, loans for small businesses, and job training. The law created the Job Corps youth training program and the VISTA (Volunteers in Service to America) program.

Johnson ran for president in 1964. He easily defeated his Republican opponent, Barry Goldwater.

1. Name two programs created by the Economic Opportunity Act.

_____

_____

BUILDING THE GREAT SOCIETY; REFORMS OF THE WARREN COURT (Pages 688–692)
How did the Great Society and the Warren Court change America?

President Johnson had a grand vision for America. He called it the **Great Society.** Throughout his term, Johnson introduced legislation to help him create his Great Society. Among other things, these laws:

- provided federal aid for schools to purchase textbooks and library materials;
- created **Medicare and Medicaid** to ensure health care for the aged and poor;
- funded the building of public housing units and created the cabinet-level Department of Housing and Urban Development (HUD);
- lifted restrictions on immigration through the **Immigration Act of 1965**—which opened the door for many non-European immigrants to settle in the United States;
- required efforts to ensure clean water, through the Water Quality Act of 1965;
- offered increased protection to consumers, through the Wholesome Meat Act of 1967;
- established safety standards for automobiles and tires.

The wave of liberal reform that characterized the Great Society also affected the Supreme Court. Chief Justice Earl Warren took an active role in promoting more liberal policies. The **Warren Court** ruled school segregation unconstitutional. The court also banned prayer in public schools and strengthened the right of free speech.

The Warren Court also changed the area of congressional **reapportionment**. This is the way in which states redraw their election districts. The Court ruled that election districts within each state had to have roughly the same number of people in them. Because so many people lived in the cities, the court's ruling led to the creation of many new urban districts. As a result, political power shifted from the countryside to the cities.

The Warren Court strengthened the rights of people accused of crimes. The Court ruled police had to read suspects their rights before questioning them. These rights are known as Miranda rights.

2. Name one result of the Great Society and one result of the Warren Court.

_____

_____

IMPACT OF THE GREAT SOCIETY (Page 693)
How successful was the Great Society?

The Great Society and the Warren Court changed America. People disagree on whether these changes left the nation better or worse off than before. On one hand, Johnson's antipoverty measures helped reduce the suffering of many people. However, many of Johnson's proposals did not achieve their stated goals. Most people agree on one point: No president since World War II increased the power and reach of federal government more than Lyndon Johnson.

Eventually, some Americans began to question the increased size of the federal government. They also wondered about the effectiveness of Johnson's programs. Across the country, people became disillusioned with the Great Society. This led to the rise of a new group of Republican leaders.

3. How did the Great Society affect the size of the federal government?

_____

_____

As you read, note what each program or law did or was intended to do.

Program or Law	Objectives or Results
1. Tax-cut bill of 1964	
2. Civil Rights Act of 1964	
3. Economic Opportunity Act of 1964	
4. Elementary and Secondary Education Act	
5. Medicare	
6. Medicaid	
7. Immigration Act of 1965	

Note how the Court ruled in each case or what the decision accomplished.

Court Cases	Results
1. *Brown* v. *Board of Education*	
2. *Baker* v. *Carr*	
3. *Mapp* v. *Ohio*	
4. *Gideon* v. *Wainright*	
5. *Escobedo* v. *Illinois*	
6. *Miranda* v. *Arizona*	

Civil Rights

Taking on Segregation

Terms and Names

Thurgood Marshall African-American lawyer who led the legal challenge against segregation

Brown v. ***Board of Education of Topeka*** Supreme Court case in which segregated schools were ruled unconstitutional

Rosa Parks Woman who helped start Montgomery bus boycott

Martin Luther King, Jr. Leader of the civil rights movement

Southern Christian Leadership Conference (SCLC) Civil rights organization

Student Nonviolent Coordinating Committee (SNCC) Civil rights organization formed by students

sit-in Protest tactic in which blacks occupied whites-only seats at lunch counters

Before You Read

In the last section, you read about President Johnson's Great Society.
In this section, you will read how African Americans challenged the
nation's policies of segregation and racial inequality.

As You Read

Use a spider diagram to take notes on the tactics, organizations, leaders,
and Supreme Court decisions of the civil rights movement up to 1960.

THE SEGREGATION SYSTEM
(Pages 700–702)
How did World War II help start the civil rights movement?

By 1950, most African Americans were still considered second-class citizens. Throughout the South, Jim Crow laws remained in place. These were laws aimed at keeping blacks separate from whites.

During the 1950s, however, a civil rights movement began. This was a movement by blacks to gain greater equality in American society.

In several ways, World War II helped set the stage for this movement. First, the demand for soldiers during the war had created a shortage of white male workers. This opened up many new jobs for African Americans.

Second, about 700,000 African Americans had served in the armed forces. These soldiers helped free Europe. Many returned from the war ready to fight for their own freedom.

Third, during the war, President Franklin Roosevelt outlawed racial discrimination in all federal agencies and war-related companies.

World War II had given American blacks a taste of equality and respectability. When the war ended, many African Americans were more determined than ever to improve their status.

1. Name two ways in which World War II helped set the stage for the civil rights movement.

_____

_____

CHALLENGING SEGREGATION IN COURT (Pages 702–703)
What was important in the case of *Brown* v. *Board of Education?*

Even before the civil rights movement began, African-American lawyers had been challenging racial discrimination in court. Beginning in 1938, a team of lawyers led by **Thurgood Marshall** began arguing several cases before the Supreme Court.

Their biggest victory came in the 1954 case known as *Brown* v. *Board of Education of Topeka,* Kansas. In this case, the Supreme Court ruled that separate schools for whites and blacks were unequal—and thus unconstitutional.

2. What did the Supreme Court rule about separate schools for whites and blacks?

_____

_____

REACTION TO THE *BROWN* DECISION; THE MONTGOMERY BUS BOYCOTT (Pages 703–705)
Where did African Americans fight racial segregation?

Some Southern communities refused to accept the *Brown* decision. In 1955, the Supreme Court handed down a second *Brown* ruling. It ordered schools to desegregate more quickly.

The school desegregation issue reached a crisis in 1957 in Little Rock, Arkansas. The state's governor, Orval Faubus, refused to let nine African-American students attend Little Rock's Central High School. President Eisenhower sent in federal troops to allow the students to enter the school.

School was just one place where African Americans challenged segregation. They also battled discrimination on city buses. In Montgomery, Alabama, a local law required that blacks give up their bus seats to whites. In December 1955, Montgomery resident **Rosa Parks** refused to give her seat to a white man. Parks was arrested.

After her arrest, African Americans in Montgomery organized a yearlong boycott of the city's bus system. The protesters looked for a person to lead the bus boycott. They chose **Dr. Martin Luther King, Jr.,** the pastor of a Baptist Church.

The boycott lasted 381 days. Finally, in late 1956, the Supreme Court ruled that segregated buses were illegal.

3. Name two places that African Americans targeted for racial desegregation.

_____

_____

MARTIN LUTHER KING AND THE SCLC; THE MOVEMENT SPREADS (Pages 705–707)
Where did King get his ideas?

Martin Luther King, Jr. preached nonviolent resistance. He termed it "soul force." He based his ideas on the teachings of several people. From Jesus, he learned to love one's enemies. From the writer Henry David Thoreau, King took the idea of civil disobedience. This was the refusal to obey an unjust law. From labor organizer A. Philip Randolph, he learned how to organize huge demonstrations. From Mohandas Gandhi, King learned that a person could resist oppression without using violence.

King joined with other ministers and civil rights leaders in 1957. They formed the **Southern Christian Leadership Conference (SCLC)**. By 1960, another influential civil rights group emerged. The **Student Nonviolent Coordinating Committee (SNCC)** was formed mostly by college students. Members of this group felt that change for African Americans was occurring too slowly.

One protest strategy that SNCC ("snick") used was the **sit-in.** During a sit-in, blacks sat at whites-only lunch counters. They refused to leave until they

were served. In February 1960, African-American students staged a sit-in at a lunch counter at a Woolworth's store in Greensboro, North Carolina. The students sat there as whites hit them and poured food over their heads. By late 1960, students had desegregated lunch counters in 48 cities in 11 states.

4. Name two people from whom Martin Luther King, Jr. drew his ideas.

_____

_____

As you read, answer questions about important events in the civil rights movement.

1875	Civil Rights Act is passed. →	1. What did the Civil Rights Act of 1875 do?	
1883	Supreme Court rules 1875 Civil Rights Act unconstitutional. →	2. How did the Court rule in *Plessy*?	
1896	*Plessy* v. *Ferguson*		
1945	World War II ends. →	3. In what three ways did World War II help set the stage for the modern civil rights movement?	
1946	*Morgan* v. *Virginia* outlaws mandatory segregation on interstate buses.		
1950	*Sweatt* v. *Painter* declares that state law schools must admit black applicants. →	4. Who argued *Brown's* case?	5. What did the *Brown* ruling declare?
1954	*Brown* v. *Board of Education*		
1955	Supreme Court orders school desegregation. → Emmett Till is murdered. Rosa Parks is arrested.	6. What organization was formed to support Rosa Parks?	7. What did it do?
1956	Supreme Court outlaws bus segregation.		
1957	Little Rock faces school desegregation crisis. →	8. How did President Eisenhower respond to the Little Rock crisis?	
	Southern Christian Leadership Conference (SCLC) is formed. →	9. Who was the president of SCLC?	10. What was SCLC's purpose?
1960	Student Nonviolent Coordination Committee (SNCC) is formed. →	11. What did SNCC accomplish, and how?	

Civil Rights

Section 2

The Triumphs of a Crusade

Terms and Names

freedom riders Civil rights activists who tried to end segregation on national buses

James Meredith African American who won enrollment to the all-white University of Mississippi

Civil Rights Act of 1964 Law that outlawed racial discrimination

Freedom Summer Name of project to win voting rights for Southern blacks

Fannie Lou Hamer Prominent voting rights activist

Voting Rights Act of 1965 Act that struck down state laws intended to keep blacks from voting

Before You Read

In the last section, you read how African Americans began challenging the nation's racist systems. In this section, you will read how civil rights activists broke down many racial barriers and prompted landmark legislation.

As You Read

Use a chart to take notes on the steps taken to challenge segregation from 1962 to 1965.

RIDING FOR FREEDOM
(**Pages** 710–711)
Who were the freedom riders?

 Freedom Riders were protesters who rode buses with the goal of integrating buses and bus stations. In 1961, a bus of Freedom Riders was attacked in Anniston, Alabama, where a white mob burned the bus. Another instance occurred when a group of Nashville students rode into Birmingham, Alabama, where they were beaten.

 Attorney General Robert Kennedy ordered a reluctant bus company to continue to carry the freedom riders. When freedom riders were attacked in Montgomery, Alabama, the federal government took stronger action. President Kennedy sent 400 U.S. marshals to protect the freedom riders. The

Interstate Commerce Commission banned segregation in all travel facilities including waiting rooms, rest rooms, and lunch counters.

 1. Name two ways the government tried to help the freedom riders.

  _____

  _____

STANDING FIRM (**Pages** 711–714)
What happened in Birmingham?

 Civil rights workers soon turned their attention to integrating Southern schools. In September 1962, a federal court allowed **James Meredith** to attend the all-white University of Mississippi. However, Mississippi's governor refused to admit him. The Kennedy administration sent in U.S. marshals. They forced the governor to let in Meredith.

Another confrontation occurred in 1963 in Birmingham, Alabama. There, King and other civil rights leaders tried to desegregate the city. Police attacked activists with dogs and water hoses.

Many Americans witnessed the attacks on television. They were outraged by what they saw. Eventually, Birmingham officials gave in. They agreed to end segregation in the city.

The growing civil rights movement impressed President Kennedy. He became convinced that the nation needed a new civil rights law. Kennedy called on Congress to pass a sweeping civil rights bill.

2. What was the outcome of the demonstrations in Birmingham?

_____

_____

MARCHING TO WASHINGTON
(Page 714)
What did the Civil Rights Act of 1964 do?

President Kennedy's civil rights bill outlawed discrimination based on race, religion, national origin, and gender. It also gave the government more power to push for school desegregation. Civil rights leaders wanted Congress to pass the bill. So they staged a massive march on Washington, D.C.

On August 28, 1963, more than 250,000 blacks and whites marched into the nation's capital. There, they demanded the immediate passage of the bill.

Dr. Martin Luther King, Jr., spoke to the crowd. He called for peace and racial harmony in his now-famous "I Have a Dream" speech.

Several months later, President Kennedy was assassinated. Lyndon Johnson became president. He won passage in Congress of Kennedy's **Civil Rights Act of 1964.**

3. Name two things the Civil Rights Act of 1964 did.

_____

_____

FIGHTING FOR VOTING RIGHTS
(Pages 715–716)
Where did workers try to register African Americans to vote?

Civil rights activists next worked to gain voting rights for African Americans in the South. The voting project became known as **Freedom Summer.** The workers focused their efforts on Mississippi. They hoped to influence Congress to pass a voting rights act.

Meanwhile, civil rights activists challenged Mississippi's political structure. At the 1964 Democratic National Convention, SNCC organized the Mississippi Freedom Democratic Party (MFDP). The new party hoped to unseat Mississippi's regular party delegates at the convention.

Civil rights activist **Fannie Lou Hamer** spoke for the MFDP at the convention. She gave an emotional speech. As a result, many Americans supported the seating of the MFDP delegates. However, the Democratic Party offered only 2 of Mississippi's 68 seats to MFDP members.

In 1965, civil rights workers attempted a voting project in Selma, Alabama. They met with violent resistance. As a result, Martin Luther King, Jr. led a massive march through Alabama. President Johnson responded by asking Congress to pass a new voting

Guided Reading Workbook

Section 2, *continued*

rights act. Congress passed the **Voting Rights Act of 1965.** The law eliminated state laws that had prevented African Americans from voting.

4. Name two states where civil rights workers tried to register blacks to vote.

_____

_____

As you read this section, take notes to answer the questions about the time line.

1961 Freedom riders travel through the South. ⟶	1. What was the goal of the freedom riders?	2. What was the Kennedy administration's response?
1962 James Meredith integrates Ole Miss.		
1963 Birmingham and the University of Alabama are integrated.		
Kennedy sends civil rights bill to Congress.		
Medgar Evers is murdered.	3. What was the goal of the march on Washington?	4. Who attended the march?
March on Washington ⟶		
Birmingham church bombing kills four girls.	5. What was the goal of the Freedom Summer project?	6. Who volunteered for the project?
Kennedy is assassinated.		
1964 Freedom Summer ⟶		
Three civil rights workers are murdered.	7. What role did the violence shown on television play in this march?	8. What did the march encourage President Johnson to do?
Civil Rights Act is passed.		
1965 March from Selma to Montgomery ⟶		
Voting Rights Act is passed. ⟶	9. What did the Voting Rights Act outlaw?	10. What did the law accomplish?

Section 3

Challenges and Changes in the Movement

Terms and Names

de facto segregation Segregation by custom or practice

de jure segregation Segregation by law

Malcolm X African-American civil rights leader

Nation of Islam Group headed by Elijah Muhammad

Stokely Carmichael Leader of Black Power movement

Black Power Movement that stressed black pride

Black Panthers African-American group founded to combat police brutality

Kerner Commission Commission that reported on race relations in America

Civil Rights Act of 1968 Act that banned discrimination in housing

affirmative action Program aimed at hiring or including minorities

Before You Read

In the last section, you read about the triumphs of the civil rights movement. In this section, you will read about challenges and changes to the movement and how it ultimately left a mixed legacy.

As You Read

Use a time line to take notes on the key events of the civil rights movement.

AFRICAN AMERICANS SEEK GREATER EQUALITY (Pages 717–719)
What problems did African Americans in the North face?

The biggest problem in the North was **de facto segregation**—segregation that exists by practice and custom. De facto segregation can be harder to fight than **de jure segregation**—segregation by law. Eliminating de facto segregation requires changing people's attitudes rather than repealing laws.

De facto segregation increased as African Americans moved to Northern cities after World War II. Many white people left the cities. They moved to suburbs. By the mid-1960s, many African Americans in the North lived in decaying urban slums. There, they dealt with poor schools and high unemployment.

The terrible conditions in Northern cities angered many African Americans. This anger led to many episodes of violence.

1. Name two problems African Americans in the North faced.

_____

_____

NEW LEADERS VOICE DISCONTENT
(Pages 719–721)
What did new leaders call for?

During the 1960s, new African-American leaders emerged. They called for more aggressive tactics in fighting racism.

One such leader was **Malcolm X.** Malcolm preached the views of Elijah Muhammad. Muhammad was the head of the **Nation of Islam,** or the Black Muslims. Malcolm declared that whites were responsible for blacks' misery. He also urged African Americans to fight back when attacked.

Eventually, Malcolm changed his policy regarding violence. He urged African Americans to use peaceful means—especially voting—to win equality. In February 1965, he was assassinated.

Another new black leader was **Stokely Carmichael.** He introduced the notion of **Black Power.** This movement encouraged African-American pride and leadership.

In 1966, some African Americans formed a political party called the **Black Panthers.** The party was created to fight police brutality. They urged violent resistance against whites. Many whites and moderate African Americans feared the group.

2. Name two new civil rights leaders.

_____

_____

1968—A TURNING POINT IN CIVIL RIGHTS (Page 721)
Who was killed in 1968?

In April 1968, a gunman shot and killed Martin Luther King, Jr., in Memphis, Tennessee. Many leaders called for peace. But anger over King's death led many African Americans to riot. Cities across the nation erupted in violence.

A bullet claimed the life of yet another leader in 1968. In June, a man shot and killed Senator Robert Kennedy. Kennedy was a strong supporter of civil rights. The assassin was a Jordanian immigrant. He allegedly was angry about Kennedy's support of Israel. Kennedy had been seeking the Democratic nomination for president when he was killed.

3. Name two of the nation's leaders killed in 1968.

_____

_____

LEGACY OF THE CIVIL RIGHTS MOVEMENT (Pages 722–723)
Why is the legacy of the civil rights movement considered mixed?

Shortly after taking office, President Johnson formed a group known as the **Kerner Commission.** The commission's job was to study the cause of urban violence. In March 1968, the commission issued its report. It named one main cause for violence in the cities: white racism.

What, then, did the civil rights movement achieve? The movement claimed many triumphs. It led to the passage of important civil rights acts. This included the **Civil Rights Act of 1968.** This law banned discrimination in housing.

The movement had also led to the banning of segregation in education, transportation, and employment. It had also helped African Americans gain their full voting rights.

Yet many problems remained. Whites continued to flee the cities. Throughout the years, much of the progress in school integration reversed. African Americans continued to face high unemployment.

The government continued steps to help African Americans—and other disadvantaged groups. During the late 1960s, federal officials began to promote **affirmative action.** Affirmative-action programs involve making special efforts to hire or enroll minorities.

4. Name one goal the civil rights movement achieved and one problem that remained.

_____

_____

As you read this section, make notes to answer the questions.

1. What is the main difference between de facto and de jure segregation?
2. How did the ideas of SNCC differ from those of the Nation of Islam?
3. How did the early views of Malcolm X differ from his later ideas?
4. What changes took place in Stokely Carmichael's membership in civil rights organizations?
5. How did the ideas of SNCC differ from those of the Black Panthers?

6. What gains were made by the civil rights and Black Power movements? Identity four.

a.	b.	c.	d.

Moving Toward Conflict

Terms and Names

Ho Chi Minh Leader of North Vietnam

Vietminh Communist group led by Ho Chi Minh

domino theory Eisenhower's explanation for stopping communism

Dien Bien Phu Major French outpost captured by the Vietminh

Geneva Accords Peace agreement that split Vietnam in two

Ngo Dinh Diem Leader of South Vietnam

Vietcong Communist rebel group in South Vietnam

Ho Chi Minh Trail Network of paths running between North and South Vietnam

Tonkin Gulf Resolution Resolution that allowed President Johnson to fight in Vietnam

Before You Read

In the last section, you read about the legacy of the civil rights movement. In this section, you will read how the United States became involved in Vietnam.

As You Read

Use a chart to take notes on the Vietnam policies of presidents Truman, Eisenhower, Kennedy, and Johnson.

AMERICA SUPPORTS FRANCE IN VIETNAM (Pages 730–732)
Why did the U.S. get involved?

Vietnam is a long, thin country on a peninsula in southeast Asia. From the late 1800s until World War II, France ruled Vietnam. The French treated the Vietnamese badly. As a result, the Vietnamese often rebelled. The Communist Party in Vietnam organized many of the rebellions. The group's leader was **Ho Chi Minh.**

In 1941, Japan conquered Vietnam. That year, the Vietnamese Communists combined with other groups to form an organization called the **Vietminh.** The Vietminh's goal was to achieve independence for Vietnam. In 1945,

Japan was defeated in World War II. As a result, the Japanese left Vietnam. The Vietminh claimed independence for Vietnam.

However, France wanted to retake control of Vietnam. French troops moved back into the country in 1946. They conquered the southern half of Vietnam. The Vietminh took control of the North. For the next eight years, the two sides fought for control of the entire country.

The United States supported France during the war. America considered the Vietminh to be Communists. The United States, like other western nations, was determined to stop the spread of communism. President Eisenhower explained his country's policy with what

became known as the **domino theory.**
Eisenhower compared many of the world's
smaller nations to dominoes. If one nation
fell to communism, the rest also would fall.

The Vietminh defeated the French. The
final blow came in 1954. That year, the
Vietminh conquered the large French
outpost at **Dien Bien Phu.**

Several countries met with the French
and the Vietminh to negotiate a peace
agreement. The agreement was known as
the **Geneva Accords.** It temporarily split
Vietnam in half. The Vietminh controlled
North Vietnam. The anti-Communist
nationalists controlled South Vietnam. The
peace agreement called for an election to
unify the country in 1956.

1. For what reason did the United States
   support France in the war?

   _____

   _____

THE UNITED STATES STEPS IN
(Pages 732–734)
Who were the Vietcong?

Ho Chi Minh ruled North Vietnam. **Ngo
Dinh Diem** led South Vietnam. When it
came time for the all-country elections,
Diem refused to take part. He feared that
Ho would win. And then all of Vietnam
would become Communist.

The United States supported Diem's
decision. The U.S. government provided
aid to Diem. America hoped that Diem
could turn South Vietnam into a strong,
independent nation. Diem, however,
turned out to be a terrible ruler. His
administration was corrupt. He also
refused to allow opposing views.

By 1957, a rebel group had formed in the
South. The group was known as the
Vietcong. It fought against Diem's rule. Ho
Chi Minh supported the Vietcong from the

North. He supplied arms to the group along
a network of paths that ran between North
and South Vietnam. Together, these paths
became known as the **Ho Chi Minh Trail.**

John Kennedy became president after
Eisenhower. Kennedy continued America's
policy of supporting South Vietnam. He,
like Eisenhower, did not want to see the
Communists take over Vietnam.

Meanwhile, Diem's government grew
more unstable. The Vietcong rebels were
gaining greater support among the
peasants. The Kennedy administration
decided that Diem had to step down. In
1963, military leaders overthrew Diem.
Against Kennedy's wishes, they executed
Diem.

Two months later, Kennedy himself
was assassinated. Lyndon Johnson became
president. The growing crisis in Vietnam
was now his.

2. Who were the Vietcong fighting?

   _____

   _____

PRESIDENT JOHNSON EXPANDS
THE CONFLICT (Pages 734–735)
What was the Tonkin Gulf Resolution?

South Vietnam did not improve after
Diem's death. A string of military leaders
tried to rule the country. Each one failed to
bring stability. Johnson, however,
continued to support South Vietnam. The
president was determined to not "lose"
Vietnam to the Communists.

In August 1964, Johnson received
reports of an incident in the Gulf of
Tonkin off North Vietnam. A North
Vietnamese patrol boat allegedly had fired
torpedoes at a U.S. destroyer. President
Johnson responded by bombing North
Vietnam.

Guided Reading Workbook

He also asked Congress for special military powers to stop any future North Vietnamese attacks on U.S. forces. As a result, Congress passed the **Tonkin Gulf Resolution.** The resolution granted Johnson broad military powers in Vietnam. In February 1965, President Johnson used his new power. He launched a major bombing attack on North Vietnam's cities.

3. What did the Tonkin Gulf Resolution grant President Johnson?

_____

_____

As you read this section, take notes to answer questions about how the
United States slowly became involved in a war in Vietnam.

1941	**Vietminh is formed.**	→ 1. What did the Vietminh declare as its main goal?
1945	**Japan is forced out of Vietnam.**	→ 2. What did Ho Chi Minh declare after Japan was forced out?
1946	**French troops return to southern Vietnam.**	→ 3. How did Ho Chi Minh respond to the return of the French?

1950	**U.S. begins its involvement in the Vietnam struggle.**	→ 4. Whom did the U.S. support?	5. What aid did the U.S. provide?
		6. Why did the U.S. get involved in the struggle?	

1954	**Eisenhower introduces domino theory.**	→ 7. What did Eisenhower compare to a row of dominoes?
	Vietminh over-runs Dien Bien Phu.	→ 8. What did this Vietminh victory cause the French to do?
	Geneva Accords are reached.	→ 9. How did the Geneva Accords change Vietnam?
1956	**Elections are canceled.**	→ 10. Who canceled the Vietnamese elections? Why?
1957	**Vietcong begins attacks on Diem government.**	
1963	**Diem is overthrown.**	11. What authority did the Tonkin Gulf Resolution grant to the U.S. president?
1964	**U.S. Congress adopts Tonkin Gulf Resolution.**	→
1965	**Operation Rolling Thunder is launched.**	→ 12. What did Operation Rolling Thunder do in North Vietnam?

Guided Reading Workbook

Section 2

U.S. Involvement and Escalation

Terms and Names

Robert McNamara Secretary of defense under Johnson

Dean Rusk Secretary of state under Johnson

William Westmoreland Commander of U.S. troops in Vietnam

Army of the Republic of Vietnam (ARVN) The South Vietnamese military forces

napalm Gasoline-based explosive

Agent Orange Chemical that destroyed jungle land

search-and-destroy mission Tactic in which U.S. troops destroyed Vietnamese villages

credibility gap Situation in which the U.S. public no longer believed the Johnson administration

Before You Read

In the last section, you read how the United States became involved in Vietnam. In this section, you will read about the war America fought in Vietnam.

As You Read

Use a chart to take notes on the key military tactics and weapons used by the Vietcong and the Americans.

JOHNSON INCREASES U.S. INVOLVEMENT (Pages 736–737)
Who supported Johnson's decision to send U.S. troops to Vietnam?

In 1965, Johnson began sending U.S. troops to Vietnam to fight the Vietcong. Some of Johnson's advisers had opposed this move. They argued it was too dangerous.

But most of the president's advisers supported sending in troops. They included Secretary of Defense **Robert McNamara** and Secretary of State **Dean Rusk.** These men believed that America had to help defeat communism in

Vietnam. Otherwise, the Communists might try to take over other countries.

Much of the public also agreed with Johnson's decision. Many Americans believed in stopping the spread of communism.

By the end of 1965, the United States had sent more than 180,000 troops to Vietnam. The American commander in South Vietnam was General **William Westmoreland.** Westmoreland was not impressed by the **Army of the Republic of Vietnam (ARVN)** as a fighting force. He asked for even more troops. By 1967, almost 500,000 American soldiers were fighting in Vietnam.

1. Name two groups that supported Johnson's decision to use troops in Vietnam.

_____

_____

FIGHTING IN THE JUNGLE
(Pages 738–740)
Why **did the war drag on?**

The United States believed that its superior weaponry would lead to a quick victory over the Vietcong. However, several factors turned the war into a bloody stalemate.

The first factor was the Vietcong's fighting style. The Vietcong did not have advanced weapons. As a result, they used hit-and-run ambush tactics. The Vietcong struck quickly in small groups. They then disappeared into the jungle or an elaborate system of tunnels. These tactics frustrated the American troops.

The second factor was the Vietcong's refusal to surrender. Throughout the war, the Vietcong suffered many battlefield deaths. However, they continued to fight on.

The third factor was the American troops' inability to win the support of the Vietnamese peasants. In fighting the Vietcong, U.S. troops ended up hurting the peasants as well. For example, U.S. planes dropped **napalm,** a gasoline-based bomb that set fire to the jungle. They did this to expose Vietcong tunnels and hideouts. They also sprayed **Agent Orange.** This was a leaf-killing chemical that destroyed the landscape. Both of these weapons wounded villagers and ruined villages.

American soldiers also turned the peasants against them by conducting

search-and-destroy missions. During these missions, soldiers destroyed villages they believed supported the Vietcong.

The frustrations of fighting the war caused the morale of American soldiers to sink. Soldiers endured great hardships, especially prisoners of war captured by the North Vietnamese.

2. Name two reasons why the U.S. failed to score a quick victory against the Vietcong.

_____

_____

THE EARLY WAR AT HOME
(Pages 740–741)
How **did the war affect Johnson's domestic programs?**

The number of U.S. troops in Vietnam continued to increase. So did the cost of the war. As a result, the nation's economy began to suffer. In order to pay for the war, President Johnson had to cut spending for his Great Society programs.

By 1967, many Americans still supported the war. However, the images of the war on television began to change that. The Johnson administration told the American people that the war was going well. But television told the opposite story. Each night, Americans watched the brutal scenes of the war on their television screens. This led to a **credibility gap** in the Johnson administration. A growing number of people no longer believed what the president was saying.

3. How did the war affect Johnson's Great Society?

_____

_____

Name _____ Class _____ Date _____

As you read about the escalation of the war, take notes to answer the questions.

1. What role did each of the following play in the decision to escalate U.S. military involvement in Vietnam?
Lyndon B. Johnson
Robert McNamara
Dean Rusk
William Westmoreland
U.S. Congress
American public opinion

U.S. military strategies result in a bloody stalemate.

2. What military advantages did the Americans have over the Vietcong?	3. What military advantages did the Vietcong have over the Americans?
4. What military strategies did the Americans use against the Vietcong?	5. What military strategies did the Vietcong use against the Americans?

Public support for the war begins to waver as a "credibility gap" grows.

6. What role did each of the following play in this change of public support?
The U.S. economy
Television
The Fulbright hearings

Guided Reading Workbook

Section 3

A Nation Divided

Terms and Names

draft System for calling people to military service

New Left Name given to the youth movement of the 1960s

Students for a Democratic Society (SDS) Prominent group of the New Left

Free Speech Movement New Left group that attacked business and government

dove American individual who called for America to withdraw from Vietnam

hawk American individual who supported the war effort

Before You Read

In the last section, you read about America's war effort in Vietnam. In this section, you will read about how the United States became divided over the war in Vietnam.

As You Read

Use a tree diagram to take notes on student organizations, issues, and demonstrations of the New Left.

THE WORKING CLASS GOES TO WAR (Pages 742–744)
Who fought the war?

Most soldiers who fought in Vietnam were called into combat under the country's Selective Service System, or **draft.** Because the war was growing unpopular, thousands of men tried to avoid the draft.

One of the most common ways to avoid the draft was to attend college. Most men enrolled in a university could put off their military service.

Many university students during the 1960s were white and financially well-off. As a result, a large number who fought in Vietnam were lower-class whites or minorities. Nearly 80 percent of American soldiers came from lower economic levels. Thus, Vietnam was known as a working-class war.

Early on, a high number of African Americans served and died in Vietnam. During the first several years of the war,

20 percent of American soldiers killed were black. Blacks, however, made up only about 10 percent of the U.S. population. This situation prompted protests from many civil rights leaders, including Martin Luther King, Jr. Many African-American soldiers also endured racism within their units.

The U.S. military in the 1960s did not allow women to serve in combat. However, nearly 10,000 women served in Vietnam as army and navy nurses. Thousands more volunteered in the American Red Cross and the United Services Organization (USO). This organization provided entertainment to the troops.

1. Name two groups of Americans who did most of the fighting early on in Vietnam.

_____

_____

THE ROOTS OF OPPOSITION
(Pages 744–745)
What were the New Left groups?

By the 1960s, American college students had become politically active. The growing youth movement of the 1960s was known as the **New Left.** The group took its name from the "old" left of the 1930s. That movement had tried to push the nation toward socialism. The New Left did not call for socialism. However, it did demand sweeping changes in American society.

One of the better known New Left groups was **Students for a Democratic Society (SDS).** This organization called for greater individual freedom in America.

Another New Left group was the **Free Speech Movement** (FSM). This group was formed at the University of California at Berkeley. It grew out of a fight between students and administrators over free speech on campus. FSM criticized business and government institutions.

The strategies of the SDS and FSM eventually spread to colleges throughout the country. There, students protested mostly campus issues. Soon, however, students around the nation found one issue they could protest together: the Vietnam War.

2. Name two New Left groups.

_____

_____

THE PROTEST MOVEMENT EMERGES (Pages 745–747)
How did the hawks and doves differ?

Across America, college students rose up in protest against the war. They did so for various reasons. The most common reason was that the conflict in Vietnam was a civil war between the North and South. Thus, the United States had no business being there. Others believed that the war kept America from focusing on other parts of the world. Still others saw the war as morally unjust.

In April 1965, SDS helped organize a march on Washington, D.C. About 20,000 protesters participated. In November 1965, a protest rally in Washington drew about 30,000 protesters. Eventually, the antiwar movement reached beyond college campuses. Small numbers of returning veterans protested. Musicians took up the antiwar cause. Many protest songs became popular.

By 1967, Americans were divided into two main groups. Those who wanted the United States to withdraw from the war were called **doves.** Those who supported the war were called **hawks.** Other Americans took no stand on the war. However, they criticized doves for protesting a war in which U.S. troops were fighting and dying.

3. Briefly explain the positions of the hawks and doves.

_____

_____

Guided Reading Workbook

As you read this section, take notes to answer the questions.

Avoiding the War
1. What were some of the ways that young American men avoided military service in Vietnam?
2. In what sense was the Vietnam War a "working-class" war? How did it become one?

Opposing the War
3. What organizations and groups of Americans tended to oppose the war?
4. What were some of the reasons that "doves" opposed the war?
5. In what ways did they show their opposition to the war?

Defending the War
6. By 1967, how did most Americans feel about U.S. involvement in the Vietnam War?
7. Why did "hawks" criticize the Johnson administration's policies in Vietnam?

Section 4

1968: A Tumultuous Year

Terms and Names

Tet offensive Series of Vietcong attacks during the 1968 Tet holiday

Clark Clifford A Lyndon Johnson adviser who became his secretary of defense

Robert Kennedy A Democratic candidate for president in 1968

Eugene McCarthy A Democratic presidential candidate who ran on antiwar platform

Hubert Humphrey The 1968 Democratic nominee for president

George Wallace A third-party candidate in the 1968 presidential election

---

Before You Read

In the last section, you read how the Vietnam War divided America.
In this section, you will read about the shocking events that made 1968
one of the most explosive years of the decade.

As You Read

Use a time line to take notes on the major events of 1968.

THE TET OFFENSIVE TURNS THE WAR (Pages 748–750)
How did the Tet offensive affect America?

January 30 was the Vietnamese equivalent of New Year's Eve. It was the beginning of festivities known as Tet. During the Tet holiday in 1968, a week-long truce was called. Many peasants crowded into South Vietnam's cities to celebrate the holiday.

However, many of the peasants turned out to be Vietcong rebels. The rebels launched a massive attack on nearly 100 towns and cities in South Vietnam. They also attacked 12 U.S. air bases. The attacks were known as the **Tet offensive.** The offensive lasted for about a month. Finally, U.S. and South Vietnamese forces regained control of the cities.

General Westmoreland declared that the Tet offensive was a major defeat for the Vietcong. From a military standpoint, he was right. The Vietcong lost about 32,000 soldiers during the attacks. The United States and South Vietnam lost only 3,000 soldiers.

However, the Tet offensive shattered America's confidence in the war. The enemy now seemed everywhere. Many Americans began to think that the war was unwinnable. The Tet offensive also shocked many in the White House. **Clark Clifford** was the president's new secretary of defense. After Tet, Clifford decided that America could not win the war.

The Tet offensive also hurt President Johnson's popularity. By the end of February 1968, nearly 60 percent of the public disapproved of Johnson's handling of the war. In addition, nearly half the country said it had been a mistake to send troops to Vietnam.

---

1. How did the Tet offensive affect Johnson's popularity?

_____

_____

2. Name two events that shocked Americans in 1968.

_____

_____

DAYS OF LOSS AND RAGE
(**Pages** 750–751)
Which events shocked the nation?

Even before the Tet offensive, an antiwar group in the Democratic Party had taken steps to unseat Johnson. The group looked for someone to challenge Johnson in the 1968 primary election. They asked **Robert Kennedy,** a senator from New York. Kennedy declined. However, Minnesota senator **Eugene McCarthy** agreed. He would run against Johnson on a platform to end the Vietnam War.

McCarthy surprised many people by nearly beating Johnson in the New Hampshire Democratic primary. Suddenly, Johnson appeared politically weak. As a result, Robert Kennedy declared himself a presidential candidate. The Democratic Party was now badly divided.

President Johnson decided to address the nation on television. He announced that he would seek peace in Vietnam. Then he declared that he would not seek reelection as president. The country was shocked.

In the days and months ahead, several more incidents stunned the nation. On April 4, a gunman killed civil rights leader Martin Luther King, Jr. Two months later, an assassin gunned down and killed Robert Kennedy.

Meanwhile, antiwar protests continued to rock college campuses. During the first six months of 1968, almost 40,000 students on more than 100 campuses held demonstrations.

A TURBULENT RACE FOR PRESIDENT (**Pages** 751–753)
What happened in Chicago?

In August 1968, the Democrats met in Chicago for their presidential convention. There, they would choose a presidential candidate. In reality, Democratic leaders had already decided on the candidate: Vice-President **Hubert Humphrey.** This angered many antiwar activists. They favored McCarthy.

About 10,000 antiwar protesters came to Chicago. Some protesters wanted to pressure the Democrats to create an antiwar platform. Others wanted to voice their opposition to Humphrey. Still others wanted to create violence to discredit the Democratic Party.

Violence eventually erupted at a downtown park away from the convention hall. There, police moved in on thousands of demonstrators. They sprayed the protesters with Mace. They also beat them with nightsticks. Many protesters fled. Others fought back.

The violence in Chicago highlighted the Democrats' division. The Republicans were more unified. They nominated former Vice-President Richard Nixon for president.

Nixon campaigned on a platform of law and order. He also assured the American people that he would end the Vietnam War. Nixon's campaign was helped by the entry of a third-party candidate, **George Wallace.** Wallace was a former governor of Alabama. He took many democratic votes away from Humphrey. In November, Nixon won the election. It was now up to him to resolve the Vietnam crisis.

3. Name two reasons that protesters came to Chicago for the Democratic convention.

_____

_____

As you read this section, note some of the causes and effects of the events of 1968. Leave the shaded box blank.

Causes	Events of 1968	Effects
	1. Tet offensive	
	2. Johnson's poor showing in the New Hampshire primary	
	3. Assassination of Dr. Martin Luther King, Jr.	
	4. Assassination of Robert Kennedy	
	5. Disorder at the Democratic National Convention	
	6. Richard M. Nixon's presidential election victory	

Section 5

The End of the War and Its Legacy

Terms and Names

Richard Nixon President of the United States, elected 1968

Henry Kissinger Nixon adviser who helped negotiate an end to the war

Vietnamization President Nixon's plan for ending America's involvement in the war

silent majority Those mainstream Americans who supported Nixon's policies

My Lai Site of massacre of Vietnamese civilians by American soldiers

Kent State University Site of protest where National gaurd killed four students

Pentagon Papers Government documents that showed the government had no real plan for leaving Vietnam

War Powers Act Act that forbids the president from mobilizing troops without Congressional approval

Before You Read

In the last section, you read about the explosive events that occurred in 1968. In this section, you will read how the Vietnam War ended and what effect the war had on America.

As You Read

Use a web diagram to take notes on the effects of the Vietnam War on the United States.

PRESIDENT NIXON AND VIETNAMIZATION (Pages 754–755)
How did Vietnamization work?

Richard Nixon pledged to end American involvement in the Vietnam War. With National Security Adviser **Henry Kissinger,** he came up with a plan to end the war. Their plan was known as **Vietnamization.** It called for the gradual withdrawal of U.S. troops and for the South Vietnamese to do more of the fighting. By August of 1969, the first 25,000 U.S. troops had returned home. Over the next three years, the number of American troops in Vietnam

dropped from more than 500,000 to less than 25,000.

Nixon, however, did not want to lose the war. So as he pulled American troops out, he ordered a massive bombing attack against North Vietnam. Nixon also ordered that bombs be dropped on the neighboring countries of Laos and Cambodia. These countries held a number of Vietcong bases.

1. Name both aspects of the Vietnamization plan.

_____

_____

TROUBLE CONTINUES ON THE HOME FRONT (Pages 756–757)
Which events weakened support for the war?

To win support for his war policies, Nixon appealed to what he called the **silent majority.** These were mainstream Americans who quietly supported the president's strategy. Many Americans did support the president. However, the war continued to divide the country.

In November of 1969, Americans learned of a shocking event. U.S. troops had massacred more than 100 unarmed Vietnamese in the village of **My Lai.** In April 1970, the country heard more upsetting news. President Nixon announced that U.S. troops had invaded Cambodia. They had tried to destroy Vietcong supply lines there. Upon hearing of the invasion, colleges exploded in protest.

A protest at **Kent State University** in Ohio turned tragic. To restore order on the campus, the local mayor called in the National Guard. Some students began throwing rocks at the guards. The guards fired into a crowd of protesters. Four students were killed.

Nixon's invasion of Cambodia cost him public support. It also cost him political support. Members of Congress were angry that he had invaded Cambodia without telling them. As a result, Congress repealed the Tonkin Gulf Resolution. This had given the president the freedom to conduct war policy in Vietnam on his own.

Support for the war declined even further in June of 1971. That month, a former Defense Department worker leaked what became known as the **Pentagon Papers.** These documents showed that the past U.S. presidents had never drawn up any plans to withdraw from Vietnam.

2. Name two incidents that weakened support for the war.

_____

_____

AMERICA'S LONGEST WAR ENDS (Pages 758–759)
Who won the war?

1972 was a presidential election year. To win reelection, Nixon believed he had to end the Vietnam War. Nixon called on Henry Kissinger, his adviser for national security affairs. Kissinger negotiated a peace settlement with the North Vietnamese. In October 1972, Kissinger announced that peace was close at hand. A month later, Nixon was reelected president.

However, the promised peace in Vietnam did not come. South Vietnam objected to the proposed peace settlement. As a result, the peace talks broke down. Nixon responded by ordering more bombings against North Vietnam.

Eventually, the peace talks resumed. In January 1973, the warring parties signed a peace agreement. By the end of March, the last U.S. combat troops had left. For America, the Vietnam War was over.

Shortly after America left, the peace agreement collapsed. North and South Vietnam resumed fighting. In April 1975, North Vietnamese troops captured the South's capital, Saigon. Soon after, South Vietnam surrendered to North Vietnam.

3. What happened to South Vietnam after America left?

_____

_____

THE WAR LEAVES A PAINFUL LEGACY (Pages 759–761)
How did the war affect America?

The Vietnam War cost both sides many lives. In all, about 58,000 Americans died in Vietnam. Another 303,000 were wounded. Vietnamese deaths topped 2 million.

After the war, Southeast Asia continued to experience violence and unrest. The Communists imprisoned hundreds of thousands of South Vietnamese. In Cambodia, a communist group known as the Khmer Rouge took power in 1975. They attempted to transform the country into a peasant society. In doing so, they killed many government officials and intellectuals. The group is believed to have killed as many as 1 million Cambodians.

In the United States, the war resulted in several policy changes. In November 1973, Congress passed the **War Powers Act.** This law prevented the president from committing troops in a foreign conflict without approval from Congress. In a larger sense, the war made Americans less willing to become involved in foreign wars. The war also left many Americans with a feeling of mistrust toward their government.

4. Name two ways in which the war affected Americans.

_____

_____

As you read about President Nixon's Vietnam policy and the end of the war, note one or more reasons for each of the following developments during the war.

1. Nixon adopts a policy of Vietnamization.	2. My Lai massacre shocks Americans.
3. Nixon orders invasion of Cambodia.	4. First student strike in U.S. history occurs.
5. Congress repeals the Tonkin Gulf Resolution.	6. The "Christmas bombings" take place.
7. South Vietnam surrenders to North Vietnam.	8. Vietnam veterans receive a cold homecoming.
9. Cambodia erupts in civil war.	10. Congress passes the War Powers Act.
11. The draft is abolished.	12. Many Americans lose faith in their government.

Section 1

Latinos and Native Americans Seek Equality

Terms and Names

César Chávez Leader of the farm workers movement

United Farm Workers Organizing Committee Union that fought for farm workers' rights

La Raza Unida Latino political party

American Indian Movement (AIM) Group that fought for greater reform for Native Americans

Before You Read

In the last section, you read about the end of the Vietnam War. In this section, you will read about how Latinos and Native Americans fought for greater equality.

As You Read

Use a Venn diagram to take notes on the issues facing Latinos and Native Americans during the 1960s.

THE LATINO PRESENCE GROWS
(Pages 768–769)
Who are Latinos?

Latinos are Spanish-speaking Americans. During the 1960s, the Latino population in the United States tripled—from 3 million to more than 9 million.

During this time, the nation's Mexican American population grew. Many were descendants of Mexicans who stayed on the land that Mexico surrendered to the United States in 1848. Others were the children and grandchildren of the Mexicans who arrived after Mexico's 1910 revolution. Still others came as temporary laborers during the 1940s and 1950s. Mexican Americans always have made up the largest group of Latinos.

About a million Puerto Ricans have lived in the United States since the 1960s.

Most Puerto Ricans have settled in the Northeast, especially in New York City.

Many Cubans also settled in the United States during the 1960s. They had fled Cuba after the Cuban Revolution in 1959. Most Cubans settled in or near Miami.

Thousands of Salvadorans, Guatemalans, Nicaraguans, and Colombians immigrated to the United States after the 1960s. They came to escape political persecution and poverty at home. Wherever they settled, many Latinos experienced poor living conditions and discrimination.

1. Name two groups that make up the Latino community.

_____

_____

LATINOS FIGHT FOR CHANGE
(**Pages** 769–771)
Which **groups fought for change?**

In the 1960s, Latinos began to demand equal rights and respect. One such group was Mexican-American farm workers. These men and women worked on California's fruit and vegetable farms. They often worked long hours for little pay.

César Chávez was the group's leader. Chávez believed that the farm workers should organize into a union. In 1962, he helped establish the National Farm Workers Association. In 1966, Chávez merged this group with a Filipino agricultural union. Together, they formed the **United Farm Workers Organizing Committee** (UFWOC).

California's grape growers refused to recognize the farm workers union. As a result, Chávez called for a nationwide boycott of grapes. His plan worked. In 1970, the grape growers finally signed contracts with the UFWOC. The new contracts guaranteed union workers higher pay and granted them other benefits.

Latinos also wanted greater recognition of their culture. Puerto Ricans demanded that schools offer classes taught in their native language. In 1968, Congress passed the Bilingual Education Act. This law funded bilingual and cultural programs for students who did not speak English.

Latinos began organizing politically during the 1960s. Some worked within the two-party system. Others created an independent Latino political movement. José Angel Gutiérrez, for example, started **La Raza Unida** (the United People Party). The party ran Latino candidates and won positions in city government offices.

2. Name two organizations that fought to promote the cause of Latinos.

_____

_____

NATIVE AMERICANS STRUGGLE FOR EQUALITY (**Pages** 771–773)
What **problems did Native Americans face?**

Native Americans, like Latinos, are a diverse group. However, despite their diversity, most Native Americans have faced similar problems. These problems include high unemployment rates, poor health care, and high death rates.

During the 1950s, the Eisenhower administration tried to solve some of these problems. The government thought that introducing Native Americans to more aspects of mainstream culture would help them. As a result, the government moved Native Americans from their reservations to the cities.

The plan failed. Most Native Americans who moved to the cities remained very poor. In addition, many Native Americans refused to mix with mainstream American society.

Native Americans wanted greater opportunity to control their own lives. In 1961, representatives from 61 Native American groups met to discuss their concerns. They demanded the right to choose their own way of life.

In 1968, President Johnson responded to their demands. He created the National Council on Indian Opportunity. The council's goal was to make sure that government programs reflected the needs and desires of Native Americans.

Many young Native Americans were not satisfied with the government's new policies. They wanted greater reform. They also wanted it more quickly. As a result, some young Native Americans formed the **American Indian Movement (AIM).** This organization demanded greater rights for Native Americans. At times, the group used violence to make its point.

Meanwhile, Native Americans won greater rights through the court system. Throughout the 1960s and 1970s, they won legal battles that gave them greater education and land rights.

3. Name two problems that Native Americans faced.

_____

_____

As you read, fill in the chart with answers to the questions.

What did Latinos campaign for?	How did some Latino individuals and groups go about getting what they wanted?	What federal laws (if any) were passed to address these needs?
1. Improved working conditions and better treatment for farm workers		
2. Educational programs for Spanish-speaking students		
3. More political power		

What did Native Americans campaign for?	How did some Native Americans individuals and groups go about getting what they wanted?	What federal laws (if any) were passed to address these needs?
4. Healthier, more secure lives of their own choosing		
5. Restoration of Indian lands, burial grounds, fishing and timber rights		

Section 2

Women Fight for Equality

Terms and Names

Betty Friedan Author of *The Feminine Mystique*

feminism The belief that women should be equal to men in all areas

National Organization for Women (NOW) Organization that pushed for women's rights

Gloria Steinem Journalist who tried to help women gain political power

Equal Rights Amendment (ERA) Amendment to the U.S. Constitution that would prohibit discrimination against women

Phyllis Schlafly Equal Rights Amendment opponent

Before You Read

In the last section, you read how Latinos and Native Americans fought for greater rights. In this section, you will read how the nation's women also attempted to improve their status in society.

As You Read

Use a time line to take notes on the key events of the women's movement.

A NEW WOMEN'S MOVEMENT ARISES (Pages 776–778)
How did the women's movement emerge?

The theory behind the women's movement of the 1960s was **feminism.** This was the belief that women should have economic, political, and social equality with men.

The women's movement arose during the 1960s for several reasons. First, a growing number of women entered the work force. In the workplace, many women received less pay than men—even for the same job. Many women saw this as unfair.

Second, women had become actively involved in both the civil rights and antiwar movements. These movements led

women to take action on behalf of their own beliefs. In addition, many men in these groups refused to give women leadership roles. As a result, many women became more aware of their inferior status.

In 1963, **Betty Friedan** published *The Feminine Mystique*. This book expressed the discontent that many women were feeling. Friedan's book helped to unite a number of women throughout the nation.

1. Name two factors that helped launch the women's movement.

_____

_____

THE MOVEMENT EXPERIENCES GAINS AND LOSSES (Pages 778–779)
What were the movement's successes and failures?

In 1966, several women including Betty Friedan formed the **National Organization for Women (NOW).** The group's goal was to more actively pursue women's goals. NOW pushed for more child-care facilities. It also called for more educational opportunities.

The organization also pressured the federal government to enforce a ban on gender discrimination in hiring. The government responded by declaring that male-only job ads were illegal.

Women also attempted to gain political strength. In 1971, journalist **Gloria Steinem** helped found the National Women's Political Caucus. This group encouraged women to run for political office.

In 1972, Congress passed a ban on gender discrimination in higher education. As a result, several all-male colleges opened their doors to women. In 1973, the Supreme Court's decision in the case *Roe* v. *Wade* granted women the right to choose an abortion.

The women's movement also met with some failure, such as with the **Equal Rights Amendment (ERA).** The ERA was a proposed amendment to the U.S. Constitution. It would have outlawed government discrimination on the basis of sex. One prominent ERA opponent was **Phyllis Schlafly.** Schlafly called the ERA the work of radical feminists.

In addition, the women's movement angered many of the nation's conservatives. In response, these conservatives joined together to form a movement known as the New Right. This movement emphasized traditional social, cultural, and moral values. Throughout the 1970s, the New Right gained support for its social conservatism.

2. Name one success and one failure of the women's movement.

_____

_____

THE MOVEMENT'S LEGACY
(Page 780)
What was the movement's legacy?

In 1977, the ERA was close to being passed, but the New Right gained strength. In 1982, the ERA went down to defeat.

But the influence of the women's movement could be seen in the workplace as more women started careers instead of staying home with their children. In 1970, 8 percent of all medical school graduates and 5 percent of law school graduates were women. By 1998, those numbers had risen to 42 and 44 percent respectively. Women also made political gains as many ran for and were elected to office.

3. Cite two examples of how the women's movement helped women improve their standing in society.

_____

_____

As you read about the rise of a new women's movement, take notes to
explain how each of the following helped to create or advance the
movement.

1. Experiences in the workplace	2. Experiences in social activism
3. "Consciousness raising"	4. Feminism
5. Betty Friedan and *The Feminine Mystique*	6. Civil Rights Act of 1964
7. National Organization for Women (NOW)	8. Gloria Steinem and *Ms.* magazine
9. Congress	10. Supreme Court

The Equal Rights Amendment would have guaranteed equal rights under
the law, regardless of gender. Who opposed this amendment? Why?

1. Who?	2. Why?

An Era of Social Change

Section 3

Culture and Counterculture

Terms and Names

counterculture Movement whose members sought to drop out of mainstream society

Haight-Ashbury Community in San Francisco that attracted many hippies

the Beatles British rock group that helped popularize rock 'n' roll

Woodstock Massive outdoor concert that demonstrated rock 'n' roll's popularity

Before You Read

In the last section, you read about the women's movement that emerged in the United States in the 1960s. In this section, you will read about the emergence of the counterculture movement—and how the nation reacted to it.

As You Read

Use a tree diagram to take notes on the counterculture of the 1960s.

THE COUNTERCULTURE
(**Pages** 781–782)
***What* characterized the counterculture?**

During the 1960s, many young people adopted values that differed from those of mainstream society. These Americans were part of a movement known as the **counterculture.**

The movement was made up mostly of white middle-class youths. Members of the counterculture were known as "hippies." Many hippies shared some of the beliefs of the New Left. They took part in demonstrations against the Vietnam War. However, a majority of hippies chose to turn their backs on America. They wanted to establish a new society based on peace and love.

The main characteristics of the hippie culture were rock 'n' roll, colorful clothes, and the use of drugs. Many also chose to live in large groups called communes.

Many hippies moved to San Francisco's **Haight-Ashbury** district. This community was popular mainly because of the availability of drugs.

After a few years, the counterculture movement began to decline. Some aspects of the movement became violent. Many urban communes grew dangerous. The widespread use of drugs also led to the decline of the movement.

More than anything else, hippies eventually found that they could not survive outside mainstream America. They needed money to live. For many, this meant returning to mainstream society— and getting a job.

1. Name two characteristics of the counterculture.

_____

_____

A CHANGING CULTURE
(**Pages** 783–784)
How did the counterculture affect America?

The counterculture movement collapsed after only a few years. However, some aspects of it had a lasting effect on mainstream culture.

The movement affected the worlds of art and fashion. The 1960s saw the rise of popular, or pop, art.

One celebrated pop artist was Andy Warhol. His work was characterized by bright, simple, commercial-looking images such as portraits of soup cans and other icons of mass culture. These images were repeated to look mass-produced as a criticism of the times. They implied that individual freedoms had been lost to a "cookie-cutter" lifestyle.

The most lasting legacy of the counterculture movement was its music. Rock 'n' roll continues to be a popular form of entertainment. Perhaps the most influential band was **the Beatles.** The British group took America by storm and helped rock music become part of mainstream America.

A dramatic example of rock 'n' roll's popularity was an event known as **Woodstock.** This was a massive outdoor rock concert in upstate New York. It occurred during the summer of 1969. More than 400,000 people attended—far more than expected. For three days, popular bands and musicians performed. Despite the crowd, however, the festival was peaceful and well organized.

The counterculture movement affected Americans' social attitudes as well. The American media began to address the subjects of sex and violence. Before this time, few Americans discussed these topics.

2. Name two areas of society affected by the counterculture.

_____

_____

THE CONSERVATIVE RESPONSE
(**Page** 785)
Why did mainstream America attack the counterculture?

In the late 1960s, many mainstream Americans criticized the counterculture. They blamed the movement for the decline of traditional American values.

Some conservative groups called the movement a threat to law and order. They also accused members of the counterculture of being immoral.

Mainstream America's anger toward the counterculture affected the country's political scene. In 1968, the Republicans nominated Richard Nixon as their presidential candidate. Nixon ran on a platform of law and order, and conservative values. His ideas appealed to many voters. As a result, Nixon won the election. He then set the nation on a more conservative course.

3. Cite two reasons why Americans criticized the counterculture.

_____

_____

As you read this section, fill out the chart below by listing and describing various elements of the counterculture of the 1960s.

1. Members or participants	2. Beliefs about American society	3. Goals for society and for themselves
4. Movement center	5. Attitudes and activities	6. Violent episodes
7. Impact on art and fashion	8. Impact on music	9. Impact on mainstream America

Guided Reading Workbook

An Age of Limits

Section 1

The Nixon Administration

Terms and Names

Richard M. Nixon 37th president

New Federalism Plan to give federal power back to the states

revenue sharing Plan for the federal government to share money with state and local governments

Family Assistance Plan (FAP) Nixon's welfare reform proposal to give direct relief to poor families

Southern strategy Nixon's effort to attract Southern votes by opposing desegregation

stagflation Situation that occurs when unemployment and inflation rise at the same time

OPEC (Organization of Petroleum Exporting Countries) Organization of nations that export oil

realpolitik Nixon's foreign policy that attempted "realistic politics"

détente Policy aimed at easing Cold War tensions

SALT I Treaty Treaty to limit nuclear weapons

Before You Read

In the last section, you read about the counterculture. In this section, you will learn about President Nixon and his attempts to move the country in a more conservative direction.

As You Read

Use a chart to take notes on the policies of Richard Nixon that promoted change and those that slowed change.

NIXON'S NEW CONSERVATISM
(Pages 794–796)
How did Nixon pursue conservative policies?

President **Richard M. Nixon** wanted to turn the United States in a more conservative direction. He tried to decrease the power of the federal government. Nixon's plan was called **New Federalism.** Its goal was to give federal power to the states.

Nixon introduced **revenue sharing.** The federal government usually told state and local governments how to spend their federal money. Under revenue sharing, state and local officials could spend their federal dollars however they saw fit with few limits.

Nixon also wanted to reform welfare. He supported the **Family Assistance Plan (FAP).** Under this plan, every family of four with no income would receive a payment of $1,600 a year, and could earn up to $4,000 more a year. But this plan failed to pass Congress.

When Nixon first took office, he cooperated with Congress. But he soon refused to spend money that Congress wanted to spend on programs that he did not like. Federal courts ruled that Nixon's action was unconstitutional. They ordered that Nixon spend the money on the programs.

Nixon also followed "law and order" policies to stop riots and antiwar protests. He used the Central Intelligence Agency (CIA) and the Internal Revenue Service (IRS) to harass people. He created an "enemies list" and had the CIA and IRS target people on this list. The list included liberals and other opponents of his policies.

1. What conservative programs did Nixon support?

_____

_____

NIXON'S SOUTHERN STRATEGY
(**Pages** 796–798)
What **was the Southern strategy?**

Nixon wanted to make sure he would get reelected in 1972. To achieve this, he used what he called a **Southern strategy** to win the support of Southerners.

To attract white voters, Nixon tried to slow school desegregation. But the Supreme Court ordered the administration to move more quickly. Nixon also opposed the extension of the Voting Rights Act of 1965. But Congress extended the act.

Nixon believed that the Supreme Court under Chief Justice Earl Warren was too liberal. During his presidency, four justices, including Warren, left the Court. This gave Nixon an opportunity to appoint more conservative justices.

2. How did Nixon hope to win Southern support?

_____

_____

CONFRONTING A STAGNANT ECONOMY (**Pages** 798–799)
What **is stagflation?**

One of the biggest problems facing Nixon was a weak economy. Between 1967 and 1973, inflation and unemployment increased. This situation is known as **stagflation.**

Stagflation had several causes. Unemployment increased because trade competition increased. This made it harder for Americans to sell their goods overseas. The nation also had trouble finding jobs for millions of baby boomers who reached working age.

Inflation increased for two main reasons. First, more government spending on social programs and the war in Vietnam raised prices. The second cause was the nation's need for foreign oil. The United States received much of its oil from the Middle East. Many of these countries belonged to a cartel called **OPEC (Organization of Petroleum Exporting Countries).** During the 1960s, OPEC gradually raised oil prices. Then, in 1973, a war broke out, with Israel against Egypt and Syria. The United States sent military aid to Israel.

The OPEC nations sided with Egypt and Syria. They stopped selling oil to the United States. This led to problems in the United States. Between the fall of 1973 and March 1974, motorists faced long lines at the gas stations. Some factories and schools closed. When OPEC started selling oil to the United States again, the price had quadrupled.

3. How did OPEC affect the U.S. economy?

_____

_____

NIXON'S FOREIGN POLICY TRIUMPHS (Pages 799–801)
What is realpolitik?

Nixon's main foreign policy adviser was Henry Kissinger. Kissinger based his foreign policy views on a philosophy known as **realpolitik.** This meant that Kissinger dealt with other nations in a practical and flexible manner. Kissinger believed it was practical to ignore a country that was weak. But it was important to deal with strong nations.

Realpolitik was a change from the policy of containment. Nixon and Kissinger changed U.S. relations with Communist countries. They called their policy **détente.** This policy was aimed at easing Cold War tensions.

In 1972, Nixon visited Communist China. Before this, the United States had refused to recognize the Communist government. Three months later, Nixon went to the Soviet Union. Nixon and the Soviet leader signed the **SALT I Treaty.** This five-year agreement limited nuclear weapons. Nixon's successes in foreign affairs helped him win reelection.

4. How did Nixon try to ease Cold War tensions?

_____

_____

As you read about the Nixon administration, take notes to describe
President Nixon's policies toward the problems facing him.

Problems	Policies
1. Size and power of the federal government	
2. Inefficiency of the welfare system	
3. Vietnam War and domestic disorder	
4. Nixon's reelection	
5. Liberalism of Supreme Court justices	
6. Stagflation and recession	
7. U.S.–China relations	
8. U.S.–Soviet relations	

Section 2

Watergate: Nixon's Downfall

Terms and Names

impeachment The constitutional process for removing a president from office

Watergate Scandal that forced Nixon to resign

H. R. Haldeman Adviser to Nixon

John Ehrlichman Adviser to Nixon

John Mitchell Attorney general and director of Nixon's campaign

Committee to Reelect the President Nixon's campaign committee

Judge John Sirica Judge in the trial of the Watergate burglars

Saturday Night Massacre Nixon's firing of Justice Department officials, including the special prosecutor investigating Watergate

---

Before You Read

In the last section, you read about President Nixon's approach to politics and the Cold War. In this section, you will learn about the Watergate scandal.

As You Read

Use a time line to take notes on the events of the Watergate scandal.

PRESIDENT NIXON AND HIS WHITE HOUSE (Pages 802–803)
***What* was Watergate?**

In 1974, the House Judiciary Committee voted to recommend the **impeachment** of—the bringing of formal charges against—President Richard Nixon. The cause was the **Watergate** scandal which was an attempt to cover up a burglary of the Democratic National Committee (DNC) headquarters.

By the time Richard Nixon became president, the executive branch had become powerful. Nixon expanded the power of the presidency. He confided in a small group of very loyal advisers. These advisers included **H. R. Haldeman,** chief of staff; **John Ehrlichman,** chief domestic adviser; and **John Mitchell,** the

attorney general. These men helped Nixon get reelected. They also shared Nixon's desire for power. This would lead Nixon and his advisers to cover up their role in the Watergate burglary.

1. Define Watergate scandal.

_____

_____

THE DRIVE TOWARD REELECTION (Pages 803–804)
***What* was the CRP?**

Nixon campaign aides were determined to win the 1972 election. They hired five men to raid Democratic party offices in the Watergate complex in Washington, D.C. The men were caught photographing

---

Guided Reading Workbook

files and placing wiretaps on phones. The press soon discovered that the group's leader, James McCord, was a former CIA agent. He was also an official of a group known as the **Committee to Reelect the President** (CRP). John Mitchell, who had been attorney general, was the CRP's director.

Nixon and his staff tried to hide the link to the White House. Workers shredded evidence. Nixon and his staff asked the CIA to urge the FBI to stop its investigations into the burglary.

The Watergate burglary was not a big issue in the 1972 election. Only two reporters kept on the story. In a series of articles, the reporters found information that linked members of the administration to the burglary. The White House denied any connections.

2. Why did the CRP order the burglary of the Democratic National Committee headquarters?

_____

_____

THE COVER-UP UNRAVELS
(Pages 804–806)
How did Nixon get caught?

After Nixon's reelection, the cover-up began to unravel. In January of 1973, the Watergate burglars went to trial. All of the burglars except James McCord changed their pleas from innocent to guilty. McCord was found guilty by a jury. The trial's presiding judge, **Judge John Sirica,** believed that the burglars did not act alone. Then in March 1973, McCord sent a letter to Sirica, stating that he had lied under oath. He also stated that the White House was involved in the cover-up.

Soon the public interest in the Watergate burglary increased. In April

1973, three top Nixon aides resigned. The President then went on television and denied any cover-up. He announced that he was appointing Elliot Richardson as the new attorney general. He authorized Richardson to appoint a special prosecutor to investigate Watergate.

In May 1973, the Senate began its own investigation of Watergate. The Senate hearings were televised live. In the hearings, one of Nixon's aides said that Nixon knew about the cover-up. Then it was revealed that White House meetings had been tape-recorded. The Senate committee demanded the tapes. Nixon refused to release them.

Court battles over the tapes lasted a year. Archibald Cox, the special prosecutor, took the president to court in October 1973 to get the tapes. Nixon refused and ordered Richardson to fire Cox. In what became known as the **Saturday Night Massacre,** Richardson refused the order and resigned. The deputy attorney general also refused and resigned. Solicitor General Robert Bork finally fired Cox. But his replacement, Leon Jaworski, was determined to get the tapes.

3. What did Nixon do during the investigation?

_____

_____

THE FALL OF A PRESIDENT
(Pages 806–807)
How did Nixon's presidency end?

In March 1974, a grand jury charged seven Nixon aides with obstruction of justice and perjury. Nixon released more than 1,250 pages of taped conversations. But he did not release the conversations on some key dates. In July 1974, the

Supreme Court ordered the White House to release the tapes.

Three days later, a House committee voted to impeach President Nixon. If the full House of Representatives approved, Nixon would go to trial in the Senate. If Nixon was judged guilty there, he would be removed from office. When the tapes were finally released, they proved that Nixon had known of the cover-up. On August 8, 1974, before the impeachment could happen, Nixon resigned.

Watergate produced distrust about the presidency. A poll taken in 1974 showed that 43 percent of Americans had lost faith in the presidency. In the years after Vietnam and Watergate, Americans developed a deep distrust of government officials.

4. Why did President Nixon resign from office?

_____

_____

As you read about Watergate, answer the questions shown on the following
time line.

1972

June	**Break-in at DNC campaign office**	⟶

1. How were the "plumbers" connected to President Nixon?

Nov.	**Nixon wins reelection.**

1973

Jan.	**Plumbers go on trial.**	⟶

2. Who was the judge? Why did he hand out maximum sentences?

Mar.	**Mitchell and Dean are implicated.**	⟶

3. How were Mitchell and Dean connected to Nixon?

April	**Dean is fired; Haldeman and Erlichman resign.**	⟶

4. How were Haldeman and Erlichman connected to Nixon?

May	**Senate opens Watergate hearings.**	⟶

5. What did the following men tell the Senate about Nixon?

a. Dean

b. Butterfield

Oct.	**Saturday Night Massacre**	⟶

6. Who was fired or forced to resign in the "massacre"?

1974

April	**Edited transcripts of tapes are released.**	⟶

7. Why weren't investigators satisfied with the transcripts?

July	**Supreme Court orders surrender of tapes.**
Aug.	**House committee adopts impeachment articles.**

8. What did the tapes reveal?

	Unedited tapes are released.	⟶
	Nixon resigns.	

An Age of Limits

The Ford and Carter Years

Terms and Names

Gerald R. Ford 38th president

Jimmy Carter 39th president

National Energy Act Law that aimed to conserve energy

human rights Rights and freedoms that all people should enjoy

Camp David Accords Agreements between Israel and Egypt

Ayatollah Ruhollah Khomeini Iranian religious leader who led the revolution against the Shah of Iran

---

Before You Read

In the last section, you learned about Watergate. In this section, you will read about the presidencies of Gerald Ford and Jimmy Carter.

As You Read

Use a time line to take notes on the major events of the Ford and Carter administrations.

FORD TRAVELS A ROUGH ROAD; FORD'S FOREIGN POLICY
(Pages 810–811)
***What* did Ford do as president?**

Gerald R. Ford replaced Richard Nixon as president. Ford was likable and honest. But he lost public support when he pardoned Nixon.

The economy had gotten worse by the time Ford took office. Ford invited the nation's top economic leaders to the White House to discuss what to do. Ford promoted a program to slow inflation by encouraging energy conservation. This program failed. Ford then pushed for higher interest rates. This triggered the worst recession in 40 years.

In foreign affairs, Ford relied on Henry Kissinger, the secretary of state. Ford continued talks with China and the Soviet Union. In 1974, he participated in a meeting in Helsinki, Finland. There, 35 countries, including the Soviet Union, signed the Helsinki Accords. These were agreements that promised greater cooperation between the nations of Europe.

1. What did Ford do about the economy?

_____

_____

CARTER ENTERS THE WHITE HOUSE **(Page** 812)
***Why* did Carter get elected?**

Ford ran for election in 1976 against Democrat **Jimmy Carter.** Carter ran as an outsider, or someone apart from Washington politics. Carter promised he would never lie to Americans. Carter won a close election with this message.

Carter stayed in touch with the people by holding "fireside chats" on radio and

---

Guided Reading Workbook

television. But Carter did not try to reach out to Congress. He refused to take part in deal-making. As a result, he angered both Republicans and Democrats in Congress.

2. Why did Carter win the 1976 presidential election?

_____

_____

CARTER'S DOMESTIC AGENDA
(**Pages** 812–814)
How did Carter try to fix the economy?

Carter believed that energy policy should be his top priority. He signed the **National Energy Act.** It placed a tax on gas-guzzling cars. It removed price controls on oil and natural gas. It also funded research for new sources of energy.

But in 1979, violence in the Middle East caused another shutdown of oil imports. High prices made inflation worse. Carter tried voluntary price freezes and spending cuts, but these measures did not stop inflation.

Other changes in the economy caused problems in the 1970s. Greater automation meant fewer manufacturing jobs. Competition from other countries cost American jobs, too. Many companies moved their factories from the Northeast to the South and West. They were looking for lower energy costs and cheaper labor.

3. How did Carter try to solve the nation's economic problems?

_____

_____

A HUMAN RIGHTS FOREIGN POLICY (**Page** 815)
How did human rights affect Carter's foreign policy?

Carter tried to follow moral principles in his foreign policy. He believed the United States should promote **human rights.** Human rights are freedoms and liberties like those listed in the Declaration of Independence and the Bill of Rights.

Carter cut aid to countries that violated the rights of their people. He supported a treaty with Panama to give control of the Panama Canal to that country. Carter signed a nuclear arms treaty— called SALT II—with the Soviets. The treaty was opposed by the Senate. But when the Soviets invaded Afghanistan, Carter refused to fight for the treaty. It was never ratified.

4. What was Carter's foreign policy based on?

_____

_____

TRIUMPH AND CRISIS IN THE MIDDLE EAST (**Pages** 816–817)
What did Carter do about the Middle East?

In 1978, Carter arranged a meeting between the leaders of Egypt and Israel. The two nations had been enemies for years. After several days of talks, Carter and the two leaders reached agreements known as the **Camp David Accords.**

In 1979, Muslim fundamentalists and their leader **Ayatollah Ruhollah Khomeini** overthrew the shah of Iran. In October of 1979, Carter allowed the shah to enter the United States for cancer treatment. This angered the revolutionaries. On November 4, 1979, they took control of the American embassy in Tehran, Iran's capital, and took 52 Americans hostage. They demanded that the United States send the shah back to Iran in return for the hostages.

Carter refused. A long standoff followed. Carter could not get the hostages released. They were held for 444 days. The hostages were freed just minutes after Ronald Reagan was inaugurated president on January 20, 1981.

5. Name one success and one defeat in the Middle East for Carter?

_____

_____

As you read about Presidents Ford and Carter, take notes to describe the policies of each toward the problems facing them.

Problems Faced by Ford	Policies
1. Ending Watergate scandal	
2. Troubled economy	
3. Hostile Congress	
4. Cold War tensions	
5. Southeast Asia	

Problems Faced by Carter	Policies
6. Distrust of politicians	
7. Energy crisis	
8. Discrimination	
9. Human rights issues	
10. Panama Canal	
11. Cold War tensions	
12. Middle East tensions	

An Age of Limits

Environmental Activism

Terms and Names

Rachel Carson Environmentalist crusader in the U.S.

Earth Day Annual day to celebrate the environment

environmentalist Person who actively tries to protect the environment

Environmental Protection Agency (EPA) Federal agency formed to decrease pollution

Three Mile Island Site of a nuclear plant that released radiation into the air

---

Before You Read

In the last section, you learned about President Ford and President Carter. In this section, you will see how Americans addressed their environmental concerns.

As You Read

Use a web diagram to take notes on how concern for the environment grew in the United States.

THE ROOTS OF ENVIRONMENTALISM
(Pages 820–821)
What is environmentalism?

Concern for the environment was increased by the 1962 book *Silent Spring*, written by **Rachel Carson.** That book argued that pesticides were poisoning food and killing birds and fish. *Silent Spring* sold nearly half a million copies within six months.

Carson's book was an awakening to many Americans. President Kennedy set up a committee to investigate the situation shortly after the book's publication. It took several years, but Carson's work helped to outlaw the use of DDT, a harmful pesticide, in 1972.

1. How did *Silent Spring* encourage environmentalism?

_____

_____

ENVIRONMENTAL CONCERNS IN THE 1970S (Pages 821–825)
What were the key environmental issues of the 1970s?

On April 22, 1970, Americans celebrated **Earth Day** for the first time. Earth Day became a yearly event to highlight environmental issues.

Richard Nixon was not an **environmentalist**—someone who takes an active role in protecting the environment. But he did recognize the nation's concern over the environment. In 1970, he created the **Environmental Protection Agency (EPA).** This agency had the power to regulate pollution caused by emissions standards and to conduct research.

Nixon also signed the 1970 Clean Air Act. This law required industry to reduce pollution from factories and automobiles. Other new laws to protect the environment also passed.

Guided Reading Workbook

In 1968, oil was found in Alaska. Oil companies began building a pipeline to carry the oil 800 miles across the state. The discovery of oil and the construction of the pipeline created many new jobs and increased state revenues.

But the pipeline raised concerns about Alaska's environment and the rights of Alaska's native peoples. In 1971, Nixon signed the Alaska Native Claims Settlement Act. This law gave millions of acres of land to the state's native tribes.

In 1978, President Carter set aside 56 million more acres in Alaska as national monuments. In 1980, Congress added another 104 million acres to Alaska's protected conservation areas.

In the 1970s, some people believed that nuclear energy was the energy of the future. They believed that it was cheap, plentiful, and safe.

Others opposed nuclear energy. They warned that nuclear plants were dangerous to humans and the environment. These people also feared accidents and nuclear waste.

On March 28, 1979, the concerns of opponents of nuclear energy appeared to come true. An accident caused one of the nuclear reactors on **Three Mile Island,** in Pennsylvania, to release radiation into the air. An investigation showed that workers at the plant had not been properly trained. It also showed that some safety measures were not taken. Afterwards, the government strengthened nuclear safety regulations.

2. What did the government do after the accident at a nuclear reactor on Three Mile Island?

_____

_____

A CONTINUING MOVEMENT
(**Page** 825)
Have the goals of the environmental movement changed?

The debate over the environment continues today. The struggle is between proponents of economic growth and conservationists. Environmental regulations sometimes block economic development and cause a loss of jobs for workers. Though there is conflict, it is clear that environmental concerns have gained increasing attention and support.

3. What issue faces Americans today regarding the environment?

_____

_____

Name _____ Class _____ Date _____

Section 4, *continued*

As you read about the nation's efforts to address environmental problems, take notes to describe how American attitudes were affected by each event or how the event affected the environment itself.

Events	Effects on Attitudes or Environment
1. Publication of Rachel Carson's *Silent Spring* →	
2. Celebration of Earth Day →	
3. Creation of the Environmental Protection Agency →	
4. Passage of the new Clean Air Act →	
5. Passage of the Alaska Native Claims Settlement Act →	
6. Nuclear accident at Three Mile Island →	

A Conservative Movement Emerges

Terms and Names

entitlement program Program that guarantees benefits to particular people

New Right Alliance of conservative groups to support conservative ideas

affirmative action Programs that required special consideration for racial and ethnic minorities and women

reverse discrimination Discrimination against whites to make up for past discrimination against others

conservative coalition Alliance of business interests, religious people, and dissatisfied middle-class voters to support conservative candidates

Moral Majority Organization formed to fight for traditional values

Ronald Reagan 40th president

Before You Read

In the last section, you read about the environmental movement. In this section, you will learn about the growth of the conservative movement leading up to 1980.

As You Read

Use a web diagram to take notes on the issues that interested Conservatives.

THE CONSERVATIVE MOVEMENT BUILDS (Pages 830–832)
Why did conservatism grow?

American conservatism had been gaining support since Barry Goldwater's run for the presidency in 1964. Many people were questioning the power of the federal government.

Many Americans resented the cost of **entitlement programs.** These are programs that guaranteed benefits to particular groups. By 1980, one out of every three households was receiving benefits from government programs. Americans were unhappy paying taxes to support these benefits.

Some people also became frustrated with the government's civil rights policies. The Civil Rights Act of 1964 was meant to end racial discrimination. But over the years, some court decisions extended the act. Some people opposed laws that increased minority opportunities in employment or education. During the 1970s, right wing, grass-roots groups emerged to support single issues. Together these groups were known as the **New Right.** Among the causes they supported were opposition to abortion and school busing, blocking the Equal Rights Amendment, and supporting school prayer.

Many in the New Right were critical of **affirmative action.** This was the policy that required employers to give special consideration to women, African Americans, and other minority groups.

The New Right called this **reverse discrimination,** discrimination against white people and specifically white men.

Right-wing groups tended to vote for the same candidates. These voters formed the **conservative coalition.** This was an alliance of some intellectuals, business interests, and unhappy middle-class voters.

Members of the conservative coalition shared some basic positions. They opposed big government, entitlement programs, and many civil rights programs. They also believed in a return to traditional moral standards.

Religious groups, especially Christian fundamentalists, played an important role in the conservative coalition. Some of these groups were guided by television preachers. Some of them banded together and formed the **Moral Majority.** They interpreted the Bible literally. They also believed in absolute standards of right and wrong. The Moral Majority criticized a decline in national morality. They wanted to bring back what they saw as traditional American values.

1. What basic positions did members of the conservative coalition share?

_____

_____

CONSERVATIVES WIN POLITICAL POWER (Pages 832–833)
Why was Reagan popular?

The conservatives found a strong presidential candidate in **Ronald Reagan.** He won the 1980 nomination and chose George Bush as his running mate.

Reagan had been a movie actor and a spokesman for General Motors. He won political fame with a speech for Barry Goldwater during the 1964 presidential campaign. In 1966, Reagan was elected governor of California. He was reelected in 1970.

In the 1980 election, Reagan ran on a number of issues. Supreme Court decisions on abortion, the teaching of evolution, and prayer in public schools all upset conservative voters. Reagan also had a strong anticommunist policy.

Reagan was an extremely effective candidate. High inflation and the Iranian hostage crisis also helped Reagan. Reagan easily won the 1980 election. The election also gave Republicans control of the Senate.

2. What factors helped Reagan win the presidential election in 1980?

_____

_____

Guided Reading Workbook

As you read about the conservative movement that swept the country, note the individuals, groups, and institutions that fueled it. Then identify issues the New Right emphasized as well as the interests it promoted.

1. Individuals	2. Groups and institutions

3. Issues and interests

Identify four factors that contributed to Ronald Reagan's victory.

1.	3.
2.	4.

Conservative Policies Under Reagan and Bush

Terms and Names

Reaganomics Reagan's economic policies

supply-side economics Economic theory that tax cuts will increase jobs and government revenues

Strategic Defense Initiative Proposed system to defend the United States against missile attacks

Sandra Day O'Connor First woman Supreme Court justice

deregulation The cutting back of federal regulation of industry

Environmental Protection Agency (EPA) Agency established in 1970 to fight pollution and conserve natural resources

Geraldine Ferraro Democratic vice-presidential candidate in 1984

George Bush Reagan's vice president elected president in 1988

Before You Read

In the last section, you saw how conservative power grew before the presidential election of 1980. In this section, you will read how President Reagan put in place conservative policies.

As You Read

Use a chart to take notes on the effects of Reaganomics.

"REAGANOMICS" TAKES OVER
(Pages 834–836)
What was Reaganomics?

Reagan tried to reduce the size and power of the federal government. He wanted to make deep cuts in government spending on social programs. He convinced Congress to lower taxes. This approach was called **Reaganomics.**

Reaganomics depended on **supply-side economics.** This theory said that cutting taxes would motivate people to work, save, and invest. More investment would create more jobs. More workers would mean more

taxpayers, which would cause government revenues to increase.

Reagan also increased military spending. Between 1981 and 1984, the Defense Department budget almost doubled. In 1983, Reagan asked the country's scientists to develop a defense system that would keep Americans safe from enemy missiles. The system became known as the **Strategic Defense Initiative,** or SDI.

The economy grew. Interest rates and inflation rates dropped. Government revenues, however, did not increase as much as Reagan hoped. So the federal government ran up huge budget deficits. During the Reagan and Bush years, the size of the government debt more than doubled.

1. What was the main idea of Reaganomics?

_____

_____

JUDICIAL POWER SHIFTS TO THE RIGHT (Page 836)
What kind of judges did Reagan and Bush nominate?

Regan nominated Antonin Scalia, Anthony M. Kennedy, and **Sandra Day O'Connor** to fill seats in the Supreme Court left by retiring judges. O'Connor was the first woman appointed to the Court. Reagan also nominated Justice William Rehnquist to the position of chief justice.

President George Bush later made the Court more conservative when he nominated David H. Souter to replace the retiring justice William Brennan. He also nominated Clarence Thomas to take the place of Thurgood Marshall. In many decisions, the Court moved away from the more liberal rulings of the previous 40 years. The Court restricted a woman's right to an abortion, put limits on civil rights laws, and narrowed the rights of arrested persons.

2. What was the result of Reagan's and Bush's appointments to the Supreme Court?

_____

_____

DEREGULATING THE ECONOMY (Page 837)
What was deregulation?

Reagan tried to reduce the power of the federal government through **deregulation.** Reagan removed price controls on oil and gas. He deregulated the airline industry and ended government regulation of the savings and loan industry.

Reagan also reduced environmental regulation. He cut the budget of the **Environmental Protection Agency (EPA).** He ignored requests from Canada to reduce acid rain. Reagan appointed opponents of environmental regulation to oversee the environment.

James Watt, Reagan's secretary of the interior took many actions that were questioned by environmentalists. He sold millions of acres of public lands to private developers, allowed drilling for oil and gas in the continental shelf, and encouraged timber cutting in national forests.

3. What actions did James Watt take that hurt the environment?

_____

_____

CONSERVATIVE VICTORIES IN 1984 AND 1988 (Pages 837–838)
Who won the elections of 1984 and 1988?

By 1984, Reagan had the support of conservative voters who approved of his policies. These voters helped Reagan win the 1984 election. He defeated Democrat Walter Mondale. Mondale chose Representative **Geraldine Ferraro** of New York as his running mate. Ferraro became the first woman on a major party's presidential ticket.

In 1988, Vice-President **George Bush** ran for the presidency. He won the

Guided Reading Workbook

Republican nomination. The Democrats nominated Massachusetts governor Michael Dukakis.

During the campaign, Bush built on Reagan's legacy of low taxes by saying, "Read my lips: no new taxes." Most Americans saw little reason for change. George Bush won the election with 53 percent of the popular vote and 426 electoral votes.

4. What did the presidential elections of 1984 and 1988 show about the mood of the country?

_____

_____

_____

As you read, note the results of "Reaganomics" and of actions taken to achieve important goals of the conservative movement.

Goal: Stimulate the economy
1. Cut government spending on social programs and lowered income taxes   →   Result(s):
2. Increased military spending   →   Result(s):

Goal: Promote traditional values and morality
3. Named conservative judges to the Supreme Court and other federal courts   →   Result(s):

Goal: Reduce the size and power of the federal government
5. Cut the Environmental Protection Agency budget and appointed EPA administrators sympathetic to business   →   Result(s):

The Conservative Tide

Section 3

Social Concerns in the 1980s

Terms and Names

AIDS (acquired immune deficiency syndrome) Fatal disease with no known cure, that became a U.S. and world-wide epidemic

pay equity Situation in which women and men receive equal pay for equal work

L. Douglas Wilder Nation's first African-American governor

Jesse Jackson Civil rights leader and presidential candidate

Lauro Cavasos Appointed secretary of education by President Reagan

Dr. Antonia Coello Novello Named Surgeon General by President Bush

Before You Read

In the last section, you read about the conservative policies of Reagan and Bush. In this section, you will learn about the social problems that existed in the 1980s.

As You Read

Use a chart to take notes about social issues during the 1980s and how the government responded to them.

HEALTH, EDUCATION, AND CITIES IN CRISIS (Pages 839–841)
What problems did Americans face in the 1980s?

A scary health issue that arose in the 1980s was **AIDS (acquired immune deficiency syndrome).** The disease is caused by a virus that destroys the immune system that protects people from illness. Most of the victims of AIDS were either homosexual men or intravenous drug users who shared needles. Many people also contracted AIDS through contaminated blood transfusions.

AIDS began spreading throughout the world possibly as early as the 1960s. It quickly became an epidemic in the U.S. and threatened much of the public blood supply.

Another issue that concerned Americans was abortion. In the 1973 *Roe* v. *Wade* decision, the Supreme Court said women had the right to have an abortion. Opponents of legalized abortion described themselves as "pro-life." Supporters of legalized abortion called themselves "pro-choice."

Battles over abortion rights often competed for attention with concerns over rising drug abuse. The Regan administration declared a war on drugs. Reagan supported laws to catch drug users and drug dealers.

Education remained an important issue. In 1983, a report entitled *A Nation at Risk* criticized the nation's schools. The report showed that American students' test scores lagged behind those of students in other nations. Many people agreed that the nation's schools were not doing a good job. But they did not agree on solutions.

Guided Reading Workbook

The nation's cities were also in crisis. Many poor and homeless people lived in cities. Budget cuts had eliminated earlier federal programs to aid the cities. Welfare payments to the poor had not kept up with rising prices.

1. How did Americans respond to the problems of the 1980s?

_____

_____

THE EQUAL RIGHTS STRUGGLE
(Pages 842–843)
Did women's lives improve in the 1980s?

Women continued to try to improve their lives. Women's groups were unable to get the Equal Rights Amendment ratified. But more women were elected to Congress.

By 1992, nearly 58 percent of all women had entered the work force. But women still earned only 76 cents for every dollar a man earned. New divorce laws and social conditions increased the number of single women heading a household. Many of these women lived in poverty.

Women's organizations and unions called for **pay equity.** This was an idea to make sure that women would earn the same pay as men doing the same work.

Under the pay equity system, jobs would be rated according to the skills and responsibilities they required. Employers would set pay rates to reflect each job's requirements. Women also called for benefits to help working mothers.

2. What political losses and gains did women have in the 1980s?

_____

_____

THE FIGHT FOR RIGHTS CONTINUES (Pages 843–845)
How did minority groups fight for their rights?

Members of many minority groups achieved greater political power during the 1980s. Hundreds of communities had elected African Americans to serve in public offices. In 1990, **L. Douglas Wilder** of Virginia became the first African-American governor in the United States. The Reverend **Jesse Jackson** ran for the Democratic presidential nomination in 1984 and in 1988.

But the income gap between white Americans and African Americans was larger in 1988 than it was in 1968. In addition, Supreme Court rulings further limited affirmative action.

Latinos became the fastest growing minority group during the 1980s. Like African Americans, Latinos gained political power during the 1980s.

In 1988, President Reagan appointed **Lauro Cavasos** secretary of education. In 1990, President Bush named **Dr. Antonia Coello Novello,** to the post of Surgeon General.

Native Americans faced cuts in federal aid. Some opened casinos on their reservations to earn money. Asian Americans made economic advances but did not gain much political power.

Asian Americans were the second fastest growing minority in the United States during the 1980s. In 1976, an organization called Asian Women United (AWU) was founded to help Asian American women.

During the 1970s and 1980s, homosexual men and women worked for laws to protect their rights. By 1993, seven states and 110 communities had outlawed discrimination against homosexuals.

3. What were some political and social gains made by Latinos during the 1980s?

_____

_____

As you read, identify specific issues in each of the following areas that
concerned Americans in the 1980s.

1. Health	2. Education	3. Cities

Take notes about the gains, losses, and chief concerns of each of the
following groups.

1. Women	2. African Americans	3. Latinos
4. Native Americans	5. Asian Americans	6. Gays and lesbians

The Conservative Tide

Section 4

Foreign Policy After the Cold War

Terms and Names

Mikhail Gorbachev Last leader of the Soviet Union

glasnost Gorbachev's policy of openness in discussing problems in the Soviet Union

perestroika Gorbachev's policy of reforming the economy in the Soviet Union

INF Treaty Treaty to reduce nuclear weapons

Tiananmen Square Place in Beijing where Chinese protesters demonstrated against the Communist government

Sandinistas Communist rebel group that took power in Nicaragua

Contras Rebel forces supported by Ronald Reagan to overthrow the Sandinistas

Operation Desert Storm The 1991 U.S. attack on Iraq to force the Iraqis out of Kuwait

Before You Read

In the last section, you learned about some of the social issues Americans faced in the 1980s. In this section, you will see how American foreign policy changed after the Cold War.

As You Read

Use a chart to take notes about U.S. foreign policy in different regions of the world.

THE COLD WAR ENDS
(Pages 848–850)
What ended the Cold War?

In March 1985, **Mikhail Gorbachev** became the leader of the Soviet Union. He started talks with the United States to lessen Cold War tensions. Gorbachev thought this would allow the Soviets to cut their military spending. It would also let them reform their economy.

Gorbachev supported *glasnost* (openness in discussing social problems) and *perestroika* (economic restructuring) in the Soviet Union. He let private citizens own land. He also allowed more free speech and held free elections.

Talks led to the **INF Treaty** (Intermediate-Range Nuclear Forces Treaty). Reagan and Gorbachev signed the treaty in December 1987. The Senate ratified it in May 1988.

The weakness of the economy and Gorbachev's reforms led to the collapse of the Soviet Union. All the republics that were in the Soviet Union became independent nations. Then they formed a loose confederation called the Commonwealth of Independent States.

The collapse of the Soviet Union ended the Cold War. In January 1993, Russia and the United States signed the START II treaty. This treaty cut both nations' nuclear weapons by 75 percent.

Communists were knocked from power throughout Eastern Europe. Germany reunited. Other Eastern European nations enacted democratic reforms.

Students in China demanded freedom of speech. In April 1989, protesters held marches to voice their demands. The marches grew into large demonstrations in Beijing's **Tiananmen Square.** The Chinese military crushed the protesters. Soldiers killed hundreds of them and arrested others. People all over the world watched these actions. They were upset by what they saw.

1. What events in the Soviet Union led to the end of the Cold War?

_____

_____

CENTRAL AMERICAN AND CARIBBEAN POLICY (Pages 851–852)
How did the United States act toward its neighbors?

In 1979, *Sandinista* rebels overthrew the Nicaraguan government. President Carter sent aid, as did the Soviet Union and Cuba. In 1981, President Reagan charged that the Sandinista government was Communist. He supported the *Contras,* a group trying to defeat the Sandinistas. After years of conflict, a peace agreement was signed and free elections were held in 1990.

Reagan sent U.S. troops to Grenada in 1983. He feared its government had ties with Cuba. The U.S. troops overthrew the pro-Cuban government. They set up a pro-American government in its place.

In 1989, President Bush sent more than 20,000 U.S. troops to Panama. He wanted to overthrow Panamanian

dictator Manuel Noriega. He also wanted to arrest him for drug trafficking. Noriega was taken by the American military. They took him to Miami. He was tried, convicted, and sentenced to 40 years in prison.

2. How did the United States influence affairs in Grenada?

_____

_____

MIDDLE EAST TROUBLE SPOTS
(Pages 852–855)
How did the United States act toward the Middle East?

In 1983, terrorists linked to Iran took some Americans hostage in Lebanon. Reagan condemned Iran. He called on U.S. allies not to sell Iran weapons for its war against Iraq.

Three years later, the American people found out that Reagan was breaking his own policy. Some of his staff had sold missiles to Iran. They were trying to free the hostages in Lebanon. Also, some of the profits from the sale were sent to the Contras in Nicaragua. These illegal activities were called the Iran-Contra affair.

In the summer of 1987, Congress investigated Iran-Contra. Some of Reagan's staff were convicted of crimes in the scandal. In 1992, President Bush pardoned some of these people.

In 1990, Iraq invaded Kuwait. On January 16, 1991, with the support of Congress and the United Nations, President Bush launched **Operation Desert Storm** to fight Iraq and to free Kuwait.

The United States and its allies staged air strikes against Iraq. On February 23, they also launched a ground attack. On February 28, President Bush announced a cease-fire. The Persian Gulf War was over. Kuwait was freed.

3. What was the purpose of Operation Desert Storm?

_____

_____

As you read about the end of the Cold War, note key persons, events, and trends involved in the nations listed below. Concentrate on political and economic developments as well as on U.S. relations with those countries. Leave the shaded boxes blank.

Nations	Key Individuals	Key Events and Trends
1. Soviet Union		Events: Trends:
2. Poland		Events: Trends:
3. Germany		Events: Trends:
4. Yugoslavia		Events: Trends:
5. China		Events: Trends:
6. Nicaragua		Events: Trends:
7. Panama		Events: Trends:
8. Iran		
9. Iraq		

Section 1

The 1990s and the New Millennium

Terms and Names

William Jefferson Clinton 42nd president

H. Ross Perot Texas billionaire who was a third-party candidate in 1992 election

Hillary Rodham Clinton First Lady and health-care reformer

NAFTA Trade agreement between Canada, Mexico, and the United States

Newt Gingrich Speaker of the House of Representatives

Contract with America Republican plan for political reform

Al Gore Clinton's vice-president, and Democratic candidate in 2000 election

George W. Bush 43rd president of U.S.

Barack Obama 44th president

Before You Read

In the last section, you learned about American foreign policy at the end of the Cold War. In this section, you will read about the presidencies of Bill Clinton and George W. Bush and the election of Barack Obama.

As You Read

Use a time line to take notes on major actions taken by President Clinton during his two terms in office.

CLINTON WINS THE PRESIDENCY; MODERATE REFORM AND ECONOMIC BOOM (Pages 860–862)
***What* was the important issue in the 1992 election?**

Governor **William Jefferson Clinton** of Arkansas was the first member of the baby-boom generation to win the presidency. Clinton defeated President George Bush and Texas billionaire, **H. Ross Perot** in the election. Bush's popularity, which was sky-high after the Gulf War, fell as the economy went into a recession. Clinton convinced voters he would move the Democratic Party to the political center by embracing both liberal and conservative programs.

Clinton tried to reform the nation's program for health care insurance. He appointed First Lady **Hillary Rodham Clinton** to head the team creating the plan. Congress never voted on the plan after Republicans attacked its promotion of "big government." Clinton was more successful in balancing the budget. The economy began to produce surpluses for the government and the economy boomed.

Guided Reading Workbook

1. Why did George Bush's popularity fall after the Gulf War?

_____

_____

CRIME AND TERRORISM

(**Pages** 862–863)

Where **did terrorists attack?**

Terrorism and violence raised Americans' fears during the 1990s and in the first years of the 2000s. In 1993, foreign terrorists exploded a bomb at the World Trade Center in New York City. In 1995, an American terrorist named Timothy McVeigh exploded a bomb at the Federal building in Oklahoma City. The bomb killed 168 men, women, and children.

School violence also plagued the nation. In 1999, two students at Columbine High School in Colorado killed 12 and wounded 23 classmates and a teacher before killing themselves.

In 2001, the worst attack on the United States in its history took place. Foreign terrorists hijacked airplanes and flew them into the World Trade Center and the Pentagon outside Washington, D.C. The explosions leveled the World Trade Center and severely damaged the Pentagon. Approximately 3,000 people died in the attacks.

2. What buildings were the target of two terrorist attacks?

_____

_____

NEW FOREIGN POLICY CHALLENGES; PARTISAN POLITICS AND IMPEACHMENT

(**Pages** 863–865)

Why **was President Clinton impeached?**

In the 1990s, the major foreign policy problem was in Yugoslavia where Serbs embarked on a murderous policy of "ethnic cleansing" first in Bosnia, then in Kosovo. The United States and NATO launched air strikes against the Serbs forcing them to back down.

Free trade was a goal of the Clinton administration. In 1994, the **North American Free Trade Agreement (NAFTA)** was signed into law by President Clinton. It provided for free trade between the United States, Mexico, and Canada. Critics of free trade opposed American actions by protesting at meetings of world trade groups in Seattle, Washington, and Quebec City, Canada.

President Clinton developed political troubles beginning in 1994 when the Republicans gained control of both houses of Congress. **Newt Gingrich,** who became speaker of the house, led the Republicans. The Republicans used a document they called the **Contract with America** to oppose President Clinton.

Clinton won reelection in 1996 even though he was accused of being involved in a land deal. He was then accused of lying under oath in questioning about an improper relationship with a young White House intern. The House approved two articles of impeachment against the president even though a majority of Americans approved of Clinton's job performance. The Senate trial that followed in 1999 failed to convict Clinton and he remained in office.

3. Why was President Clinton impeached?

_____

_____

THE RACE FOR THE WHITE HOUSE; THE BUSH ADMINISTRATION
(**Pages** 865–867)
How did George W. Bush confront terrorism?

The candidates in the 2000 election were Vice-President **Al Gore,** the Democratic candidate, and Texas Governor **George W. Bush,** the Republican candidate. There was confusion on election night over who won the state of Florida. Gore had won the popular vote. But whoever won Florida would win a majority of the electoral votes and the election.

Both sides sent lawyers and spokespeople to Florida to try to secure victory. Bush held a slim lead. A manual recounting of the votes began. Then the battle moved to the courts. On December 12, the U.S. Supreme Court ruled 5-4 to stop the recount. As a result, Bush won Florida and the presidency.

After the terrorist attacks on September 11, 2001, President Bush began waging a war against terrorism. The United States and coalition forces broke up the terrorist network in Afghanistan that was responsible for the September 11 attacks. Then Bush expanded the war to Iraq. Iraqi

dictator Saddam Hussein was overthrown. On the home-front, Bush faced an economy hurt by corporate scandals. He passed a $350 billion tax cut to help the economy.

4. What action did President Bush take in the war on terrorism?

_____

_____

THE 2008 PRESIDENTIAL ELECTION (Page 868)
What factors helped the Democrats to win the 2008 presidential election?

The continuing war in Iraq and a failing economy contributed to President Bush's unpopularity. The collapse of the financial markets in the fall of 2008 only made matters worse. As a result, in the 2008 presidential election, Americans voted for a change in direction by electing Democrat **Barack Obama**, U.S. senator from Illinois. Obama made history as the first African American to be elected president of the United States.

On taking office, Obama faced several problems, including an economy in recession. He pushed through an economic stimulus package to combat this. He also announced plans to end combat operations in Iraq and in Afghanistan. In addition, he worked with Congress to pass a sweeping health reform bill.

5. Why were the Democrats able to win the presidency in 2008?

_____

_____

As you read, write notes in the appropriate boxes to answer the questions.

The 1992 Presidential Election		
1. a. Who ran as a Republican?	2. a. Who ran as an independent?	3. a. Who ran as a Democrat?
b. Why did he fail to convince voters to support him?	b. What created an opportunity for this independent candidacy?	b. What helped him win?

The Clinton Administration's First Term	
4. What did Clinton achieve in domestic policy?	5. What did Clinton achieve in foreign policy?

The Republican Congress and the Contract with America	
6. What goals did the contract set for Republican leaders?	7. How did Clinton and the Senate undermine the contract?

The New Global Economy

Terms and Names

service sector The part of the economy where businesses provide services rather than material goods

downsize To reduce the number of workers on staff

Bill Gates Extremely successful owner of Microsoft, a computer software company

NASDAQ The technology-dominated stock index

dotcom Internet related business

General Agreement on Tariffs and Trade (GATT) International trade agreement

Before You Read

In the last section, you learned about the presidencies of Bill Clinton and George W. Bush. and the election of Barack Obama. In this section, you will read about the economic issues that Americans faced at the turn of the 21st century.

As You Read

Use a web diagram to take notes on the major changes in the U.S. economy during the 1990s and early 2000s.

THE SHIFTING AMERICAN ECONOMY (Pages 869–871)
What changed for American workers?

There was good news and bad news about the economy between 1993 and 2000. Millions of new jobs were created. By 2000, the unemployment rate had fallen to the lowest it had been since 1970. But wage inequality between upper-income and low-income Americans also grew.

There was an increase of jobs in the service sector. The **service sector** is the part of the economy that provides services to people. By 2000, nearly 80 percent of American workers were teachers, medical

professionals, lawyers, engineers, store clerks, waitstaff, and other service workers. The largest growth in the service sector came in jobs that paid low wages. These included jobs such as sales clerks and janitors.

Many companies **downsized**—reduced staff in order to cut costs. They hired temporary workers to replace full-time staff. This had serious consequences for the workers. Most temporary workers had lower wages, little job security, and few benefits. This led many workers to feel insecure about their jobs.

Manufacturing jobs declined sharply in the 1980s and 1990s. The loss in jobs in manufacturing led to a drop in union

Guided Reading Workbook

membership. Workers with high-paying jobs saw no need to join unions. Workers with low-paying jobs were too worried about losing their jobs to join unions.

Workers in high-tech fields such as computers, made up a growing percentage of the work force. These new high-tech jobs demanded that workers have special skills. Most workers who had high-tech jobs earned high salaries.

By the late 1990s, some people who had creative ideas about computers made fortunes. **Bill Gates** was one of these people. He founded Microsoft, a computer software company. By 2008, he had assets estimated at about $53 billion. This made him the second wealthiest individual in the world.

High-tech business traded on the **NASDAQ** (National Association of Securities Dealers Automated Quotation System) exchange grew rapidly. These Internet businesses called **dotcoms** created fortunes for their founders. But the stocks of these businesses were terribly overvalued, and beginning in 2000 the NASDAQ fell sharply. After the NASDAQ rose again to record highs in 2007, it was rocked by the global financial crisis of 2008 and 2009.

1. What were three changes in the workplace in the United States during the 1990s?

    _____

    _____

    _____

CHANGE AND THE GLOBAL ECONOMY (Pages 872–873)
What is the global economy?

Improvements in transportation and communication allowed people, goods,

and information to move around the world faster than ever. One of President Clinton's major foreign policy goals was to expand trade.

In 1994, the United States joined other nations in signing a world trade agreement called **General Agreement on Tariffs and Trade (GATT).** GATT lowered tariffs. It also set up the World Trade Organization (WTO). This organization was created to settle trade disputes.

Many people believed that GATT would be good for the U.S. economy. But many American workers feared they would lose their jobs. They thought it would help companies make products in countries where wages were low.

Many low-wage American jobs were lost as a result of NAFTA. But exports to Canada and Mexico increased. By 1997, there were 300,000 more jobs in the United States than there had been in 1993.

Around the turn of the 21st century, the global economy began to slow down. The U.S. economy also encountered problems. Both the U.S. and world economies began to reverse the downward trend by 2004. But in 2008, a global financial crisis left growth in the world's economies sluggish at best.

2. In what ways did President Clinton try to expand trade?

    _____

    _____

As you read this section, take notes to answer questions about the U.S. role
in the changing world economy.

The Domestic Economy: Good News and Bad News	
1. What was the good news?	2. What was the bad news?

The Changing Domestic Economy	
3. What trends led to explosive growth in the service sector? How were workers affected?	
4. What trends led to explosive growth in temporary work? How were workers affected?	
5. What trends led to a sharp decline in manufacturing jobs? How were workers affected?	
6. What trends led to explosive growth in the high-tech industry? How were workers affected?	

The Changing Global Economy	
7. What trends affected international trade and competition? How did those trends affect U.S. businesses and workers?	

Technology and Modern Life

Terms and Names

information superhighway Popular name for a proposed computer network

Internet Worldwide computer network

telecommute The ability of people to work out of their homes

Telecommunications Act of 1996 Controversial law to reform the communications industry

genetic engineering Method of changing the genes of living cells

Before You Read

In the last section, you saw how the American economy changed at the turn of the 21st century. In this section, you will learn how technology has changed Americans' lives.

As You Read

Use a chart to take notes on the technological changes described in this section and how these changes have affected life in the United States.

THE COMMUNICATIONS REVOLUTION (Pages 876–878)
***How* have new technologies affected communications?**

President Clinton wanted to create an **information superhighway.** This would be a computer network that would link people around the world. The network would link cable, phone, and computers to provide entertainment and information.

Clinton appointed VicePresident Gore to oversee the government's role in creating the information superhighway. They wanted private entrepreneurs to build the network. But they believed the government should protect people's rights to use it.

Most people took part in the information superhighway through the **Internet,** a worldwide computer network.

By 2009, nearly 228 million Americans used the Internet regularly to send e-mail, to network, to share music, or to browse through pages on the Web.

New technologies let many Americans **telecommute,** or work out of their homes instead of going to an office every day.

The changes in communications caused the growth of many communications companies. Congress passed the **Telecommunications Act** of 1996 to make sure people would receive good service. The law allowed telephone and cable companies to enter each others' industries. One of the results of the law was an increase in mergers. This cut the number of competing companies.

The communications industry liked the Telecommunications Act. But some people believed that the law allowed a small number of people to control the media. Civil rights activists thought the Communications Decency (passed as part of the Telecommunications Act) Act limited free speech. Parts of these laws were struck down in court. Since the early 2000s, the issue of network neutrality has created considerable controversy.

1. How did the Internet and cable television affect Americans?

_____

_____

SCIENTIFIC ADVANCES ENRICH LIVES (Pages 878–881)
How does technology affect daily life?

In addition to telecommunications, great progress was made in robotics, space exploration, and medicine. Visual imaging and artificial intelligence were combined to provide applications in industry, medicine, and education. Flight simulators helped train pilots. Doctors have been able to better explore within the body. Architects and engineers have used virtual reality to build visual models of buildings and structures.

In space, *Pathfinder* and *Sojourner* transmitted live pictures from the surface of Mars. Shuttle missions began building the *International Space Station (ISS)*. The Hubble Space Telescope was used to discover new planets.

Enormous progress was made in the field of biotechnology. The Human Genome Project announced in 2000 that it had mapped the genes of the human body. Molecular biologists hoped this genetic map of DNA would help them to develop new treatments for inherited diseases. But the applications of this new information or "biotechnology" was controversial. Many people were concerned about animals that were cloned from single cells. The use of **genetic engineering,** the artificial changing of the molecular biology of organisms' cells to alter an organism, aroused concern. Scientists used genetic engineering to alter food crops like corn. Consumer groups resisted the practice, and it was restricted in some places.

Applications of technology helped medical progress. New treatments for cancer and AIDS helped many patients. The use of magnetic resonance imaging (MRI) helped doctors with medical diagnoses.

Environmental concerns rose through the decade. People looked for ways to reduce the use of fossil fuels and the production of acid rain. Americans also improved recycling efforts.

2. What were some important technological advances in the United States?

_____

_____

As you read about the impact of technological advances on life in the
United States, note inventions, trends, and efforts relating to each field
listed below.

1. Communications
2. Health care
3. Genetic engineering
4. Entertainment
5. Education
6. Space exploration
7. Environment

The Changing Face of America

Terms and Names

urban flight Movement of people away from cities

gentrification The rehabilitation of old neighborhoods and displacement of lower income people

Proposition 187 California law which cut benefits to illegal immigrants

Before You Read

In the last section, you learned about the ways technology affects modern life. In this section, you will read about the changes facing Americans at the start of the 21st century.

As You Read

Use a chart to take notes on demographic changes in the United States.

URBAN FLIGHT (Pages 882–884)
Why did people move to suburbs?

Between 1950 and 1970, America experienced a pattern of **urban flight,** where Americans left the cities and moved to the suburbs. By the early 2000s, after years of decline, some major cities had increased their population or slowed the rate of decline.

There were several causes of urban flight. Overcrowding in cities was one. Overcrowding helped cause increased crime and decaying housing. Many city dwellers who could afford to, moved to the suburbs for better schools and safer neighborhoods. Cities lost taxes and downtown shopping districts lost business to suburban malls.

By the mid-1990s, people began to return to the city. In a process known as **gentrification,** they bought and

rehabilitated old houses and neighborhoods. Neighborhoods came back, but low-income residents were displaced by rising housing costs.

Many suburban workers commuted to the city for work. But suburbs competed for business and industry. Suburbs offered tax breaks to get business to locate there and then saw their tax revenues decline as a result.

1. How did urban flight change the nation's cities?

_____

_____

_____

Guided Reading Workbook

THE AGING OF AMERICA
(Pages 884–885)
How will aging affect America?

The U.S. Census Bureau documents that in 2008 Americans were older than ever before. The median age, 36.8 years, was four years older than the median age in 1990. The cause was simple: people were living longer and the large baby boom generation was getting older. This trend put pressure on programs for the elderly. Social Security was stressed because there were fewer younger workers paying into the system and retirees were living longer.

In 1996, three workers made Social Security contributions to support every retired person. But experts expect that by 2030, there will be only two workers to support each retired person. Social Security will begin to pay out more than it takes in. As a result, some people want to reform the Social Security system.

2. How does the increase in the number of elderly people affect Social Security and Medicare?

_____

_____

THE SHIFTING POPULATION
(Pages 885–887)
How has immigration affected America?

Over the years, the pattern of immigration to the United States has changed. The large numbers of immigrants who entered the country before and just after 1900 came from Europe. In contrast, since the 1960s the majority of immigrants have come from Asia and the Western Hemisphere—mostly from Mexico.

Census Bureau data show that these are changing the country's ethnic and racial makeup. By 2001, for example, California had become a majority-minority state, with Asian Americans, Latinos, African Americans, and Native Americans making up more than half its population. By 2009, three other states—Hawaii, New Mexico, and Texas—had also become majority-minority states. A number of other states, including Arizona, are close to majority-minority status.

The presence of such a large number of immigrants has led to debate over U.S. immigration policies. Many Americans believe that their country can't absorb more immigrants. Many illegal immigrants arrived from Latin America, Canada, Poland, China, and Ireland. They took jobs many Americans turned down, as farm workers and domestic servants. By 2009, an estimated 10.8 million illegal immigrants resided in the United States.

Hostility toward illegal immigration has increased in California and Arizona, two states with high percentages of immigrants. In 1994, California passed Proposition 187, which cut all education and nonemergency health benefits to illegal immigrants. By March 1998, Proposition 187 was ruled unconstitutional. In 2010, Arizona passed a law that enhanced local and state police power to enforce federal immigration laws. These efforts to control immigration inspired political participation among Hispanic voters, who saw themselves as targets.

As more immigrants make their way to the United States and the nation's ethnic composition changes, debates about immigration will continue.

Native Americans continued to struggle. In 2007, about 25 percent of Native Americans lived below the poverty line. Throughout the 1990s, Native Americans strived to improve their lives through building casinos and using the courts to gain greater recognition for their tribal ancestry and land rights.

Guided Reading Workbook

3. How is immigration changing the United States?

_____

_____

AMERICA IN A NEW MILLENNIUM
(Page 887)
***What* challenges do Americans face in the 21st century?**

America entered the 21st century with several concerns, old and new. For

example, environmental concerns have become a global issue and have gained importance. Poverty is a major concern, as is curbing acts of terrorism that threaten Americans both at home and abroad.

4. What challenges faced Americans at the turn of the 20th century?

_____

_____

Guided Reading Workbook

As you read this section, note three facts or statistics concerning each of the following important trends in the late 20th century.

URBAN FLIGHT	1.
	2.
	3.
BABY BOOMERS	4.
	5.
	6.
IMMIGRATION	7.
	8.
	9.

Note one challenge the United States will face in each of the following areas during the 21st century.

1. Urban and Suburban Life	
2. Aging Population	
3. Immigration Policy	